D1520333

UNLIKELY STORIES

UNLIKELY STORIES

Causality and the Nature of Modern Narrative

Brian Richardson

DELAWARE

Newark: University of Delaware Press
London: Associated University Presses

4-24-98 dmi

PR
478
.C38
R53
1997

© 1997 by Associated University Presses, Inc.

All rights reserved. Authorization to photocopy items for internal or personal use, or the internal or personal use of specific clients, is granted by the copyright owner, provided that a base fee of $10.00, plus eight cents per page, per copy is paid directly to the Copyright Clearance Center, 222 Rosewood Dr., Danvers, Mass. 01923. [0-87413-609-1/97 $10.00 + 8¢ pp, pc.

Associated University Presses
440 Forsgate Drive
Cranbury, NJ 08512

Associated University Presses
16 Barter Street
London WC1A 2AH, England

Associated University Presses
P.O. Box 338, Port Credit
Mississauga, Ontario
Canada L5G 4L8

The paper used in this publication meets the requirements of the American National Standard for Permanence of Paper for Printed Library Materials Z39.48-1984.]

Library of Congress Cataloging-in-Publication Data

Richardson, Brian, 1953–
     Unlikely stories : causality and the nature of modern narrative / Brian Richardson.
         p.   cm.
     Includes bibliographical references and index.
       ISBN 0-87413-609-1 (alk. paper)
       1. English literature—20th century—History and criticism.
     2. Causation in literature. 3. American literature—20th century-
     -History and criticism. 4. Necessity (Philosophy) in literature.
     5. Postmodernism (Literature). 6. Coincidence in literature.
     7. Modernism (Literature). 8. Narration (Rhetoric). I. Title
     PR478.C38R53   1997
     820.9'384—dc20   96-30906
                                                                              CIP

PRINTED IN THE UNITED STATES OF AMERICA

CANISIUS COLLEGE LIBRARY
BUFFALO, N.Y.

The unpredictable and the predetermined unfold
together to make everything the way it is. . . .
The future is disorder

—Tom Stoppard, *Arcadia*

Contents

8   Contents

Acknowledgments

I wish to thank the Division of Sponsored Research at the University of Florida for a summer grant that enabled me to work uninterruptedly on this manuscript. I also thank the editors of *Style, Essays in Literature,* and *The Faulkner Journal* for permission to use previously published material.

I also wish to thank the following scholars whose generous comments on various chapters proved extremely helpful: Donald Kartiganer, Leroy Searle, Evan Watkins, Kathleen Blake, Miceal Vaughn, Gary Handwerk, Karen Shabetai, Ann Goodwyn Jones, Linda Macri, and R. B. Kershner. Alan Richardson discussed many of the texts and theoretical issues with me at great length over many years; he deserves extensive and continued thanks. Hazard Adams read most chapters more than once, always with exemplary acuity and remarkable promptness, for which I remain very grateful. I also wish to thank my colleagues at the University of Maryland for the rich and congenial intellectual community they provide. I thank my parents, David and Paula Richardson, for unstintingly supporting a project they only imperfectly understood—a circumstance that makes their generosity all the more impressive.

Finally, I wish to thank my wife, Sangeeta Ray, for her unflagging support, brilliant advice, astute pragmatism, and boundless love; she deserves far more appreciation than an acknowledgment can ever contain or express. To her I dedicate this book, and much, much more.

UNLIKELY STORIES

Introduction:
Conceptualizing Causation

Near the beginning of the sixteenth chapter of *Bleak House*, Dickens interrupts the narrative to ask the reader teasingly:

> What connexion can there be, between the place in Lincolnshire, the house in town, the Mercury in powder, and the whereabout of Jo the outlaw with the broom, who had that distant ray of light upon him when he swept the church-yard step? What connexion can there have been between many people in the innumerable histories of this world, who, from opposite sides of great gulfs, have, nevertheless, been very curiously brought together!

Like many authors before and since, Dickens here specifically draws attention to the subject of causal connection. Implicit in such a query is the unwritten assumption that the different story lines, despite their apparent independence, are nevertheless somehow conjoined; by deferring the moment of intersection, Dickens plays with the reader's normal expectation of some sort of convergence. This passage also asks the reader to speculate about what particular type of causation will emerge to bring the divergent events together. At this point in the text, it is equally plausible to assume that the connection will be brought about by any of the following agencies: divine providence, sheer coincidence, unknown natural causes, or authorial intervention. Dickens's lines thus announce a kind of hermeneutical challenge that embraces the connection between multiple story lines, the interpretation of the text, the sequencing of episodes, and the causal system governing the world of the fiction.[1] It is this cluster of intersecting issues and their ideological underpinnings that will be examined in *Unlikely Stories*.

Cause is one of the most significant and fundamental aspects of narrative; surprisingly, it is also one of the most neglected and under-theorized topics of narrative theory and criticism.[2] To be sure, one can find many excellent studies of certain aspects, types, or subdivisions of causal agency, such as fortune, determinism, chance, fate, coincidence, probability, the fantastic, or providence; nevertheless, there is no compre-hensive, general theory of causality in narrative capable of embracing and contrasting more local varieties.[3] Cause is an extremely protean relation and can operate at different levels within a fictional world as well as in the arrangement of the text. A primary goal of this study is to delineate the systems of probability that govern the connection between events within fictional worlds. I pay particular attention to innovative modern constructions that foreground the play of chance, coincidence, the random, the absurd, and the logically impossible. Since the causal dynamics of fictional worlds are frequently related to the connections, ruptures, and disjunctions between independent narrative segments of a text, it is necessary to look into what might be called the poetics of narrative sequencing. Similarly, important literary deployments of cau-sation need to be juxtaposed with corresponding developments in philo-sophical discourse: it is no coincidence that the role of chance becomes prominent in fiction at the same time that theories of probability begin to emerge.

Roland Barthes has observed, "Everything suggests, indeed, that the mainspring of narrative is precisely the confusion of consecution and consequence, what comes *after* being read in narrative as what is *caused by*; in which case narrative would be a systematic application of the logical fallacy denounced by Scholasticism in the formula *post hoc, ergo propter hoc*—a good motto for Destiny. . . ." (1977, 44). This elo-quent statement, quoted approvingly by Todorov in his own discus-sion of causality (1981, 42) is worth probing, since it compresses and conflates so many of the heterogeneous elements subsumed under the rubric of cause. To begin with, Barthes equates causation with textual sequence, even though critics beginning with Aristotle have censured episodic tales for failing to possess the "illusory" causality Barthes at-tributes to all narratives; nor is it clear how Barthes could respond to Dickens's deliberate (though temporary) strategy of opposing narra-tive sequence to causal connection. On the other hand, Barthes's im-plicit critique of the anthropomorphic teleology inherent in the appeal to destiny encourages us to look critically at the philosophical theories and ideological values concealed within metaphysical conceptions of causation. It is of great significance whether events proceed from the hand of God, the motion of history, or the roll of the dice, and it is usually in the interests of hegemonic powers to obscure these relations.

It is unfortunate that Barthes's statement tends to obscure important differences between, say, fate in *Oedipus Rex*, the determinism of *L'Assommoir*, the unlikely profusion of coincidences in *Ulysses*, and the metafictional imperialism of Nabokov, not to mention the apparently random adventures of the varied protagonists of Apuleius, Le Sage, or Céline. It is also important to observe that the reader's customary expectations of an unambiguous causal framework can be mirrored by characters themselves struggling to discover the causal laws of the world they inhabit, and that the audience's demands for causal connection can, as we have seen, be provoked and frustrated by authors who defer or destabilize the unity of the events they narrate.

The theoretical part of this study attempts to disentangle, clarify, and reconceptualize the varied strands of causality in literature. The first chapter critically analyzes and takes issue with the positions of earlier theorists such as Paul de Man, Roland Barthes, and Roy Jay Nelson. Building on the work of Wolfgang Iser and others, I go on to suggest the ways in which the same interpretive dilemmas that perplex characters can also confront the reader, and I note some of the paradoxes involved in the narrative embodiment of philosophical theories of cause. Since every narrative includes (along with space and time) some system of causation as part of its setting, it needs to be determined just what the fictional deployment of a philosophical theory of cause precisely means. Here too the ideological valences inscribed within the notions of fate, destiny, necessity, and luck are disinterred and scrutinized.

The second chapter sifts through the range of causal settings—fate, providence, determinism, fortune, chance, necessity—and outlines four basic types of probability that govern fictional worlds: supernatural, naturalistic, chance, and metafictional systems of causation. Since these systems are mutually exclusive, close attention is brought to bear on the hermeneutical dilemmas and ideological contests that arise as competing conceptions of cause are expressed and tested in the fictional universe. Fantastic literature, as Todorov has pointed out, relies on an epistemological tension between supernatural and naturalistic explanations of unusual events. I argue that such interpretive confrontations appear (and are often explicitly debated) when any incompatible causal systems are made to collide: too great a proliferation of chance occurrences, for example, will subvert both naturalistic and supernatural positions. This chapter is intended to be a contribution to narrative poetics, complementing existing theories of narrative space and temporality. At the same time it constitutes a genealogical inquiry chronicling the rise, development, and supersession of dominant paradigms: to outline a range of possible causal agencies in narrative is to discover an underlying, if oscillating, historical trajectory.

The third chapter moves from fictional worlds to narrative segments, examining causal connection, disjunction, deferral, and rupture in various narrative sequences while reflecting on the theoretical stances of Aristotle, Forster, and Chatman. It goes on to contrast the two most prominent concepts of narrative: one based on temporal succession (Prince, Rimmon-Kenan), the other stressing causal ties between narrative segments (Tomashevsky, Bordwell and Thompson). Close analysis of the interplay between the deviously independent story lines of *Mrs. Dalloway* and the apparently unconnected speeches in Pinter's *Landscape* suggests that both of these "limit texts" foreground and ultimately depend upon some form of causal connection, and thus point toward a revisionary model of narrative.

The second part of this study offers critical readings of some notoriously ambiguous novels from the vantage point of the theoretical framework established in part 1. In Conrad's *Nostromo*, the characters continuously attempt to comprehend and narrativize the order of the events that surround them. All such attempts prove futile, as the logic of "material interests" contradicts the notions of providence and progress variously articulated by the novel's characters: Viola, for one, is correct in suspecting that he will never be "able to understand the ways of Divine justice" (1960, 38). Conrad goes on to temper the force of this emerging determinism by strong infusions of chance and coincidence, thereby mounting an implicit critique of the relentless chains of cause and effect typical of naturalistic fiction. The ontological instabilities that result increase the pressures for consistent if inaccurate narratives; these fabrications in turn go on to engender significant material consequences.

In *Light in August*, Faulkner's personae regularly employ the rhetoric of various forms of fatalism: Nathaniel Burden refers to a "curse which God put on a whole race of people" and states that "none can escape it" (1972, 239). The action of the novel, however, shows a different and opposite causal pattern at work: in every case, the characters' actions are not fated, but only believed to be so; each finally chooses to be subject to his or her own doom—one that is invariably based on a prior fiction. In this novel, to escape one's "fate" is to recognize it as a fiction. A somewhat analogous situation is present in *Invisible Man*, where the narrator must uncover the genuine pattern governing his experience while resisting both Mr. Norton's invocations of "destiny" and the Brotherhood's historical teleology. ("What if history was a gambler, instead of a force in a laboratory experiment?" [1972a, 431].) Ellison's protagonist must learn to read society's master codes, and then respond with a counternarrative of his own that can include otherwise marginalized elements of his existence.

Molloy is composed of two similar narratives, one of which embodies a Humean causal skepticism, while the other sets forth and deconstructs a Cartesian causal schema. Molloy is unable to discern the simplest causal progressions, while Moran continually affirms connections that do not in fact exist. The precise relation between the two parts is thoroughly ambiguous; the disjunctions and convergences of the two textual units alternately suggest and deny causal connection ("for all things run together, in the body's long madness, I feel it" [1965, 56]), thus raising interesting questions of the work's status as a single narrative. In addition, the ontological status of the fictional world(s) of the text is inherently unstable and in constant danger of being reduced to an avowed fabrication.

The question of causal agency has urgency for writers whose cultural heritage includes non-Western traditions. The act of prophecy, which fascinated Sophocles, Shakespeare, and Calderón, has emerged as a major topos in narratives of modern Asia, Egypt, the postcolonial world, the African diaspora, and in the work of U.S. ethnic authors. Prophecy is a crucial site for testing the rival claims of indigenous supernatural traditions, Western notions of Christian providence, and a naturalistic skepticism. In a chapter devoted to these clashes, I outline the function, truth value, and metafictional implications of prophecy in a number of writers including Achebe, Narayan, Soyinka, al-Hakim, Lu Hsun, Maxine Hong Kingston, and Charles Johnson. Although a wide spectrum of positions are set forth, a surprising number of these texts end up rejecting traditional supernatural metaphysics even as they critique Western political and cultural imperialism. For many of these authors, causal investigation leads to ontological skepticism, although the rejected supernatural beliefs are often recalled nostalgically as part of a lost totality, or reinscribed as metaphorically true if literally false, or transmuted into effective postmodern allegories.

Contemporary authors of fiction and drama are as intrigued by causal arrangements as were their predecessors, and this fascination appears in a number of forms in narratives written in the past twenty-five years. Particularly interesting are Stanislaw Lem's *The Chain of Chance* and Iris Murdoch's *An Accidental Man*, works that explore the furthermost limits of the range of chance events that can be encompassed within a naturalistic framework. Both works show just how powerful chance can be in the world of our experience. Postmodern writers, on the other hand, often prefer to load the dice in favor of chance, piling one unlikely event upon another until any pretense of mimesis evaporates. This practice reveals the paradox of chance in fictional narratives: its absence indicates a specious causalism that fabricates an unusual chain of appropriate causes and predictable effects; its presence, however, always reveals authorial intervention, since chance in literature is never a chance occurrence. In very different ways, Tom Stoppard, Bharati Mukherjee, and Angela Carter reanimate the dynamics of causation, as chance structures are variously pitted against naturalistic progressions, the intertextual pressures of antecedent works, and the conventional rules of established genres. In *Rosencrantz and Guildenstern Are Dead*, the forces of chance and will struggle confusedly against the power of the scripted words of *Hamlet* that the titular characters are doomed to act out; in Carter's *Wise Children*, the play of chance is ubiquitous and the characters (including Dora Chance and Sir Melchior Hazard) inhabit a world beyond the realm of the probable that oscillates between unmotivated good fortune and random catastrophe.

Mukherjee's *Jasmine* is particularly interesting in this context, since its pages reenact the general progression of the history of narrative from the supernatural, through the naturalistic, to the chance realm of unlikely accidents and improbable coincidences. Ironically, *Jasmine*'s investigation into causality has been commonly misread as a failure to observe the laws of probability, a charge frequently leveled against female writers who tamper with conventional sequences of cause and effect, as Nancy K. Miller, Joanne Frye, and others have shown. Feminist narrative theory helps provide both a better insight into the intersections of ideology and narrative technique, and an alternative interpretation of Mukherjee's suggestive text.

Each of the works analyzed in the second part of this study explicitly thematizes the idea of cause and usually foregrounds modern notions of chance at the expense of older, totalizing systems. Most of these texts also embody or parody philosophically articulated theories of causality, and each features characters who attempt to comprehend the causal laws of the world they inhabit—often mirroring the reader's own confusion in the face of the apparently random or strangely conjoined events of the narrative. In addition, these works contain elaborate metafictional patternings that serve to problematize causal settings, as subterranean dramas of the power of words, names, and narratives accompany and contest the ostensible stories of the protagonists' actions.

In the conclusion I summarize the findings of the critical readings, suggesting that modern literary history can be seen as a causally connected (though nonteleological) narrative that features the rise and profusion of probabilistically unlikely stories and a corresponding increase in more explicit metafictional strategies. With the end of modernism we also see a challenge to the role of chance, as the ontological instability typical of the multiple worlds of postmodern fiction threatens to preclude genuinely random events except where innovative causal interactions reanimate the play of chance and restore its destabilizing power.

Throughout this book, my primary concern is with the typically modern deployment of causation, which by and large did not exist before the advent of romanticism. To fully delineate the modernist achievement, it is necessary to contrast it with earlier and later modes, note significant precursors, and explain why modern strategies of causation did not or could not occur earlier. As a result, this investigation covers a large and heterogeneous terrain, touching on the plays of Shakespeare and Aphra Behn, the rise of probability theory, the prefaces of Walter Scott, the philosophy of Hume, the decline of popular belief in supernatural agents and interventions, and the incorporation of insurance companies after London's great fire of 1666. Nevertheless, my emphasis remains fixed on the role of causality as explicit theme, ideological construct, and narrative setting in fiction of the twentieth century.

A number of critical and theoretical surprises turn up in the course of this investigation. I argue against common perceptions of Conrad as a determinist, Faulkner as a fatalist, and Mukherjee as a failed realist. This study uncovers Beckett's debt to Hume and Ellison's skeptical engagement with notions of destiny; it enters into current debates on the nature of narrative, the origins and scope of postmodernism, and the collapse of the distinction between fiction and nonfiction in recent theory. To provide a manageable focus, I have drawn most of my examples from novels written in English, though I have also tried to identify significant texts from other literatures (notably French) and genres (especially drama). Causality is one of the most difficult, confused, and neglected topics of literary theory; it is also, as this book attempts to reveal, an indispensable critical concept for narrative analysis, interpretation, and critique.

The Fortunes of Chance: Historical Contexts of Modern Causal Strategies

Before proceeding further, I would like to provide a brief overview of some key moments in the often curious history of the concept of chance in Western literature and discourse. The following should perhaps be read more as a chronicle than a narrative history, sequentially setting forth some of the main issues and major players that will be recontextualized in different ways in the chapters that follow.[4] The key issues to be observed are the systematic official suppression of the notion of chance for most of Western history, the difficulties early expositors encountered as they tried to formulate a discourse appropriate to encompass it, and the general transformation in the language that attempts to describe the real or imagined relations between ostensibly interconnected events.

The notion of chance as a major force in the unfolding of events is a relatively recent idea, and it only begins to emerge toward the end of the Enlightenment. There is a very good reason why this would be the case: the existence of chance defies virtually every thoroughgoing variety of theism and can also severely problematize traditional conceptions of materialism. Pagan ideas of fate and destiny as well as Christian beliefs in providence and design do not allow for the possibility of chance: all events are instead posited as forming part of a larger, meaningful narrative of human history.[5] In the ancient Greek worldview, all events are governed by a preexisting fate. The apparent vagaries of fortune are entirely determined by the dictates of fate, and chance, *tyche*, does not exist, as Sophocles, we will soon see, demonstrates so effectively.

Boethius, in the *Consolation of Philosophy*, synthesizes standard classical Greek and Roman beliefs with early, classically inflected Christian precepts. In particular, his attack on chance summarizes and anticipates several centuries of assiduous polemic. This position proved so influential for the millennium after his death that his basic formulations need to be identified at the outset. Fortune rules nothing, he affirms, but is ultimately directed by God, who "must dispose everything according to the good. He is, in a manner of speaking, the wheel and the rudder by which the vessel of the world is kept stable and undamaged" (1962, 71). Fate, which arranges fortune, is in turn governed by providence: "Everything which is subject to fate is also subject to Providence, and . . . Fate itself is also subject to Providence" (92). Not surprisingly, this cosmology leaves no room for chance: "If chance is defined as an event produced by random motion and without any sequence of causes, then I say there is no such thing as chance. . . . I consider it an empty word" (104).[6]

However unjust the vicissitudes of one's luck may seem, poly- and monotheists continually aver that the wheel of fortune is conscientiously turned by the hand of providence. Some pre-Christian notions of doom and nemesis are admittedly more harsh than the theology that superseded them, but they are equally insistent concerning the unalterable nature of divinely ordained events. To the pagan mind, whatever happened was what was destined to occur; it was always preordained in the stars, woven by the Parcae, or decreed since the beginning of time— the original meaning of the word "fate" (from the Latin *fatum*) is "that which is spoken," and even the gods of antiquity were subject to its doom. In the Icelandic sagas, even the notion of luck *(lukke)* is charged with supernatural implications. As Magnus Magnusson explains, "Good luck or ill luck was inherent in every individual, and ultra-sensitive men, like Njal or Hrut, could detect it in others, like an aura. Skarp-Hedin is 'ill-starred,' but Karl is 'lucky'. . . . One's luck was an inescapable part of the complex pattern of fate" (1960, 16).

Non-Calvinistic Christianity generally insists on the element of free will, but never at the expense of a providential teleology that may or may not be clearly made manifest on earth. The possibility of random or uncaused events was systematically suppressed, and fortuitous occurrences were never allowed to be considered truly fortuitous: divine vengeance, inscrutable providence, the whims of the goddess Fortuna, or the textile handiwork of the fates was invariably called on to provide a narrative order to the flux of experience. In the nineteenth century, this position was still frequently invoked: Father Picard tells Julien Sorel he must never speak of chance, but only of providence (*The Red and the Black*, bk. 2, chap. 1).

To be sure, various independent minds occasionally formulated doctrines of chance. Democritus believed that chance happenings first established cosmic order out of the aboriginal chaos, Aristotle acknowledged the existence of accidents as causes, Epicurus posited a causeless swerve in the trajectory of atoms, and Simplicius argued that fortune *(tyche)* was an all-embracing power ultimately steering all things. In the Renaissance, Montaigne and Bacon seem at times to adumbrate modern notions of chance, and Spenser, in the Mutability Cantos, offers a compelling account of the rule of the random before reinscribing it within a larger cosmic order.

Machiavelli and Shakespeare were more thoroughgoing, however. Leo Strauss argues that Machiavelli personifies the notion of fortune the better to reduce it to mere extrinsic accident (1959, 213–18), and Hanna Pitkin notes that "Fortune is like luck or chance; indeed, Machiavelli repeatedly equates them" (1984, 164). Such a conception also governs the world of *Antony and Cleopatra:* for man's participation in a world of change, "Shakespeare's dominant image is appropriately the game of chance," Michael Lloyd remarks (1962, 552). He continues:

> When Brutus predicts that men will fall "by Lottery" (J.C., II.i.137), he is referring to a game of chance played with a wheel like fortune's own [cf. also *Antony and Cleopatra* 2.2.281–82]. . . . The soothsayer had put Antony's relationship with Octavius in the context of the game, with the odds in Antony's favour; and Antony extends the view (II.iii.31, 43). It is as such a gaming contest that Cleopatra sees their opposition at Antony's death: "The oddes is gone" (IV.xv.83).

Here, an entirely modern notion of chance is set forth: arbitrary, random occurrences devoid of any providential purpose or mechanistic necessity, the simple result of an undetermined lot. Furthermore, the typical modernist fusion of a chance universe and a meddling, metafictional creator appears in *Antony and Cleopatra*, as the hero wonders whether the author of his destiny hasn't stacked the deck against him (Lloyd 1962, 553–54).

In lines reminiscent of Bacon's claim that "chiefly the mould of a man's fortune is in his own hands" ("On Fortune"), Thidias affirms:

> Wisdom and fortune combatting together,
> If that the former dare what it can,
> No chance may shake it.
>
> (*Antony and Cleopatra* 3.13.96–98)

But Antony of course continually sacrifices wisdom for the demands of passion, and for this reason he is particularly susceptible to the turn of events brought about by Octavius. In this play, "there is a tide in the affairs of men,/ Which, taken at the flood, leads on to fortune" (4.3.248–49), but Antony invariably seems to miss the boat. The wheel of fortune is here reduced to an arbitrary lottery devoid of any larger teleology, though capable of being affected by individual volition. These incursions into the ontological significance of the random, it must be emphasized, were quite uncommon; popular desires to perceive a larger order, along with ecclesiastics' efforts to maintain their ideological sway, worked assiduously against the subversive doctrine of chance.

During the Renaissance other forces were set in motion that would ultimately displace the concepts of fate, providence, and fortune. The concomitant rise of experimental science, the Reformation, and nontheological philosophy were finally responsible for a general decline in belief in the supernatural. The revolution in the educated Englishmen's *Weltanschauung* can be suggested by noting the shifting response to ghosts. In 1597, King James published his popular *Daemonologie*, which classified the types of unearthly spirits, noted their peculiarities, and offered advice on how to resist their powers. This work was quite representative of popular belief and was, if anything, more skeptical than most contemporary accounts. By 1765, however, Samuel Johnson, writing on *Macbeth*, found it necessary to explain the former prevalence of the "universal error" of the credulous belief in ghosts and witches, noting in Shakespeare's defense that "the scenes of enchantment, however they may now be ridiculed, were both by himself and his audience thought awful and affecting" (1960, 102).

On the Continent, the situation was similar: the historical Wallenstein (1583–1634), like many of his contemporaries, was a firm believer in astrology. When Schiller composed a drama about him (1798), the author despaired of making his hero's superstition credible, and in letters to Goethe confessed his own repugnance toward such "silliness."[7] A radical change in consciousness had occurred; the supernatural was no longer thought to be present in everyday existence. It is worth noting that Fielding's call for the suppression of the supernatural (*Tom Jones* , bk. 8, chap. 1) not only alluded to Horace's aesthetic pronouncement (73) but also responded to the practical, empiricist sensibilities of the growing middle class.

The notion of "special" (that is, interventionary) providence declines, and the modern meanings of "fortune," "destiny," and "necessity" become entwined, all connoting that which happens to occur, rather than that which has been preordained (see Barfoot 1982, 176–88). During this paradigm shift, chance replaces fortune in narrative discourse, the notion of providence is displaced by the concept of probability, and the status of coincidence shifts from the unnatural and inartistic to the ordinary and unremarkable.[8] In medieval, Renaissance, and Restoration texts, fortune had generally been viewed in relation to individual desires and ambitions, and it invariably implies a larger, governing (though often obscure) supernatural design. Chance, on the contrary, is impersonal, arbitrary, and subject to statistical quantification, while its effects on human aspirations are random and incidental. Major metaphors of fortune are the wheel, the moon, the tides, and a fickle woman; the dominant trope of chance, whether couched in terms of dice, cards, or lotteries, typically comes from gambling. (It is perhaps no coincidence that speculation on joint-stock companies, an extremely proper and profitable form of gambling, emerges around the same time.)

The end of the seventeenth century was the setting of seminal developments of the theory of probability in England. Earlier work on the subject had been rudimentary and as often as not conjoined to the supernatural: Geronimo Cardano had speculated on probabilities relating to games of chance (1564; pub. 1663) but had also written on astrology, magic, and occult divination; Blaise Pascal both formulated a "geometry of the die" *(aleae geometrica)* and worked out a foolproof wager with God. After 1660, nontheological investigations burgeoned, as mathematical probability theory emerged and the word "statistics" was invented. Hacking and Patey have meticulously traced the origins and development of the concept of probability; Hacking, following Foucault, goes so far as to assert that "as a matter of historical fact epistemic probability did not emerge until people thought of measuring it" (1975, 73), which was first done, he asserts, in the Port-Royal *Logic* of 1662. While Hacking may be overstating his case,[9] the proliferation of writings on the statistical probability of the occurrence of chance events— whether losing ships at sea, winning at dice games, or being struck by a lightning bolt—was truly impressive, especially in England.

In 1686, Aphra Behn's comedy of probability, *The Lucky Chance*, was performed on the London stage. The play's title refers both to the happy implausibility that opens the drama—the hero's chance interception of a revealing letter addressed to another—and also to a climactic game of dice that allows him, despite the odds, to attain in the end the woman he loves. In 1690, Sir William Petty's *Political Arithmetic* was published; three years later Edmund Halley's *Estimate of the Degrees of Mortality of Mankind* appeared, providing newly flourishing insurance companies

(Lloyd's was founded shortly after the great fire of 1666) with a mathematical basis for actuarial rates.

Although these researches were strictly arithmetical they were not felt to conflict with established religion. Abraham de Moivre's *The Doctrine of Chances* (translated into English in 1718) attempted to use the theory of probability to demonstrate the existence of God's design,[10] while Dr. Arbuthnot felt it necessary to aver that it was "no Heresy to believe" that providence allows ordinary matters to be subject to the rule of chance (Patey 1984, 73). In 1733, Pope could still postulate a happy correspondence between the laws of nature and the wisdom of divinity; eloquently promulgating Shaftesbury's synthesis of the competing claims of science and religion, Pope affirmed:

> All Nature is but Art unknown to thee;
> All chance direction, which thou canst not see
> (*Essay on Man* 1.10.289–90

Such an easy solution, or dissolution, of the problem of chance could not last. The literature of the middle of the eighteenth century explicitly addresses causal themes and explores their complexities and contradictions. Voltaire's *Candide* attacks many of the notions promulgated by Pope, while his "Zadig, or Providence" affirms the existence of inscrutable cosmological designs. *Roderick Random* confronts the issues of randomness and pattern in a narrative not nearly as desultory as is generally averred.[11] Laurence Sterne, despite inveighing against the notion of chance in a sermon, includes a chapter on chances in *Tristram Shandy*,[12] and Diderot amplifies and exacerbates Shandean notions of order and chaos in *Jacques le fataliste*, as Geoffrey Bremner has pointed out (1983, 170–87).

The contradictions between a providential ordering of events and the random workings of improbable chance, adumbrated by the novelists just mentioned, were formalized philosophically in Hume's work and mathematically by Laplace. In his discussion of miracles, Hume single-handedly demolished earlier attempts to infer God's design from the existence of unlikely or miraculous events by pointing out that no testimony was sufficient to establish a miracle, unless the testimony were of such a kind that its falsehood would be more miraculous than the fact that it purported to establish. Laplace, advocating a strictly determinist worldview, left no room for either God or chance; every

possible event in nature could be infallibly predicted down to the mi-
nutest detail by a sufficiently informed intelligence ("Laplace's demon").
This outlook, which seemed to be the logical conclusion of previous
speculation on statistical probability, resulted in the most comprehensive work on the subject up to that time—his *Theorie analytique des
probabilités* (1812).

Outside imaginative literature, which in the hands of many romantics flirted with various types of indeterminism, deterministic systems
in philosophy and the sciences moved to completely supplant the teleological Christian *Weltanschauung* that was no longer tenable. Logically minded anti-idealists have always been as suspicious of mere
chance as of divine orderings, and theorists from Democritus and
Aristotle to Voltaire, Laplace, and J. S. Mill have generally advocated
some form of causalism, the doctrine that denies the possibility of uncaused events and affirms the existence of unbroken chains of cause
and effect from the beginning of time to the end of eternity.[13] For them,
a chance event is either the intersection of two independent causal chains
or an effect the cause of which is unknown at the time. This alternative
conception is every bit as all-encompassing as theistic models and once
again no event is left uncaused or unexplained; a pandeterminism simply replaced supernatural teleology, and purposeless mechanism supplanted guiding deities. The model of the universe was still a perfectly
ordered one, but the machinery of nature no longer called for a divine
engineer.

Even Hume felt bound to acknowledge this general stance: "Though
there be no such thing as *Chance* in the world; our ignorance of the real
cause of any event has the same influence on the understanding and begets
a like species of belief or opinion" (1902, 56). While this implicitly affirms
the unprovable postulate of universal chains of causal connection interweaving all events that ever occurred, it also lays the foundations
for a strictly probabilistic account of the relations between events in
which cause and chance simply refer to strong and weak probabilities
of the appearance of a given event. In addition, Hume, by demolishing
the idea of a necessary first cause, laid the groundwork for the refutation of the principle that every effect must have a cause.[14] Despite
Hume's critique, the powerful deterministic models of the late-eighteenth
and early-nineteenth centuries paved the way for causal explanation of
apparently random phenomena throughout nature and society. In narrative literature, these scientific revolutions were often reflected by re-

lentless causal progressions in realist and naturalist fiction that left no place for supernatural designs or chance occurrences.

Though repeatedly ignored, denied, or suppressed, the notion of chance never entirely vanished and started to be reconceptualized in conjunction with other ideas previously thought to preclude its existence. In 1812 Hegel affirmed that the accidental both was caused and was causeless, that necessity determines itself as chance, and that chance is absolute necessity (*Logic* 2, bk. 3, sec. 2). Near the middle of the nineteenth century, an increasing number of figures drawing directly or indirectly on Hegelian ideas began to set forth a series of roughly comparable formulations. Friedrich Engels stated that chance and necessity are not mutually exclusive, but rather "both exist side by side in nature" (1940, 230), and that what is chance at one level of explanation can become necessity at another level, as demonstrated by Darwin's theory of natural selection. Somewhat earlier (1860), Emerson, in a rather different vein, similarly noted the interpenetration of these purportedly antithetical concepts. "[S]ee how fate slides into freedom, and freedom into fate, observe how far the roots of every creature run, or find, if you can, a point where there is no thread of connection" (1983, 961). It is precisely this thread Melville extends in Ishmael's well-known metaphysical commentary on Queequeg's mat weaving:

> [I]t seemed as if this were the Loom of Time, and I myself were a shuttle mechanically weaving and weaving away at the Fates. . . . this savage's sword, thought I, which thus finally shapes and fashions both warp and woof; this easy, indifferent sword must be chance—aye, chance, free will, and necessity—no wise incompatible— all interweavingly working together. The straight warp of necessity, not to be swerved from its ultimate course—its every alternating vibration, indeed, only tending to that; free will still free to ply her shuttle between given threads; and chance, though restrained in its play within the right lines of necessity, and sideways in its motions modified by free will, though thus prescribed to by both, chance by turns rules either, and has the last featuring blow at events. (1983, 1021–22)

Friedrich Nietzsche, an admirer of Emerson and enemy of Hegel, was soon to mount a more radical critique of causality. He frequently castigated what he considered false causal attributions (such as the idea of free will) and regularly drew attention to the neglected concepts of chance and chaos.[15] In a representative aphorism he states that supreme fatalism is nonetheless identical with chance and creative activity.[16] More importantly for the subsequent development of European philosophy, Nietzsche continually emphasizes the inherent unknowability of the noumenal world, and the subsequent fictionality of most discourse on causation. In a frequently cited passage he asserts: "[B]etween two utterly different spheres, as between subject and object, there is no causality, no accuracy, no expression, but at the utmost an *aesthetical* relation, I mean a suggestive metamorphosis, a stammering translation into quite a distinct foreign language. . . ." (1965, 510–11).

By 1885, C. S. Peirce was developing his doctrine of tychism, which contends that absolute chance is present in the universe, except where evolution gradually imposes natural laws on experience. In fiction, William Dean Howells in *The World of Chance* and *A Hazard of New Fortunes* pursues realism into the realm of chance, as necessity and the accidental struggle for explanatory supremacy. This arena of contestation was also attracting other authors, most notably George Eliot, Thomas Hardy, Joseph Conrad, and Theodore Dreiser. William Newton has drawn attention to Hardy's "counter-pointing of determinism with an uncanny concatenation of events that no determinist would think of owning to" (1951, 173). With some qualifications, this assessment would also apply to the other authors just mentioned. All, moreover, might very well agree with Dreiser's speculations on chance, cause, and effect that appear in his notebooks, where he suggests that spiders' webs and traps are simultaneously excellent illustrations *both* of the law of cause and effect and of the operation of chance:

> [W]e can truly say that any effect springs from a given cause and, more, that there is no such thing as a cause without an effect. At the same time, it is also true that involved with the probability of a given effect is the element of chance. That is, the cause of a probable effect can be arranged for or determined, although the probability of a given effect within a given time cannot always be even approximately indicated. In other words, any effect in connection with a pre-arranged cause may be indefinitely postponed, may not even occur. (1974, 43)

At this point, the notion of chance, always a stubborn presence in American fiction, had thoroughly pervaded even the works of authors who might have been expected to oppose it most vigorously. Subsequent deployments of ironic accidents in Faulkner, West, Hawkes, and

Pynchon are not innovations so much as additions to a long and rich tradition.

The early-twentieth century witnessed the first major cracks in the mechanistic causal models so diligently constructed by scientists of the preceding generations. Poincaré, in his *Calcul des probabilités*, had hedged away from Laplacian determinism, noting varieties of contingency, the impossibility of prediction when confronted by fortuity, and most importantly that the knowledge of the laws of probability does not eliminate chance. The last thesis is best illustrated by his example of an omniscient physician who, knowing when each client would die, could remove the ignorance of an insurance-company director, though this knowledge would not alter at all the dividends of the firm, since all the premiums were calculated according to statistical regularities. Chance events could no longer be attributed to an ignorance of causes, since one may, like Poincaré's hypothetical physician, know all causes and still need to invoke chance as part of the explanation of a course of events.

Henry Adams helped to inaugurate the suspicion toward seamless causal attribution that now is a commonplace among historiographers. "Historians undertake to arrange sequences,—called stories, or histories—assuming in silence a relation of cause and effect. These assumptions," Adams continues, "have been astounding, but commonly unconscious and childlike"; he himself is able only to perceive sequences of heterogeneous events, devoid of the causal cement that purports to connect them (1961, 382). Adams here mounts a critique of the implied causality of historical narratives that is analogous to Hume's attack on the notion of cause in metaphysics.

The notion of chance also proved central to dada and surrealist artists and writers. As Harriett Watts observes, "For Duchamp, chance was the tool by which one could break completely with aesthetic taste, with perceptual habits. Tzara tried to achieve a state of total indeterminacy where all predictable patterns . . . would have been rendered impossible" (1980, 156). Breton's *Nadja* is filled with wildly unlikely coincidences that nevertheless suggest a larger, mysterious order. It embodies the doctrine of *hasard objectif*, while his *Les Vases Communicants* investigates what happens to time, space, and the principle of causality in dreams as it asserts that dream states and waking life insistently permeate each other. Similarly, Aragon sought to reproduce in *Le Paysan de Paris* "the marvels of chance meetings and daily chance events that transformed ordinary living" (Balakian 1959, 106).

Newtonian physics, the paradigm for mechanistic, billiard ball-style causal theories, was overthrown in the first decades of the twentieth century through the work of Einstein, Planck, Heisenberg, and others, as is well known. William A. Wallace points out: "In 1958, a year before his death, Friedrich Waismann lectured at Oxford University on the subject 'The Decline and Fall of Causality,' and pinpointed 1927 [the year Heisenberg propounded his uncertainty principle] as the year that 'saw the obsequies' of causality in contemporary science" (1972, 163). As the investigation into subatomic particles has progressed, all intuitive presuppositions have become suspect; recent hypotheses have postulated the appearance of new particles ex nihilo, irregular and intermittent causal workings, and even a kind of negative causality that works backward in time.

Among the first to respond philosophically to the new developments in the physical sciences, Bertrand Russell (1910) devised a "force-field" theory of causation independent of chronology, in which cause and effect are seen as two aspects of the same process, rather than a temporally sequential relation connected by some causal glue (Russell did nevertheless admit that it sounds odd to say, as his theory demands, that the breaking of a window is the cause of the brick thrown through it as much as the hurled brick caused the pane to break).[17] A little earlier, Bergson had asserted the radical contingency of the external world and the subjective nature of all attributions of causality, a position modified and developed by Whitehead. Both metaphysicians believed they were providing a philosophical basis for the ongoing revolution in physics that seemed to corroborate their ideas.[18]

Other sciences gradually integrated the notion of chance. In developmental psychology, Piaget has documented the importance of the child's acquisition of the concept of the random and analyzed the stages of its evolution. Johan Huizinga, in his study of the central role of play in culture, *Homo Ludens*, identified chance as a defining component of play. In biology, Jacques Monod stressed the fundamental importance of what he termed "absolute coincidences," those that "result from the intersection of two totally independent chains of events" (1972, 114). This notion is essential in his account of the profound significance of chance mutations:

> The initial elementary events which open the way to evolution in the intensely conservative systems called living beings are microscopic, fortuitous, and utterly without relation to whatever may be

their effects upon teleonomic functioning. . . . In effect natural selection operates *upon* the products of chance and can feed nowhere else. . . ." (118)

Probability theory—that is, the science of chance—still continues to flourish and expand. The second half of the twentieth century saw the development of dynamic systems theory, fuzzy set theory, and the now rather discredited "catastrophe theory"—all early attempts to calculate the indeterminable that helped engender chaos theory.[19] Jung's concept of synchronicity, Freud's notion of the uncanny, and Derrida's revival of Epicurus's idea of the *clinamen* (uncaused swerve) have further integrated indeterminacy into the human sciences. Einstein, always skeptical about the bases of quantum mechanics, devoted most of his adult life to the development of a unified field theory that would not leave the basic structure of the universe to what he termed a dice-throwing God. He died without having achieved this aim. Einstein's failure nevertheless points toward—and backward to—earlier literary uses of gaming metaphors to describe the vicissitudes of human existence and the operation of natural forces. In this respect, nature seems to have come to imitate art.

Part One

Theory

1

Philosophical Systems, Fictional Worlds, and Ideological Contestations

At a very general level, the most fundamental interpretive questions we may ask of a narrative are causal ones. The frequent tensions between motive and action, word and deed, and intention and result are familiar to every student of fiction and drama. Similar dilemmas concerning the elusive roles of fortune, chance, necessity, providence, and metafictional impersonations of destiny also abound. Other related critical issues arise once we analyze causal connections between successive episodes in nonlinear texts, asking just what causes the events of chapter 4 to be narrated after those of chapter 3. Questions like these are so basic that they are easily overlooked; on the other hand, attempts to articulate such complex and confusing topics can quickly make the overzealous theorist feel like one of Milton's fallen angels, who

> apart sat on a hill retir'd,
> In thoughts more elevate, and reason'd high
> Of Providence, Foreknowledge, Will, and Fate,
> Fix'd Fate, Free Will, Foreknowledge Absolute,
> And found no end, in wandring mazes lost.
> *(Paradise Lost* 2.557–61)

The fact that Milton—like Dickens and a number of authors to be discussed—explicitly raises these issues in his work makes our theoretical task all the more urgent: for centuries, creative writers have unambiguously and at times provocatively thematized questions of causation in literary texts, but on this subject, criticism has for the most part been strangely silent. In fact, causality has been so undertheorized that most practicing critics may—very understandably—have no precise idea of just what a causal analysis of a work of fiction might entail. Still worse, the word "cause" does in all probability conjure up a series of largely unexamined associations that need to be adjusted or dispelled. Consequently, this chapter must to some extent function as a kind of disclaimer, specifying what will not appear in this book, and explaining why many common critical assumptions are in need of substantial revision. We will see that causal questions arise in many unexpected areas, and often fail to appear, at least in familiar guise, in other more conventional loci.

In this book, my working definition of cause will be one from common usage: a condition that occasions a change in events.[1] To effectively address the causal self-situating of authors of notoriously difficult texts, four distinctions should be kept in mind: (1) the causes of characters' behavior, (2) the embodiment or parody of metaphysical theories of causality within a literary work, (3) causal connection between successive episodes, segments, or story lines of a narrative text, and 4) the causal laws that govern a fictional world. Though conceptually distinguishable, these modes of causal construction are frequently interwoven, as my studies of individual texts should reveal. Nevertheless, these issues are logically independent, and conflating them can lead to reductionism, overgeneralization, or needless confusion.

Since this work focuses on the conceptually largest and most basic issues, I will not spend much time addressing the more local topics of the causes of characters' action except to point out cases where putative sources of behavior are rendered impossible by more general laws that are unknown to the characters. Jocasta, for example, believes she inhabits a world ruled by chance *(tyche)*, only to learn that fate ultimately governs all of her actions. Because of this focus, I will refer to Poe's "The Angel of the Odd," which recounts the terrible ordeal of a man who scoffs at the belief in improbable coincidences, but I must forgo "The Imp of the Perverse," which charts a similar progression through the maze of individual psychology. Modern incarnations of Poe's themes will suffer a similar fate: the surrealists' *hazard objectif* is an essential item in the intellectual history of chance, while the Gidean *acte gratuite*, on the other hand, applies only to individuals.

Philosophical theories of cause at times are parodied by authors of fiction and occasionally are embodied in literary texts. While the literary treatment of metaphysical notions of time, the self, and ontology frequently appear and are frequently discussed in criticism, the analogous subject of causality is almost never addressed. There are compelling reasons why this should be the case, as will be discussed later in this chapter, the most pressing of which is that at first glance it is not entirely clear in what ways a narrative that embodies a specific theory of causality would differ from any other narrative. To clarify this issue we must first identify the causal settings that ground every narrative; afterwards we may discern the unique contributions of philosophically minded novelists.

At this point it should be helpful to contrast the direction of this work with that taken by R. S. Crane in his 1952 essay, "On the Concept of Plot and the Plot of *Tom Jones*." Here Crane argues for a more expansive notion of plot that embraces action, character, and thought. The element missing from Crane's otherwise capacious account—setting— is what I wish to examine, particularly as it interacts with the sequencing of the work's events and the often mistaken perspectives of both character and narrator. Instead of an expanded notion of plot, I will be scrutinizing naked sequences of events. Neither am I interested in pursuing the moral questions Crane states are implicit in his concept. For these reasons, and because so many other theorists have felt a need to redefine yet again the idea of "plot," I will avoid whenever possible the use of the term in the rest of this work.

Among literary theorists, the word "cause" is most often used to describe the connection between successive events in a narrative. From Aristotle to E. M. Forster to Gerald Prince, critical theory has posited a distinction between narratives that are casually connected and those that are not. In the third chapter, I will suggest that this is an unfortunate distinction that obscures more than it reveals; the roots of causal connection extend much deeper and appear in more guises than is generally recognized. I argue that causal connection, however intermittent, deferred, or oblique, is a necessary condition of narrativity. At the same time, I try to show how various authors, alert to this condition, play on the boundaries of narrative by postponing or transgressing causal ties. Certain narratives, in fact, are so constructed that the ambiguity of the causal relations within the fiction are reproduced for the audience to experience, as the reader's interpretation of the text becomes an analogue of the protagonists' understanding of the world they inhabit.

The Causal Parameters of Fictional Worlds

The three aspects of causality just described all imply or refer back to the causal laws that regulate fictional worlds. As Meir Sternberg has explained (1978), the world depicted within a fiction always contains both a spatial and temporal setting, and a canon of probability peculiar to it.[2] I will suggest that there are three major types of causation that operate in a fictional world: supernatural (as in *Paradise Lost*), naturalistic (*Madame Bovary*), and the chance universes found in modern works like Borges's "The Lottery of Babylon." There is also a kind of meta-literary fourth dimension, present whenever a narrator or implied author tampers with the causal laws already established in the narrative. Furthermore, some of the most intriguing and compelling interpretive tensions arise whenever incompatible causal systems are made to collide. This may occur within the fiction, as when different characters offer competing explanations of the same events. In Pushkin's "The Queen of Spades," a young man, Tomskii, tells some fellow gamblers a story of his grandmother's ability to predict the cards that will win at faro. Upon hearing the strange tale, the men make the following comments:

> "Mere chance!" said one of the guests.
> "A fairy tale!" remarked Hermann.
> "Perhaps they were powdered cards," joined in a third.
> "I don't think so," Tomskii replied in a serious tone.
>
> (1983, 213)

All but Tomskii are operating on largely naturalistic assumptions, and in doing so they indicate the alternative types of causal worlds in which such events are possible. The first guest invokes coincidence; statistically unlikely events do occasionally occur, and this was one of them, though if the feat could be repeated, the notion of chance—or of the world in which such "chance" reigns—would have to be modified. Hermann questions the factuality of the events to be explained; in his opinion, such a concatenation of happenings can only occur in the supernatural world of the fairy tale; he believes it is more likely that his friend's story is false than that the laws of nature can be controverted so easily. The third man is the most insistently naturalistic. For him, the events can be explained by cunning, not accident: the cards were simply doctored. There is no mystery at all.

Tomskii's doubts, however, are troublesome. After all, he knows more about the events and character of this incident than the skeptics that surround him. Because of this, the interpretive burden shifts to the reader. We are now confronted with what Todorov terms a fantastic tale, and as the "coincidences" mount until they can no longer be coincidences, the reader must decide whether the causal world of the fiction is supernatural or naturalistic. The same dialectic is also present when naturalistic and chance worlds are contested in modern texts. Finally, it needs to be mentioned that whenever a character in a fantastic tale refers to events as a fairy tale, and the work itself is by a self-conscious author who admired Sterne, we must be alert to possible metaliterary meanings. And sure enough, this "fairy tale" in fact obsesses Hermann, driving him to the brink of madness—until a final preternatural stroke of fortune makes him permanently insane. In a very important respect, the subject of Pushkin's tale is the interpretation, verification, and reenactment of Tomskii's original narrative.

Within a single, consistent causal world characters will have different powers, intentions, hidden drives, and interpretive outlooks. Demigods may be pitted against larger cosmic forces, or individual desires may be eroded by economic necessity. In the Book of Joshua, the miracles of Jehovah triumph over those of Baal; the causal setting is a supernatural one, though many of the assembled personages do not know until the end the identity of the reigning divinity. In the nineteenth century the different deterministic systems of Marx, Darwin, and Freud jostled for explanatory supremacy of the social world within the confines of naturalism. In the realist works of Thomas Mann, Bernard Shaw, and the later Eugene O'Neill, the exegetical battleground is largely the same, and the choice of possible causal agencies is narrowly regulated. The same is true of character motivation: in the works of such authors, conscious and subconscious desires are pitted against biological forces and the logic of history. Despite the differences in causal agency, all these contests occur within a single naturalistic order and thereby form subdivisions within the larger conceptual framework of possible causal systems. A major aim of this study is to draw attention to the interpretive clashes between *incompatible* causal systems, rather than focusing on rival agencies within a single causal framework. Operating within such parameters, perhaps little will be lost, since traditional criticism has thoroughly explicated rival theological systems and the varieties of social determinism within individual texts. It is, once again, the most fundamental levels of causation that require exploration.

All four forms of causal setting appear in most periods of literary

history, though in different periods (and genres) a single type is frequently predominant. A glance at some prominent causal arrangements
over the last few centuries will reveal interesting developments and
variations. Fictional narratives of the sixteenth century and much of
the seventeenth century typically adhered to an aesthetic of the unexpected. These works were valued for their imaginative presentation of
extraordinary events, surprising encounters, preternatural occurrences,
and outlandish realms. Barnaby Rich, in the preface to his collection of
tales *Farewell to Military Profession* (1581), states that most of its stories
"are tales that are but forged only for delight, neither credible to be
believed, nor hurtful to be perused." This statement applies equally
well to most prose fiction of the period. In the supernatural setting of
the moral allegory and pastoral romance as well as the naturalistic world
of the picaro, voyager, or criminal, improbability was embraced and
the connection between successive events was often lax.

In the eighteenth century, the balance shifted from the extraordinary to more diurnal notions of probability. Henry Fielding was one of
the most forceful proponents of what was then called fidelity to nature
and justness of design, and he invented the term "comic epic in prose"
to designate the kind of novel he preferred to write, in which the supernatural was banished, the ordinary and probable were enfranchised,
and successive events were directly caused by the actions that preceded
them. Skillful plotting replaced flights of fancy, and Fielding was careful to inform his reader of this fact. Toward the end of *Jonathan Wild*,
after the generous Mr. Heartfree unexpectedly finds his death sentence
commuted, the author addresses his reader precisely to "endeavour to
show him that this incident, which is undoubtedly true, is at least as
natural as delightful; for we assure him we would rather have suffered
half mankind to be hanged than have saved one contrary to the strict-
est rules of writing and probability" (177). Fielding's causal synthesis
is more rich than I have indicated; as the passage just quoted should
suggest, dictates of poetic justice and the desires of the audience are
also fulfilled. More significantly, the larger demands of the notion of
providence are upheld: it always reserves for men like Wild a special
end—the noose of a rope; concerning the altruistic Heartfrees, we are
assured that "Providence will sooner or later procure the felicity of the
virtuous and innocent" (201).

The happy union of probability, verisimilitude, and providential
design could not be sustained. Romantic authors loosened the connec-

tion between events to include interstices for the mysterious and the fortuitous, as well as the perfectly timed (indeed operatic) arrival of the hero in the nick of time. Possible causal agencies proliferated and the fantastic emerged as a major genre of the period. This new attitude toward causation is forcefully expressed and defended by Walter Scott who, in his preface to *The Monastery*, goes so far as to assert that the presence of unknown and mysterious causes is more realistic than carefully arranged causal skeins:

> For whatever praise may be due to the ingenuity which brings to a general combination all the loose threads of a narrative, like the knitter at the finishing of her stocking, I am greatly deceived if in many cases a superior advantage is not attained by the air of reality which the deficiency of explanation attaches to a work written on a different system. In life itself many things befall every mortal of which the individual never knows the real cause or origin; and were we to point out the most marked distinction between a real and a fictitious narrative, we would say that the former in reference to the remote causes of the events it relates is obscure, doubtful, and mysterious, whereas in the latter case it is a part of the author's duty to afford satisfactory details upon the causes of the events he has recorded, and, in a word, to account for everything.

The rise of nineteenth-century realism led to the suppression of providential teleology and the marginalization of chance. Supernatural orderings were superseded by the workings of material forces, and characters' sentimental or religious glossings of events were frequently revealed to have all-too-human origins and motives. The play of chance, including the Romantics' opportunistic overuse of the "fortunate coincidence" to keep the plot moving, was rigorously curtailed. Robert Louis Jackson's careful study of chance and design in *Anna Karenina* discloses the ways in which Tolstoy introduces ostensible coincidences that later in the novel turn out to be probable or even inescapable occurrences. All the apparently "chance" events are shown to be "very far from *pure chance*" (324) and are instead the result of predilection, compulsion, inevitability, or skillful plot construction. From this kind of fiction divine intervention and fortunate coincidences are equally excluded so that the extensive effects of social and biological forces can be shown in all their complexity and self-sufficiency: within this aesthetic, there is little place for any other explanatory principle.

By contrast, many twentieth-century works assert the objectivity of chance and the arbitrariness of human destinies. Marcel Proust's *Remembrance of Things Past* is arguably the high-modernist novel par excellence, and it is certainly a paradigmatic text for the analysis of causation in modern fiction. Chance events and unexpected coincidences appear throughout the novel, analogical correspondences between parallel story lines displace direct causal connections between events, subtle but insistent metafictional dramas permeate the text, and Bergsonian notions of causality are assiduously embodied in the structure of incidents. But Proust's most fascinating achievement may well be his manipulation of tangentially conjoined episodes: the most wildly heterogenous occurrences, however abrupt, disjointed, or arbitrary, always seem finally to coalesce into a tenuous, circuitous, but undeniable pattern. As Genette observes, Marcel's meeting with Gilberte's daughter, Mlle. de Saint-Loup, provides him with

> the opportunity for a general "replay" of the main episodes of his existence, episodes which until then were lost to insignificance because of their dispersion and are now suddenly reassembled, now made significant by being bound all together amongst themselves, because all are bound now to the existence of this child who was born Swann and Guermantes. . . . chance, contingency, arbitrariness all wiped out, his life's portrait now suddenly "captured" in the web of a structure and the cohesiveness of a meaning. (1980, 56–57)

In a typical Proustian antithesis, the arbitrary, unconnected, and chance events that interpenetrate Marcel's life (and the lives of those around him) form a coherent aesthetic design in—and only in—the book he will write.[3] Swann's life, his frustrated love for Odette, and his uncompleted monograph on Vermeer never constitute part of a direct causal chain with the other events of the novel, but function as a negative analogy of Marcel's transformation of his own life and failed loves into a finished artwork, as what is experienced as chance becomes reinscribed as compositional design. The moral of this modernist stance is that the coherence and significance sought in life can only exist in an avowed fiction.

This brief sketch of causal developments is only intended to serve as a rough outline and does not imply any teleology; in the pages that follow I will suggest that the periods of literary history were considerably less homologous than is necessarily implied by such an overview, and even that some of the representative examples adduced above are more complicated than I have specified here.[4] Nevertheless, it is to be hoped that this account will help identify the issues that need to be clarified, as well as suggest the historical framework of the construction of causation in fictional narratives.

CAUSALITY, INTERPRETATION, AND THE ACT OF READING

In many respects, interpretation and causality are two sides of the same coin. Confronted by multiple and mutually exclusive explanatory options, characters and readers alike are impelled to weigh the evidence, take hermeneutical stands, and adjust prior expectations to meet anomalous incidents. The more ambiguous, unlikely, or contradictory the causal agency appears to be, the greater the demand for interpretive accuracy becomes. In didactic narratives like medieval morality plays and what Susan Suleiman refers to as "authoritarian fictions," the audience is expected to identify the governing causal logic, even as the characters struggle to make sense of the ordering of their world. In other kinds of works, a more sustained ambiguity reigns, one which can lead to a number of intriguing intersections between protagonists' struggles to understand the causal laws of the world they inhabit and readers' attempts to interpret the text. Todorov has defined the fantastic tale as a work that is suspended between naturalistic and supernatural interpretations for readers as well as characters, and an analogous kind of uncertainty is shared by the protagonists and audiences of medieval dream visions and modern oneiric works (Strindberg's *A Dream Play*, Kafka's *The Castle*). In the later fictions of Samuel Beckett, precise causal relations are never fully disclosed; like the unnamed figures that crawl or hobble through these texts, the reader is led through a stark chaos of false starts, contradictory disruptions, and events that are first described and then denied. Borges's mazes, like Blanchot's dead ends, are equally designed to overwhelm the protagonist and entrap the reader.

A common feature of modernist and postmodern narratives is the tendency to interrogate the boundary between fact and fiction, lived experience and the act of reading. Often a text is constructed in such a way that the hermeneutical problems confronting a character are staged so that the reader is also forced into a similar drama of interpretation and causality, as both try to make sense of the same series of apparently unconnected or contradictory narrative fragments. As Wolfgang Iser notes, by continually altering the frame of reference, modern novelists create "a continual process of transformation that leads back into itself and not into a composite image of reality. The result of this process, triggered and arranged by the serial arrangement of perspectives, is that the reader, in striving to produce the aesthetic object, actually produces the very conditions under which reality is perceived and comprehended" (1978, 102–3). In other words, readers are given the raw material out of which narratives are formed and must use their own interpretive acumen to determine the existence and direction of causal connection, as we do in the more dubious confusions of our lives, not knowing what context, if any, to locate indecipherable actions within.

It is worth pausing to examine a more local example of the interplay between the characters' and readers' interpretations of events. Near the end of *The House of the Seven Gables*, the following sequence of events occurs: Judge Pyncheon summons his cousin Clifford in order to blackmail him. The two are alone in the drawing room. Clifford leaves, the judge is found dead, and Clifford then flees. A supernatural reading will view this as the latest effect of Maule's curse, which has been "haunting" the Pyncheons for centuries. A naturalist will suspect foul play, postulating an efficient cause (namely, Clifford's fingers) between their private meeting and the judge's asphyxiation. A reader impressed by chance, which strikes frequently in this novel, will write the incident off as a particularly devious coincidence. On the other hand, a metaliterary reader will note a very suspicious series of narrative repetitions that defy coincidence or probability and strongly suggest that Hawthorne is very much taking fate into his own hands.

The original death of Colonel Pyncheon occurred the same way, and so did old Jaffrey Pyncheon's, for whose "murder," we are informed, Clifford was unjustly sent to prison on merely circumstantial evidence. What Hawthorne is doing is recreating similar pieces of evidence, in order to see whether the reader will come to the same erroneous conclusions as did the jurors who first sent Clifford to jail. The series of events chronicled in the text, after they are reenacted, precipitate an interpretive confrontation as the reader is forced to become an accomplice of either Clifford, his persecutors, or his creator. Moreover, the subsequent revelation of the actual circumstances can most fully corroborate only one of the possible causal stances (though Hawthorne does not definitively refute all of the others; in particular, he leaves some wiggle room for his supernatural interpreters). In this way, the reader's values, preconceptions, and hermeneutical acuity are tested by the text.

Modern narratives often conflate or provoke the balance between the actual and the fictive world. We may find this in such odd subgenres as the "nonfiction novel," autobiographical performance art, and certain hypertexts. As Linda Hutcheon observes, many recent metafictional texts make explicit demands on the reader, as a kind of cocreator, for "intellectual and affective responses comparable in scope and intensity to those of his life experience. In fact, these responses are shown to be a *part of* his life experience" (1984, 5).

Even if we feel that Hutcheon's language is a bit too strong, her thesis is certainly cogent. Comments on fiction making within a fiction often have implications for the processing of the text as well as the construal of reality. The act of interpretation, which may be to a large extent the accurate perception of genuine causal patterns, is equally at work when we piece together the events of a fiction or scrutinize the narratives that pervade our everyday lives. And, as a number of recent theorists have pointed out, the narratives we live by are frequently drawn from fiction. In this study I try to preserve the sharp edges of this dialectic to do justice to the integrity and intricacies of a fictional world without denying its many connections to the one we inhabit. Here the concept of cause is instructive: nothing could be more extrinsic than the convoluted notions of long-dead philosophers, yet the parody of or homage to such theories can often explain how a text achieves its distinctive configurations and engenders its powerful effects.

POTENTIAL OBJECTIONS

Before proceeding further, it is necessary to address the suspicion of causality that has recently emerged in some sectors of the critical community that would have us believe that the relation of cause and effect is somehow spurious, dangerous, or reactionary. To begin at the broadest level, Roy Jay Nelson has succinctly articulated the general doubts of a number critics by stating that "causation is indeed not a truth but a hypothesis, not an entity found in nature, but rather a useful perceptual grid in the minds of human observers" (1990, ix). He goes on to assert that he sees causation "as a subjective pattern, as a model of some practical utility in the specific situations of everyday life, but meaningless as a scientific or philosophical generality" (xxvii). Causal relations, however, cannot be so easily reduced to mere subjective perceptions. Consider for a moment the old story frequently related by philosophy teachers about the farmer and his wife traveling by train to the city. The farmer sees another passenger eating a small orange fruit and asks what it is. "A kumquat," the passenger responds, offering one to both husband and wife. The farmer bites into his just as the train enters a tunnel; he quickly shouts, "Don't eat it Marge—it'll make you go blind!" Here we do indeed have a subjective attribution of causal connection, a hypothetical grid or pattern in the mind of a human observer, but this particular causal hypothesis is false: the eating of kumquats (unlike the drinking of tainted moonshine) does not cause loss of vision. The same distinction is articulated by the narrator of Geoffrey Wolff's *Providence* as he describes the mental operations of the character Skippy: "He was like a person throwing a light switch just as a volcano erupts, thinking he has done it. . . . Cause and effect were just rumors where Skippy dwelled" (1991, 177). We need the notion of accurate and inaccurate causal attribution to function in the world and to analyze fictional texts that play with or problematize real and imaginary causal progressions.

Several feminist theorists have also questioned the concept of cause and suggested it is an integral part of an oppressive patriarchal master narrative. Gayle Greene summarizes and quotes representative statements on this subject:

> Pearson and Pope describe the "assumption that life occurs in a logical, linear order" and is "determined by linear, causal relationships" as fundamentally patriarchal (pp. 216–217). Patricia Tobin links time as a line, an irreversible arrow whose trajectory is determined by original intention, the causality of past event controlling future, to "the genealogical imperative.". . . "the prestige of cause over effect . . . is analogous to the prestige of the father over the son" (p.7). (1991, 15)

These and similar statements, many of them much more sweeping, contain an important truth and also, I believe, obscure a significant distinction. The rigorous and ruthless "marriage plot," complete with its limited possibilities for female behavior, narrow causal progressions, and definitive closure—in which the female protagonist was invariably left married, dead, or in anguished isolation—is indeed a primary oppressive force, as are the constricting, patriarchal teleologies that accompanied it. The problem is not the concept of cause, but the false causes and enforced progressions of events determined by the patriarchy. Indeed the idea of causation is essential to feminist discourse and all human discourse. Suspected causal links between pornography and violence against women, the causes of the neglect of significant female writers through history, the search for the cause of toxic shock syndrome, the socioeconomic causes of the origin of patriarchy in ancient Greece—these are important and fundamental questions that must be investigated, not pseudoissues that must be rejected as hopelessly contaminated by the phallogocentric discourse of causation. The idea of cause, like the concept of number or the notion of space, is in itself gender neutral and ideologically indifferent, even though historical individuals have repeatedly invoked false causes, skewed various numbers, and delimited public spaces in order to suppress women. Causality must not be reduced to or confused with teleology, naturalistic notions of probability, or patriarchal master codes, all of which do indeed presuppose causation, but none of which is entailed by the concept of cause.

Several recent French theorists have attacked or attempted to deconstruct the notion of cause; these attempts in turn have engendered significant critical responses, some of which are not as well known as they deserve to be. Roland Barthes, it will be remembered, suggested that "the mainspring of narrative is precisely the confusion of consecution and consequence, what comes *after* being read in narrative as what is *caused by*; in which case narrative would be a systematic application of the logical fallacy denounced by Scholasticism in the formula *post hoc, ergo propter hoc*" (1977, 44). The implication that causal attribution is somehow inherently fallacious, dispensable, and suspicious is open to a number of objections, as we have already seen. It might further be noted that in the *Poetics* Aristotle stresses the importance of the distinction between mere sequence and causally connected sequence that Barthes attempts to elide: "It makes all the difference whether any given event is a case of *propter hoc* or *post hoc*" (1971, 54). Mieke Bal, in what may be a direct response to Barthes' statement, demonstrates the importance of distinguishing between consecution and consequence: "It is a frequent misconception that chronological and causal sequences are always interrelated. It is true, of course, that one can only kill one's father after having been engendered. One may even do so because one is engendered by one's father; but there may also be entirely different reasons" (1985, 42). This example, I believe, effectively refutes Barthes's claim.

Paul de Man, in *Allegories of Reading*, attempts to find a deconstruction of the principle of cause and effect in a passage from *The Will to Power* that de Man claims is characteristic of Nietzsche's later work. Focusing on Nietzsche's mention of the *"chronological reversal* which makes the cause reach consciousness later than the effect," de Man dubiously derives that, for Nietzsche, "the objective, external cause is itself the result of an internal effect" (1979, 107). Here de Man seems to be confusing the sequence of cause and effect with the sequence of one's discovery of the cause of an already perceived effect—a confusion Nietzsche is himself careful to avoid in the way he has phrased this distinction. It is easy to quarrel with de Man's exegesis on many grounds: he never mentions the main thrust of Nietzsche's paragraph from which the line is extracted (it is a critique of phenomenalism, not causality), he ignores other related passages in *The Will to Power* that could clarify Nietzsche's meaning, and he fails to mention any of the sustained, intriguing, and at times contradictory discussions of causality throughout Nietzsche's published work.[5] Nor are these hard to find: *The Twilight of the Idols* contains an entire chapter on "the four great errors" of causal discourse and attribution, and the fourth section of this chapter elaborates on most of the ideas mentioned in the passage de Man scrutinizes. It is difficult not to be skeptical of the conclusion of this idiosyncratic reading, that the "two sets of polarities, inside/outside and cause/effect, which seemed to make up a closed and coherent system (outside causes producing inside effects) has [*sic*] now been scrambled into an arbitrary, open system in which the attributes of causality and of location can be deceptively exchanged, substituted for each other at will" (107–8). For Nietzsche, cause and effect are not arbitrary, scrambled, or reversible—it is individual *perceptions* of real and imagined causes that are faulty.

But this kind of criticism may be missing the larger point. De Man after all is "not primarily interested in [the passage's] specific 'thesis' but rather in the manner in which the argument is conducted" (107). Perhaps this is not a mere but a major misreading, a necessary blindness that leads to significant insight. Instead of dismissing it as faulty scholarship, we should examine de Man's thesis on its own merits. Here we may turn to the work of Jonathan Culler, who extends and elaborates de Man's position to explain the "deconstruction of causality." Building on the passage from Nietzsche as filtered by de Man, Culler claims that an effect, such as a feeling of pain, "causes the production of a cause," namely the discovery of the pin that caused the pain (1982, 87). He goes on the affirm that deconstruction reverses the "hierarchical opposition of the causal scheme" (88) and demystifies the originary status of cause (88). In a review of Culler's book, John R. Searle points out that there is nothing in the "pain . . . pin" example to support the idea that the effect causes its cause: "The experience of pain causes us to look for its cause and thus indirectly causes the discovery of the cause. The idea that it produces the cause is exactly counter to what the example actually shows," he explains (1983, 74). Searle also denies that there is any causal hierarchy to be dismantled, "since the two are correlative terms: one is defined in terms of the other" (74).

One might speculate further on the reasoning that led Culler to identify cause rather than effect as the primary term of the binary pair. Relatively minor causes have produced catastrophic effects in Western myth, literature, and historical discourse from the abduction of Helen to Desdemona's lost handkerchief to the shot fired in Sarajevo in August 1914. Surely it is not cause but effect, with its attendant claims of necessity, teleology, closure, and the logic of history, that is uppermost in the hierarchy of a functionalist culture and most in need of vigorous deconstructive displacement.

Searle also observes that Culler uses the term "origin" in two distinct senses, the causal origin of the pain and the (epistemic) origin of our discovery of its cause; Culler's argument hinges on a confusion of these two senses. One might further observe that not all causes are temporally prior to their effects; some are simultaneous (the movements of a seesaw, the orbit of planets). Culler claims that the "distinction between cause and effect makes the cause an origin, logically and temporally prior" (88). Since we have just seen that cause is not logically and need not be temporally prior to effect, we must conclude that there is no hierarchical opposition there to deconstruct. It is easy to understand why Searle characterizes Culler's discussion as "a tissue of confusions" even as he affirms the need for careful scrutiny and criticism of "common sense" prejudices about causation (74). We may conclude that the notion of cause is far more difficult to deconstruct than is generally assumed.[6]

It is necessary to examine a final objection to the kind of analysis that will inform this study. Robert Newsom has recently propounded an intriguing conundrum he refers to as "the antinomy of fictional probability." He states that it "is logically not only unnecessary, but nonsensical" to assert that the "plot of *Oliver Twist* is too full of coincidences to be probable" (1988, 8–9). One must either enter the fictional world and accept the pretense of the fiction, or remain in the real world and recognize the fictionality of the novel. In either case, Newsom continues, "there ought to be no question of ascribing degrees of probability to the novel's plot, for from the standpoint of the world of the fiction the events it describes do not put us in doubt because they are certainly true, while from the standpoint of the real world they do not put us in doubt because they are certainly false" (9).

The inadequacy of Newsom's position becomes clear once we try to apply it to narratives governed by different canons of probability or to probabilistic statements made by narrators or characters. It does not make much sense to complain that a fairy tale, an Aristophanic comedy, or a text like *Gulliver's Travels* is improbable, since works like these are constructed independent of probabilistic concerns. *Oliver Twist*, by contrast, is a novel that adheres to the general aesthetic program of realism and is set in and around Dickens's London. Consequently, it is perfectly appropriate to attempt to determine the degree to which the causal system of the novel conforms to or diverges from the probabilities of lived experience—in fact, literary realism has historically asserted just such a congruence. Logically speaking, Newsom might just as well affirm the senselessness of referring to time or space in a novel, since these are categories by which we measure events and areas of the real world, while the events and spaces of a novel are merely fictional.

Another problem with Newsom's position is that it discourages examination of the very questions of causal agency that Dickens invokes. In the first paragraphs of *Oliver Twist*, the narrator plays with the concepts of probability and of providence; in later chapters, the notions of destiny, chance, fate, and fortune are set forth. If one accepts "the antinomy of fictional probability," both the dialectic of causality present in *Oliver Twist* and Dickens's gradual retreat from a providential causal system during the course of his career (a retreat meticulously documented by Thomas Vargish [1985, 89–162]) must remain unexplored.

If it is true that "[p]robability statements about the characters or plots in imaginative literature logically belong to a different space than do statements about the real world, and there is something fundamentally strange—or absurd—about discussions of the probability of Mr. Pickwick" (96), then what could Newsom say concerning probabilistic statements made by fictional characters? Observing the successful duping of Malvolio, Fabian remarks to Sir Toby, "If this were played upon a stage now, I could condemn it as an improbable fiction" (*Twelfth Night* 3.4.119–20). Newsom's opposition between fictional and real worlds breaks down here, since the fictional character believes he inhabits the real world, and in the real world such events are indeed implausible. The theoretical model I am employing can make sense of such statements, and even suggest that they are probably inevitable. A similar situation arises in Poe's "The Angel of the Odd," in which the narrator, perusing a newspaper story that recounts the curious death of a boy who mistakenly sucked on the wrong end of a dart blower, becomes enraged at the journalists that concocted what he feels is such a poor and obvious hoax: "These fellows, knowing the extravagant gullibility of the age, set their wits to work in the imagination of improbable possibilities—of odd accidents, as they term them; but to a reflecting intellect . . . such as I myself possess, it seems evident at once that the marvelous increase of late in these 'odd accidents' is by far the oddest accident of all" (490). The narrator thus invokes the probabilistic expectations that the reader normally applies to everyday existence and employs them to question the factuality of purportedly nonfictional accounts of dubious events. One not only can make probabilistic statements concerning fictional events; in some cases, the fictions demand that one do so.

In the end, Newsom's position depends on a near total separation between fictional worlds and the real world. But, as "possible worlds" theory has shown, there can be no such thing as a totally fictional world. As Keir Elam states concerning dramatic representation, "Dramatic worlds, to the extent that they are representable *in*. . . . the actual world of the spectators, are always accessible *to* that world. . . . The spectator assumes that the represented world, unless otherwise indicated, will obey the logical and physical laws of his own world" (1980, 103–4). And these include the laws of probability. Without such an assumption, Elam continues, it would be necessary for a drama to specify *all* the properties of its fictional world, and no reference "could be made, for example, to a 'woman' or a 'battle' without defining the referents in full" (104).[7] Imagined universes are dependent on and in constant interaction with the world of our experience, and self-conscious writers of fiction play mischievously on the shifting boundaries of connection and contamination.[8] Though Newsom's hypothesis is elegant and tempting, and is very useful in discussing the ontological status of fictional characters, I feel it must finally be rejected as needlessly limiting and ultimately implausible when extended to the causal systems of fictional worlds.

CANISIUS COLLEGE LIBRARY
BUFFALO, N.Y.

Philosophical Systems and Narrative Construction

The precise relations between philosophical constructs, ideological stances, and narrative practice are often—understandably—misconstrued, and some preliminary clarifications are indispensable. Perhaps the greatest single source of confusion is what might be called the "monistic fallacy": the idea that a character's behavior necessarily implies a type of narrative organization that in turn rests on particular metaphysical assumptions that support a specific ideology. Careful analysis will show that these complex issues cannot be lumped together so facilely. To do justice to our subject, it is necessary to scrutinize the relation between the motives of individuals and the causal setting of a fictional work, to determine what it means for a philosophical theory of cause to be incorporated into a literary narrative, and to distinguish the very different causal traditions that inform the history of philosophy, the history of literature, and the history of official ideologies in such a way as to be able to discern both idiosyncratic developments and significant convergences.

Many literary critics assume that there is always a direct and invariable connection between a given ontology and the question of free will. A naturalistic author, it is frequently averred, must deny the freedom of the will in order to be philosophically consistent.[9] But in fact no such invariant entailment exists; generally speaking, the question of the freedom of the will is logically distinct from macrocosmic ontological issues.[10] To use the terms of this study, a supernatural view is compatible with both determinism (Greek or Calvinistic fatalism) and the belief in free will (most Christian positions); a naturalistic view of the universe may embrace or deny determinism in the sphere of human actions; and modern cosmologies that affirm the uncaused, theoretically indeterminable, or random nature of subatomic particles are entirely consonant with either determinism or indeterminism on the subject of free will, as a cursory glance through any anthology of philosophical papers on this subject will quickly demonstrate. Causality at the ontological level is logically distinct from issues of the source of human behavior, and this very distinction is important to observe if we are to appreciate the drama of causation present in many of the works discussed in chapter 3. Throughout, my primary concern is with ontological systems; forays into the very different question of individual volition will only be made when it is fused in literary narratives with the larger, independent concerns of metaphysics.

It is also the case that the ties that connect the causal world within a fiction to philosophical theories of cause on the one hand and to more general ideological concerns on the other are rarely simple or direct. In both cases, the relation may be one of embodiment, parody, or the absence of any significant connection. For example, close scrutiny of Aristotle's *Poetics* and *Metaphysics* will not reveal any bond between the accounts of causality in each work. The injunction that a poet should narrate a single action rather than a series of independent ones has nothing to do with the more abstract doctrine of the varieties of possible causation. And perhaps the one cannot in principle have any consequences for the other. Metaphysical investigations into the nature of cause are so general that they must embrace all possible individual causal interactions, whatever they may be, or however they may be represented. The levels of analysis are incommensurable, so the results of one cannot usually affect the other. Whether an author writes a *Theseid* or *Iliad* can have no implications for a universal theory of causation, and the view that causality has two, four, or six components is irrelevant to poetic doctrines of the unity of action. Such an incommensurability of independent levels of analysis is more easily discerned with more familiar examples: that cellular behavior follows fixed laws does not mean that human behavior is equally deterministic, even though we are entirely composed of cells; similarly, the fact that there is an inherent indeterminability in the behavior of certain atomic particles does not prove that human behavior cannot be deterministic, even though we are, like our cells, made up of just such particles. In fact, to make such an argument about either free will or narrative causality is to commit the logical fallacy of confusing qualities of the parts with qualities of a whole, which Aristotle clarifies in the "Sophistic Elenchi," appended to the *Topics*.

For this reason, there is no need to construct a typology or history of theories of causality set forth by professional philosophers. Such a schema would be largely irrelevant to a study of literature. Though creative writers dabble with philosophical notions from time to time, very few are sufficiently Faustian to wade through volumes of highly technical quiddities. Then there is the additional problem of a philosophical theory's embodiment in a narrative. Even assuming that they were aware of and agreed with Leibnitz's attempts to revive the Aristotelian notion of final cause, how could someone like Wieland, Beaumarchais, or Samuel Richardson actually place one into the fairly rigid genres they worked within? Even in the case of Kleist, who did read

Kant and was strongly affected by his writings—poring over the *Critique of Pure Reason* almost drove him insane—even Kleist never alludes to or precisely embodies the Kantian distinction between objective and subjective causality.[11] Nor should this be surprising: if Kant's position is accurate, it will be true of every possible causal occasion, and Kleist's fictional events, insofar as they are mimetic, will describe the same world. That is, a mimetic work, by definition, will reproduce the same situations of the physical world that theoretical formulations are invented to explain. To take a different perspective, whether one prefers Aristotle's or Newton's accounts of falling bodies, a rock will fall to earth faster than a feather. In a mimetic work of any period this fact will be observed, in a nonmimetic fiction it need not be. In neither case is a particular theory of gravitation implied.

It should also be noted that in the rare cases when a philosophically acute novelist starts to play with causality, it is often at a very basic level. Once George Eliot (Feuerbach's translator) or Lewis Carroll (an Oxford logician) goes to work, it is to invert the order of cause and effect and thereby call into question the notion of cause itself. The killing of Cock Robin is remembered before it occurs in *Through the Looking Glass*, and Daniel Deronda does not learn of his Jewish origins until after he is attracted to Judaism, without any intervening agency of "genetic sympathy" being involved. This is not a question of Locke versus Berkeley, but whether an effect can precede its cause—a question philosophers wouldn't begin to ask until the middle of our own century.[12] Neither is it accurate to aver that only after Hume could such thoughts be conceived, since Shakespeare performs the same inversion of cause and effect in *Macbeth*.[13]

But most importantly, any theory of causation, philosophical or otherwise, can appear in a narrative fiction only as an explanation of or challenge to the general framework of causation that governs an invented universe. That is, every narrative has a causal setting; if a philosophical theory of cause is invoked, it can be understood only in relation to the laws of probability that govern the fictional world. This should also help to explain why narrative embodiments of specific philosophical theories of causality are infrequent and tend to be objects of parody, often in nonrealistic texts. The theories are treated not as actual descriptions of the interaction of events in the world, but as the fabulous setting of a universe that can only exist in a fiction. This may be done in three ways. In Chaucer's Tale of Melibee, Aristotle's six kinds of cause are employed to analyze a specific event in a largely mimetic world; all six are refuted by the text, written off as philosophical fictions ultimately devoid of explanatory power. Similarly, in *Tristram Shandy*, Sterne concocts the improbable connections that would have to exist if Locke's theories of associationism were correct.[14]

An analogous stratagem is vividly employed by Borges in his invention of a Berkeleyan universe in "The Circular Ruins" or the Humean inhabitants of Tlön, and by Calvino's reinscriptions of Zeno and Nietzsche in "t zero." In these works, the authors construct the fabulous universes that would have to exist if the theories of these philosophers were valid. Such a story can be viewed effectively as a highly imaginative reductio ad absurdum of the philosophical system it dramatizes. Beckett's *Molloy*, which I discuss later at some length, employs both kinds of critique: the character Molloy seems to have internalized Hume's skepticism and consequently fails to perceive genuine causal progressions. At the same time, the nature of the world he inhabits is sufficiently curious to justify a good deal of suspicion concerning apparent relations of cause and effect.

In the work of Proust and Nabokov, Bergsonian conceptions of time and cause are defended and embodied in a more serious manner within narrative structures that were invented to challenge the traditional form of the realistic novel. In *Time and Free Will*, Bergson inveighs against the intellect's fragmentation of the flow of duration, but notes:

> Now, if some bold novelist, tearing aside the cleverly woven curtain of our conventional ego, shows us under this appearance of logic a fundamental absurdity, under this juxtaposition an infinite permeation of a thousand different impressions which have already ceased to exist the instant they are named, we commend him for having known us better than we knew ourselves. This is not the case, however, and the very fact that he spreads out our feeling in a homogeneous time, and expresses its elements by words, shows us that he in his turn is only offering us its shadow. . . . (Quoted in Mendilow 1952, 152–53)

Proust of course took up Bergson's challenge, but only after two or three early attempts was he able to create the narrative form that would enclose this stance most effectively. Again, it should be emphasized that the narrative embodiment of philosophical theories of cause is relatively uncommon; when it does occur, the causal theories involved are generally selected for their susceptibility to parody and are refuted by the causal system governing the fiction, or are shown to be able to exist only in a fantastic universe, or are presented through innovative narrative forms.

Intellectual History, Popular Belief,
and Official Ideology

In considering narrative causality, four distinct traditions need to be borne in mind: popular notions of destiny and fortune, dominant causal settings in different periods of literary history, officially sanctioned ideological positions, and technical philosophical doctrines of cause. Occasionally there is a rough correspondence between all four, as when Chaucer embodies Boethian concepts approved by the church and accepted by the people in *Troilus and Criseyde*,[15] or when Proust instantiates Bergson's theories, which reflected and fueled a widespread ideological movement away from mechanistic models of causality. In many instances, however, disparity is the rule rather than the exception. There are many reasons why this would be the case. In almost every period, extremes of both skepticism and credulity can be found in all segments of a given population, and hegemonic ideologies can move swiftly to adopt and contain a potentially troublesome conceptual difference. Philosophers are notoriously skeptical of received ideas and popular wisdom, and proudly defy conventional beliefs. Literature can also be wildly untimely; often, it is more deeply rooted in literary history than in contemporary events. Modern French dramatists who would never dream of believing in the gods of the Greek pantheon nevertheless were so transfixed by the possibilities of rewriting Sophocles' plays that they instigated what André Gide described as an *"Oedipemic."* Even when large-scale intellectual paradigm shifts occur, affecting an entire culture's way of perceiving the world, there are often century-long gaps between philosophical speculation, literary practice, and popular belief. All four traditions must be closely monitored if a theory of causality in narrative is to avoid excessive formalism and simplistic reductionism. Before proceeding further, it is worth pausing to observe some specific moments of rupture and convergence in these distinct but interpenetrating arenas.

Machiavelli, who wrote passionately of fortune in the final books of *The Prince*, nevertheless took care to exclude its effects from the naturalistic world of *Il Mandragora*. In that comedy, the role of chance is minimal, and the author ridicules every belief in the efficacy of the supernatural, most obviously in the materiality of his clerics and the physiological worthlessness of the mandrake root.[16] To comprehend the causal agencies of this drama it is more important to map out its own laws, rather than pore over Machiavelli's nonfictional writings.

It is also true that topics like chance and teleology are sufficiently slippery that every period produces theorists who argue for most possible stances; furthermore, the subjects are sufficiently common that no one ever needs to go to a philosopher for advice. Aristotle and Bertrand Russell, for example, have nothing in common in their notions of cause; they are not even asking the same questions. In fact, the Aristotelian categories were abandoned by the seventeenth century, and all modern accounts start with Hume. Nevertheless, concerning chance, their positions are very similar: for Aristotle, chance is the intersection of two separate causal chains; for Russell, a chance event is one whose cause is not currently known. On the other hand, the existence of uncaused events are central in the philosophies of Epicurus, Bergson, and Derrida, and they are of paramount significance to Pyrrhus and Nietzsche. Mixed theories too, which combine chaos and teleology can be found both in Empedocles' principles of Love and Strife and in Whitehead's modern hylozoism.

Quasi-philosophical notions like fortune and destiny have found theoretical spokesmen from Pythagoras and Plutarch to Hegel and Spengler. Most modern philosophers, however, follow Kant, who argued that notions like fortune (*Glück*) and fate (*Schicksal*) are "usurpatory concepts" possessing no explanatory validity. In this he sides with Cicero, who in his essay "On Fate" denies any hidden teleological meaning behind the surface of events:

> [I]f there were no such word at all as fate, no such force, and if either most things or all things took place by mere causal accident, would the course of events be different from what it is now? What is the point then of harping on fate, when everything can be explained by reference to nature or fortune without bringing fate in? (1948, 199)

Philosophical writing has its own history—one that is singularly devoid of solutions and resistant to notions of progress, and that is also often at odds with accepted ideas and frequently irrelevant to the concerns of authors of narratives.

At the same time, it is incumbent on us to place the diverse philosophical speculations and the equally rich literary deployments of cause within the larger perspective of intellectual history. At the most general levels, we may perceive a series of changes in Western concepts of cause in both literature and ideology from indigenous notions of preordained fate, destiny, and doom to Christian beliefs of providence to eighteenth- and nineteenth-century mechanistic concepts of determinism to, most recently, relatively modern ideas of chance, randomness, and indeterminism. The outline here provided of these general transformations in the discourse of causation in the West should help to frame the many significant differences, retrograde trajectories, and unusual anomalies that will be set forth in the pages that follow.

At times, issues of causation are invested with direct political valences, and one may discern at times a rather Manichaean struggle over the interpretation of causes that runs through all periods of literary history. After all, some causal stance is explicit in every *Weltanschauung*, and literature regularly dramatizes antithetical positions. Interpretive battles between mutually exclusive causal systems are found in everyday existence as well as in formidable metaphysical systems, and these are never innocent of political implications. As Karl Marx correctly observed, a materialist is more likely to act to change oppressive material conditions and social relations, while idealists are more apt to reify, mystify, or ignore the more troubling aspects of the material world; consequently, we may infer that naturalistic causal systems are in general more progressive than supernatural ones. Similarly, the cosmic egoism exemplified by individuals convinced of their own good luck is usually illusory and probably politically retrograde. The most oppressive causal concept is that of fate—that one's earthly status is inalterable and divinely preordained. Such a notion is less an arguable philosophical tenet than a method for rationalizing and legitimizing existing power relations.

Even when the term is freed from its original theological context and used in a vaguer, modern sense, it tends to hypostatize and fictionalize experience. As John Hannay remarks, "even calling one's lot 'fate' defends against incomprehensibility by giving the illusion of naming a pattern. Such an epithet claims coherence: 'fate' implies shape to life, often despite obvious contradictions" (1986, 78). It is precisely for this reason that chance, whether in philosophical or literary texts, is potentially so destabilizing, and it helps to explain why chance has been denied, suppressed, and excluded from officially sanctioned discourse for millennia. To adapt a well-known statement of Foucault, it could be said that causal explanation is no mere verbalization of conflicts and systems of domination, it is the very object of human conflicts. Whoever controls the concept of destiny can deploy it to make its own predictions come true. In ideological struggles, one of the key causal battlegrounds has always been the conflict between naturalistic and supernatural explanations of events. No army marches into a foreign country without having first been told its historical mission, manifest destiny, or divine prerogative, and ruling classes generally foster whatever religion will best keep them in power at home.

The clash between incompatible interpretations of events is routinely depicted in literature; an especially blunt confrontation occurs as Hotspur and Glendower plot their rebellion and argue over their future spoils. The Welsh wizard claims, "I can call spirits from the vasty deep." Hotspur replies, "Why, so can I, or so can any man;/ But will they come when you do call for them?" (1 Henry IV 3.1.52–54).[17] The exposure of specious supernatural claims was a favorite practice of nineteenth-century fiction but, though it may seem an especially modern concern, its genealogy can be traced back for millennia. One thinks of the blatant fraudulence of Chaucer's pardoner, the all too human priestess of Priapus in the Satyricon, and Aristophanes' less than reverent votaries of the Thesmophoria. Sophocles' Oedipus publicly asserts that Teiresias's prophecies are deliberate lies told to weaken his authority,[18] and Agamemnon has similar suspicions about Calchas at the beginning of the Iliad. Even when naturalistic readings like Oedipus' are manifestly wrong, or when supernatural direction is present but less prevalent than certain characters aver, the struggle between incompatible explanatory systems—and the stakes involved—are more than evident.

Just as it is necessary to recognize the ideological component of some causal confrontations, it is equally important to avoid simplistic reductionism: each confrontation must be understood in its larger context. Chaucer, for example, did not abandon his skeptical fideism when writing the Pardoner's Tale. On the other hand, the ontological triumph of one system in a fictional world does not necessarily imply that the author believes the system is equally true in the real world. Goethe and Marlowe did not believe in the supernatural machinery dramatized in their versions of Faust, and we will probably never know whether Sophocles personally adhered to the concept of fate that dominates Oedipus—though no one will deny that he knew how to construct a riveting plot. But, of course, authors can (and often do) believe in the system of causation they construct in their fictions. Formalist and antiformalist dogmas are equally limiting for a study of cause: one must be alert to ideological implications whenever they are present, but at the same time recognize the cases where a fiction is simply a fiction. Although this is not primarily a political study, it will be seen (particularly in the analyses of *Nostromo*, *Light in August*, and *Jasmine*) that a thorough examination of causality and its interpretation often entails an account of the social forces that stage events and enforce explanations favorable to their material interests. In these cases we will see that, once again, the characters' reading of events and the reader's interpretation of the text are bound together by the persistence of unusual configurations and unlikely sequences of actions that are charged with ideological significance.

2

A Poetics of Probability: Systems of Causation within Fictional Worlds

THE VARIETIES OF CAUSAL SETTING

Every fictional universe created by an author operates under some set of causal laws. The system of causation in a narrative is as basic a component of its setting as are the related elements of time and place. In some stories, causal parameters are the most clearly specified aspects of narrative stage-setting: the fairy tale beginning "Once upon a time . . ." may project a fantastic geography in an indeterminable time period, but the audience generally knows that the story to come is certain to employ a mode of causation that admits preternatural powers. I suspect that many individual genres can be defined by reference to their causal systems; the often disputed nature of the American romance and of postmodern narrative, for example, can be considerably refined once agents of causation are foregrounded.

A work's causal setting—that is, the canon of probability that governs the fictional world—is extremely important, and it intersects a number of other related concerns, including reception, interpretation, ideology, and construction. Consequently, it is quite strange that little systematic attention has been devoted to these issues. As Felix Martinez-Bonati has observed, "Except for the Aristotelian distinction (of characters superior, equal, or inferior to us) developed in Northrop Frye's theory of *modes,* and the circumscribed analysis of Todorov's *Littérature Fantastique,* I know of no works on the subject of the formal ontology of fictional worlds. I think it has hardly been envisaged as a theoretical possibility" (1983, 194).[1]

Martinez-Bonati, employing some basic binary oppositions, classifies texts as containing one or several worlds that are pure or "contaminated" (e.g., intertextual), realistic or fantastic, stable or unstable. This schema eventually generates forty-four possible classes of fictional worlds. His essay is provocative and illuminating, allowing us to perceive unsuspected contiguities between one of Cervantes's exemplary novellas, *The Colloquy of the Dogs*, and Juan Rulfo's hallucinatory *Pedro Páramo*. Nevertheless (and this may be an inherent limitation of all binary systems), many of the dichotomies he proposes seem to invite disputation. His realistic/nonrealistic distinction is certainly too broad and precludes equally crucial oppositions within the category of the nonrealistic. The opposition of "pure" and "contaminated" worlds tends to minimize important similarities between pure though temporarily unknown worlds (e.g., Hoffmann's *Mademoiselle de Scudéry*) and ultimately ambiguous ones (*The Golden Pot*, also by Hoffmann). His stable/unstable division is of a different order and refers not to the ontology of a fictional world but to the reader's knowledge of that ontology, and for that reason may be unstable itself. Martinez-Bonati admits that "All of these categories, especially, of course, the concepts of *realism* and *non-realism*, admit further specification and subdivision" (194). The real danger, however, is that subdivisions may fail to stay in their proper places in the conceptual hierarchy, or so proliferate as to call into question the utility of a potentially massive typology: as the king in *Through the Looking Glass* found out, a map as large as the territory it covers is no map at all.

In what follows, I will offer a different model that roughly designates four major systems of causation: supernatural, naturalistic, chance, and metafictional. In a world ruled by supernatural causation (commonly found in myths and fairy tales), various agents such as gods, fairies, and magicians possess extraordinary causal powers, often including the ability to arrange that world's events into a teleological order. In a naturalistic fictional universe, the only functional causal system consists of familiar human and natural forces that regularly produce plausible, conventional effects. The relentless determinism of Zola is a fairly stark form of this kind of causation.[2] Chance is a relatively modern stratagem that foregrounds gaps within and between causal chains, and centers on randomness, coincidence, and accidents. It is located on the border between order and chaos, ambiguity and incredulity. In the fictional realms of Borges and Nabokov there are many causes and numerous effects; the precise relation between antecedents and consequences is often highly suspect. What I term the metafictional is a kind of causal fourth dimension appearing whenever the narrator or implied author tampers with the causal laws already established. A classic example may be found in *The Beggar's Opera*: after Macheath is taken off to be hanged, the author comes on stage and is told by an actor that such an ending is inappropriate: "The Catastrophe is manifestly wrong, for an Opera must end happily" (3.16). The author agrees, changes the script, and reverses the fates of his characters so that the play ends in comedy.

Again, it must be stressed that a system of causation is part of a narrative's setting, and may vary in different works by the same author. A writer like Shakespeare will change canons of probability from play to play: very different supernatural agencies rule *A Midsummer Night's Dream, Macbeth*, and *The Tempest*, while a naturalistic causal system governs the events of *Much Ado About Nothing, Othello*, and *King Lear*.[3] In addition, as I have already suggested, dramas like *Antony and Cleopatra* anticipate modern deployments of chance. Most of these plays also contain metafictional (or metadramatic) elements that complement or problematize the designated causal setting.

In the pages that follow it will be necessary to refer briefly to a large number of narratives. In this way, it becomes possible to appreciate the scope and variety of causal systems, to investigate overlooked achievements of well-known authors, and to do justice to the pioneering work of earlier critical investigations from the vantage point of a more comprehensive theoretical framework. The discussion of chance will be especially wide-ranging, in order to draw attention to undeservedly neglected writers who nevertheless made important contributions to this distinctive feature of modern narrative and to indicate just how pervasive this strategy has become. An all too common failure of literary history is the sweeping theory based on a paucity of examples, seemingly ripe for refutation; my own account will, if anything, err in the opposite direction. Nevertheless, only with extensive documentation is one able to avoid the pitfalls of facile generalization and set forth a conceptual model that can be useful and accurate. Extended studies of individual texts are offered in part 2; the basis of my reading of modern narratives, however, rests on the range of works about to be discussed.

SUPERNATURAL CAUSATION

The supernatural can be easily distinguished and is present whenever a divine or superhuman causal agency is present. Events are typically endowed with a larger cosmological significance, and notions of fate, destiny, and fortune are used to describe the divine or diabolical plan that is worked out in the text. This type of work is what Todorov would call a tale of the marvelous and Frye would classify it as in the mythic mode.

The governing causal power may be the playful eldritch forces of *A Midsummer Night's Dream*; more frequently, it is the comprehensive teleological patterning generally associated with a systematic religion. Supernatural causation invariably posits invisible powers behind the mechanisms of the natural world and precludes the possibility of chance or random events: in a comprehensive supernatural framework, chance is only apparent, denoting the failure of human understanding rather than any gap in the divine plan. In some cases where supernatural causality reigns, everything is possible. One of the reasons that Milton's dubious battle on the plains of heaven tends to be rather unexciting is the fact the combatants can do anything except destroy each other. Without some causal limitations, any conflict can soon become insubstantial. Many authors employing the supernatural tend to limit its power (for example, Tasso's merely plenipotent Ismeno) or they reduce the extent of its intervention: in *The Iliad*, the gods cause very little that couldn't (or wouldn't) have happened anyway, and Greek dramatists were generally careful to restrict the descents of their gods to a minimum: the deus ex machina is basically the imposition of a supernatural solution on a fundamentally human dilemma. Writers of medieval romances also recognized the artistic need to curb the reach of the marvelous. As the author of one of the versions of *Tristan and Iseult* noted: "[M]ost men are unaware that what is in the power of magicians to accomplish, that the heart also can accomplish by dint of love and bravery" (Bédier 1945, 20).

There is also a kind of secular variant of the supernatural, which I will designate the fabulous, that also follows the same logic. In most of Aristophanes' plays, *Gargantua and Pantagruel*, and some contemporary antirealistic narratives, a radical extension of ordinary human causal powers appears. Gargantua's appetite is equal to Thor's, and Aristophanes' protagonists can leave heaven or enter Hades as easily as Milton's Satan.

Within the realm of the supernatural, competing causal systems may vie for dominance. Calderón's *Life is a Dream* is a clear-cut example: notions of predestination, astrological prediction, and unalterable fate are confronted and finally displaced by a providential Christian teleology that, in the world of the play, is shown to be accurate.[4] In other narratives the supernatural, though present, is not nearly as pervasive as it is thought to be. Macbeth learns this lesson the hard way; the vatic predictions of the Weird Sisters are not an "equivocation of the fiend,/ That lies like truth" (5.5.43–44), but accurate statements whose naturalistic meaning was never suspected by him. Birnam Wood literally does come to Dunsinane, hand-carried by Malcolm's invading forces. The hags do seem to quibble "with us in a double sense,/ That keep the word of promise to our ear/ And break it to our hope." (5.8.20–22), but the problem is not so much the witches' words as it is Macbeth's uncritical supernatural gloss.[5]

Oedipus Rex, a model of the kind of predestination Calderón attacked, contains a different but equally pervasive causal battle.[6] Many of its characters believe that they live in a naturalistic world, and Oedipus gives a strictly materialist reading of Teiresias's pronouncements. Although all have taken careful actions to thwart the prophecy, Jocasta speaks for more than herself when she proudly exclaims, "[W]hy should men fear since chance is all in all / for him and he can clearly foreknow nothing?" (1959, 977–78; cf. 964–73). Of course, fate soon catches up with them. Through a series of apparent coincidences (the Destiny of the gods is perceived by mortals as chance, until its design is made evident), Oedipus's true identity is revealed and the supernatural ordering of events is manifested to all.

Thomas Vargish finds a similar dynamic at work in Jane Austen's *Emma*. In directing Harriet's destiny, Emma is

> repeatedly enchanted by the way events seem to conform to her own "prearrangement," that what she desires "should so immediately shape itself into the proper form." She has to learn the "unpardonable arrogance" of proposing "to arrange everybody's destiny," an arrogance that Austen's readers would quickly have seen as attempting to usurp the prerogatives of providence and thus as a spiritual as well as a social disorder. (1985, 49)

Needless to say, Emma is duly chastened and the omnipotent though mysterious rule of providence is affirmed.

In *Julius Caesar*, supernatural auguries become the sites of interpretive battles. Calpurnia's genuinely prophetic dream is given an alternative exegesis by Decius Brutus, who attempts to locate it within the causal world of naturalism:

> This dream was all amiss interpreted;
> It was a vision fair and fortunate.
> Your statue spouting blood in many pipes,
> In which so many smiling Romans bathed,
> Signifies that from you great Rome shall suck
> Reviving blood, and that great men shall press
> For tinctures, stains, relics, and cognizance.
> This by Calpurnia's dream is signified.
>
> (2.2.83–90)

Decius here denies the dream's literal supernatural meaning (which he knows is correct) to reduce the vision to a harmless allegory. And, by the paradoxical logic that governs oracles in literature, the prophecy is fulfilled precisely because Caesar doubts its truth and goes to the capitol. During the rest of the play, supernatural forces continue to exert their powers.[7]

In *King Lear*, precisely the opposite occurs: the major characters repeatedly invoke a supernatural agency that never appears at all. "Is there any cause in nature that makes these hard hearts?" (3.6.75–77), Lear asks, but he receives no answer. In the world of the play, teleological order and divine intervention are equally absent. Gloucester's well-known line, "As flies to wanton boys are we to th' gods; / They kill us for their sport" (4.1.86–87), readily evokes sympathy; his suggestion of a malevolent teleology, however, is as erroneous as are the other characters' asseverations that a benevolent pattern must emerge. The issue of causation is thematically highlighted by Edmund, who mocks the cosmological superstitions of those around him:

> This is the excellent foppery of the world, that when we are sick in fortune, often surfeits of our own behaviour, we make guilty of our disasters the sun, moon, and stars; as if we were villains on necessity; fools by heavenly compulsion. . . . An admirable evasion of whoremaster man, to lay his goatish disposition on the charge of a star.
>
> (1.2.115–22)

It is hard to find a more vigorous assault on predestination, or a more tragic depiction of a relentlessly naturalistic world.[8]

An intriguing twentieth-century return to this issue and the language used to debate it appears in Thornton Wilder's *The Bridge of San Luis Rey*, which revolves around a character's experiment to determine whether "we live by accident and die by accident, or we live by plan

and die by plan" (1986, 6). As the narrator goes on to state: "Some say
. . . that to the gods we are like flies that boys kill on a summer day, and
some say, on the contrary, that the very sparrows do not lose a feather
that has not been brushed away by the finger of God" (9). As we have
just seen, the origin of the first alternative is in *King Lear*; as we probably recall, the immediate source of the second is, ironically, also Shakespeare, namely Hamlet's claim "there is a special providence in the fall
of a sparrow" (5.2.208–9).

The novel's plot centers on the sudden death of five colonial Span-
iards caused by the sudden collapse of the bridge of San Luis Rey in
1714 outside of Lima. This catastrophe is witnessed by (and almost kills)
Brother Juniper, a Franciscan who had long desired to place theology
among the exact sciences. This disaster, occurring in a country where
"those catastrophes which lawyers shockingly call the 'acts of God' were
more that usually frequent" (4), seemed to provide the perfect laboratory for a scientific investigation of divine providence. By carefully examining the nature and trajectory of the life of each victim, the brother
hopes to determine exactly how timely or unjust those deaths were.
After painstaking analyses of the morality, usefulness, good works, and
future potential of each one, the cleric—like the reader—is unable to
discern the slightest pattern or meaning in the five deaths. Each appears to be entirely adventitious. The reader is also informed that, after
writing up his account, Brother Juniper is burned at the stake by the
Inquisition. Providence, this book concludes, will never be revealed by
rational inquiry—if indeed it exists at all.

Naturalistic Causation

A naturalistic system of causation within a fictional world should
not be confused with philosophical naturalism or limited to certain nineteenth-century aesthetic programs. A materialist may write a fairy tale,
and a Catholic can produce a strictly secular comedy of manners. A
naturalistic causal world simply implies that recognizable and repeat-
able actions and events engender plausible consequences, without the
intrusion of supernatural entities, causal voids, or authorial meddling.[9]
In a naturalistic universe, like that of everyday experience, a raw egg
thrown hard against a stone will break—not turn into a dove, remain
intact while shattering the stone, or be left suspended in midair as the
narrator launches into a digression on ovular symbolism. The author

of such a world, in Fielding's words, "Keeps within the bounds of possibility; and still remembers that what is not possible for man to perform,
it is scarce possible for man to believe he did perform" (*Tom Jones* , bk.
8, chap. 1).[10] Thus, *Don Quixote, The Marriage of Figaro*, and even Jules
Verne's novels all employ a naturalistic causal system.

I do not mean to imply that the boundary between the naturalistic
and the supernatural is completely clear-cut; some items (like love po-
tions) and some events (luck rituals) are viewed naturalistically by one
culture and supernaturally by another—or in different periods of the
same culture. Nevertheless, the distinctions I employ have a surprising
consistency that cuts across eras and belief. As Thomas Pavel summarizes: "In the ontology of the sacred, the plenary reality of the sacred
domain is crucially opposed to the precarious existence of the profane.
Sacred beings not only obey different laws than do sublunar creatures,
but their way of being is fundamentally different (to use Rudolf Otto's
well-known formula)" (1986, 60). Polytheists, monotheists, and agnos-
tics are often in full agreement concerning what constitutes the supernatural; they differ over who causes miracles and whether miracles exist
at all, rather than what the definitively miraculous would be. Because
of this, the causal distinctions I employ are ontologically neutral in relation to the world we inhabit.

Within a naturalistic framework, there is, to be sure, a great variety
in character motivation, general plotting, and the effects of large social
forces. The behavior of some of Boccaccio's characters often seems
motiveless, while most of Balzac's figures are compulsively driven by
some combination of greed, vanity, and sex. The degree of motivation
may vary widely, and so may the number of sources of characters' behavior. In the preface to *Miss Julie*, Strindberg takes pains to emphasize
the multiplicity of circumstances that contribute to bring about her tragic
end. It might be added that Julie's overdetermined motivation helps
make her an interesting and plausible character; an account of behavior that is too narrow quickly grows tiresome. As W. J. Harvey notes:
"We know that not *everything* is explicable in terms of our genetic
makeup or our Oedipus complex or the nature of the class struggle."
An overly reductionistic author "strains our sense of mimetic accuracy
because he offers too *simple* an explanation" (1965, 137). It might be
noted in passing that a good farce works precisely because of the obsessive, simplistic, and repetitive actions of the characters.

Within a naturalistic framework, the connection between successive events may be slight, as in picaresque novels, or direct, as in neo-

classical comedy. In many nineteenth-century fictions, the causal connection between events is so tight and characters' fates so ineluctable that comparisons have been made to classical notions of destiny. Thomas Hardy made one himself: the final paragraph of *Tess of the D'Urbervilles* begins "'Justice' was done, and the President of the Immortals, in Aeschylean phrase, had ended his sport with Tess." It hardly needs to be pointed out that the usage here is metaphorical; there are no immortal Norns or Parcae (as there are in the *Oresteia*) who weave one's fate before it happens, but only a series of interlocking naturalistic events that ultimately determine what occurs. It is important to recognize this distinction since it is often used to oppose and contest different worldviews, as the examples of *King Lear* and *Julius Caesar* suggest. One of Flaubert's archer ironies hinges on a conflation of the teleological with the naturalistic. Meeting up with Rodolphe at the end of *Madame Bovary*, Charles says philosophically that what had happened was to be blamed on fate ("C'est la faute de la fatalité" [1964, 692]). Rodolphe, on the other hand, who had engineered that fate ("qui avait conduit cette fatalité"), does not bother to correct Charles's naive interpretation.

As I have already indicated, a naturalistic framework can be used to oppose and subvert supernatural systems of explanation; it can also serve as the site where competing naturalistic theories are tested. In *Nostromo*, the putative motives of the characters include idealism (Gould), love (Decoud), republicanism (Viola), self-preservation (Hirsch), progress (Avellanos), spiritual values (Holroyd), duty (Mrs. Gould), greed (Ribera), and popular renown (Nostromo). But most of these motives are finally unmasked or subordinated; viewed from a larger perspective, every character is a tool of "material interests," part of the inexorable machinery of capitalism from which there is and can be no escape.[11]

The naturalistic system comes with its own enemies: supernaturalism, coincidence, and quasi-natural orders. It should not be surprising that within this narrative world other causal models are articulated, tested, and refuted. In nineteenth-century realistic fiction, some representative of divine teleology, usually a selfish priest or fatuous parson, is regularly brought in to comment vaguely on God's unfolding plan just as the narrative's events show an opposite and incompatible order.[12] Such scenes recur so often that they almost seem to be a kind of purification ritual by realistic authors. And perhaps this must happen, since a naturalistic causal order precludes alternative interpretations of events. Ironically, naturalistic causation is so comprehensive and self-sufficient that genuine believers were not able to work God's hand into realist fictions. "It is commonplace that the most striking thing about the clergymen of Trollope—and for that matter of Jane Austen—is their lack of interest in God; nor does the authorial commentary suggest that God is much interested in them," David Lodge observes (1977, 81), and this judgment may be extended to most authors, Christian or anti-Christian, that employ the aesthetic of naturalism.[13]

Victorian novelists tended to treat coincidence rather like sex: a small concession to its powers would induce compelling attention, though it was better to avoid such a crude and dangerous stimulant altogether. James's and Forster's theoretical positions unambiguously denigrate the improbable and the fortuitous (even though, as I will discuss shortly, the practice of these transitional figures includes modern self-conscious manipulations of coincidence). Praising the work of a contemporary naturalist, James notes, "Mr. Howells hates an artificial fable and a *denouement* that is pressed into service; he likes things to occur as they occur in life, where the manner of a great many of them is not to occur at all" (1972, 161). And Forster, in his spirited attack on the clumsiness and artificiality of Scott, repeatedly draws attention to the abrupt intrusions of romantic coincidence that permeate *The Antiquary* (1927, 51–62). The improbable, condemned in theory, also proved unfortunate for the fictional characters who gambled on its whims. In *Middlemarch*, George Eliot relentlessly castigates characters who egoistically hope for fortunate turns of events. Peter Jones explains that for the characters, "even partial awareness that one is imagining only possibilities is accompanied by the desire that some special agency might intervene in the natural course of events in order to realize those possibilities; the characteristic sign of this desire in *Middlemarch* is the occurrence of the terms 'chance,' 'luck,' and 'Providence'." Furthermore, individuals "who hope to be released from the causal web in which they find themselves enmeshed, are often partially aware that such a hope is forlorn" (1975, 36).

Like the supernatural, the fortuitous is anathema to the naturalistic system. Belief in luck is self-delusion for a character, and too great a reliance on coincidence is an unwarranted aesthetic license for an author working in this mode. Robert Louis Jackson's observations on chance and design in *Anna Karenina* apply equally well to other works of realism: "Our impression of the unplanned, however, is precisely an impression: on closer analysis it gives way to a sense of organized movement and design" (1968, 315–16). Similarly, "all the 'chance' elements we have noted are very far from being *pure* chance" (324). His conclusion is that the play of chance is more apparent than actual (324). In this, he identifies a classic gambit of the naturalistic, by which apparently chance events are introduced only to be later revealed as part of a larger causal skein. It may well be, as Balzac states in his preface to *La Comédie humaine*, that chance is the world's greatest novelist ("Le hasard est le plus grand romancier du monde"); in realist fiction, however, its play is severely restricted, as a glance at any of Balzac's mature works will confirm. (This is not to say it was entirely extirpated—some authors include an occasional coincidence in order to produce an *effet du réel*.)

This stance leads directly to intertextual considerations. Not every author employing a particular causal system will be equally faithful to its demands, and many quasi-naturalist genres, while eschewing the supernatural, nevertheless invite appropriate coincidences at crucial moments in the story. Here, a more-naturalistic-than-thou dialectic can arise. In *Don Quixote, Waverley,* and *Madame Bovary*, the protagonists come to grief for acting as if life followed the conventions of romance. Or, in the terms of Jauss, "expectations derived from reading encounter an alien reality and the pure sentiments and higher passions of poetry fail to materialize in life. . . . Some of the peak achievements of the novel took this phenomenon as their model" (1982, 7). This was an especially insistent topos of nineteenth-century realism, appearing in a variety of avatars.[14] The romance is not the only genre that rigorously mimetic authors chose to refute; literary history is full of examples of conventional improbabilities parodied by a more scrupulously naturalistic causal system. These genres—and their deflators—include Aeschylean tragedy (Euripides' *Electra*), heroic drama *(Tom Thumb)*, the Gothic *(Northanger Abbey)*, the detective novel (Faulkner's *Old Man)*, and the sentimental love story (Welles's film *The Lady from Shanghai)*. In each case, the inconsistent causal system of the genre satirized is contrasted to a more thoroughgoing naturalistic order, as chance and coincidence are exposed and suppressed.

CHANCE WORLDS

In "The Lottery in Babylon," Borges describes a preclassical world of causation, and by doing so displays his own modernity: "I have known what the Greeks did not: uncertainty," his ancient narrator asserts (1981, 131). The lottery itself, which determines power and humiliation, ecstasy and death, was instigated by the populace to interpolate chance into the order of the world. The lottery grew more baroque, secret, and barbaric until, by a typically Borgesian twist, it became only slightly more adventitious than what we consider the random disorder of ordinary existence. The modernist is completely at home in the kind of world where

> Chaos umpire sits,
> And by decision more embroils the fray
> By which he reigns: next him high arbiter
> Chance governs all.
>
> (*Paradise Lost* 2.907–10)

In the cosmology of *Paradise Lost*, chaos and chance, though undeniably powerful, are decisively relegated to a minor status in the order of things. A typical aspect of modernist fictional worlds is an inversion of Milton's painfully established harmonies. Now chance and uncertainty rule; more subversively, it often seems that no other order is possible or even desirable. The natural development from cause to effect is frequently tampered with or sabotaged in modernist worlds. Voids open between antecedent and consequent, multiple coincidences subvert probability, obscure events produce outlandish results, and familiar causal patterns are supplanted by linguistic, oneiric, or absurdist progressions.

Virginia Woolf, in her seminal essay "Modern Fiction," clearly articulates the dilemma of Edwardian authors: "The writer seems constrained, not by his own free will but by some powerful and unscrupulous tyrant who has him in thrall, to provide a plot, provide comedy, tragedy, love interest, and an air of probability embalming the whole. . . ." (1925, 153). Modern criticism has thoroughly documented the attenuation of classical plotting, the collapse of conventional genre types, and the demise of love (if not sex) in the literature of our century. The suspension of "embalming" probability still needs to be explored, however.

A glance at Henry James's treatment of the classic theme of fulfilled predictions should illuminate the modernist approach favored by Woolf. In an instructive early story, "A Problem" (1868) (itself a refinement of Hawthorne's "The Prophetic Pictures"), a pair of newlyweds, having their fortune told by an old Indian woman, is informed that they will have a daughter and that she will die very young. The husband, contemptuous of superstition, openly scoffs; his wife is considerably more credulous. The woman does give birth to a daughter who later falls seriously ill, but soon recovers. The crisis over, the wife confesses that she had been disturbed by another prophecy, made by an old Italian with a deck of cards, that she would marry twice. Her husband is startled into a parallel discovery—years before, it had been predicted that he too would marry twice. The husband reflects that "the oddity was not in his having been predestined, according to the young lady, to marry twice; but in poor Emma having drawn exactly the same lot. It was a conflict of oracles" (1973, 1:269). The emphasis is not on the supernatural but the coincidental, as the tension shifts from fate to chance. Emma's response mirrors her husband's: "She had laughed at the folly of the Indian's threat; but she found it impossible to laugh at the extraordinary coincidence of David's promised fate with her own. That it was absurd and illogical made it only the more painful" (270). Here James strikes a characteristic note of modernism.

Despite the literal falseness of the old Indian's prophecy, both are haunted by the newly disclosed forecasts—which they do not believe can occur—and their marriage is ultimately destroyed by this obsession. Now James increases the irony. After they separate, the child dies. Mutual grief brings them back together, and each is figuratively said to have become "married" for the second time. The literal and metaphorical do not match up, so the supernatural is discredited by the events of the story, and despite the fact that belief in the double contradictory prophecy causes it to become "true," a strictly naturalistic account cannot explain the uncanny accuracy of the opening prediction. Instead of a facile romantic coincidence, the reader is presented with something much more problematic, a coincidence of coincidences, as it were. It is precisely the kind of event that James the theorist might deprecate as "tending not to occur at all," a kind of exacerbation of chance. The reader of this tale is left hovering in a fictional world where the accidental can neither be trusted nor ignored; and because the improbability is acknowledged and the depiction is mimetic, we are invited to see this world as a possible version of the one we inhabit.[15]

I will employ the admittedly limited term "chance" to cover the range of modern subversions of the naturalistic causal system. Strictly speaking, "chance" is too narrow a word to embrace the problematizing and interruption of familiar causal progressions. A more accurate term might be "contingency," but its very breadth makes for vagueness.

Typically, one of four tactics is followed: coincidences proliferate uncannily, statistically unlikely events abound, ordinary causes fail to engender typical effects, or alternative connections displace naturalistic ones. That is, one may find causes producing too many effects, too few effects, or the wrong effects altogether. In each case, we are confronted by a causal system that is neither supernatural nor naturalistic. More precisely, we are given worlds in which systematic causal systems are interrupted, contested, or parodied.

It should be useful to demarcate some prominent modernist topographies at this point. The examples I will adduce are not distinct types but varying tendencies that often merge with contiguous strategies. And this is as it should be: it would be odd if a world that defies causality could be located within logically distinct categories. Nevertheless, we may identify several clusters of narratives that foreground chance in comparable ways. Among the milder forms of contingency, which problematize rather than overthrow the naturalistic model, we may begin with ambiguous worlds like that of James's "A Problem," in which naturalistic and coincidental patterns alternate as the governing causal setting of the fictional world. Conrad's *Chance*, Forster's *A Room with a View*, Cortázar's *Hopscotch*, Rushdie's *Midnight's Children*, David Lodge's *Small World*, and Angela Carter's *Wise Children* extend and amplify this strategy. Chance plays a leading role, even though many coincidences prove inconsequential and numerous apparently fortuitous events turn out to have naturalistic explanations.[16]

Ulysses and the works of Dorothy Richardson and Virginia Woolf contain sequences of events apparently devoid of causal connection.[17] Todorov articulates a common viewpoint when he states "the most striking example of submission to the temporal order is *Ulysses*. The only, or at least the main, relation among the actions is their pure succession: we are told, minute after minute, what happens in a certain place or in the mind of the character" (1981, 42). This is clearly an impoverished account and better describes the work of Richardson than Joyce, though it does accurately portray the impressions of a casual reader. Texts like *Ulysses* disguise and defer causal connections, and replace them with parallel episodes in independent story lines. Furthermore, the many coincidences in *Ulysses*, by eroding the naturalistic setting, underline authorial design. As Hazard Adams observes, this novel is "a book of accidents and coincidences, and at the level of story, it tells us that such things are what hold our lives together. Further, at the level of arrangement, we see not the coincidence of events or things, but the coincidence of words." And at this level, "of course, there are no coincidences" (1990, 104–5).[18]

Strindberg, most notably in *A Dream Play*, uses the logic of dreams instead of the ordinary causal progressions of waking life. Many other writers have continued in this direction, and the one that generally comes to mind first is Franz Kafka. Closer scrutiny however discloses a more complex problematic. Thomas Pavel states that in *The Castle*, "contradictory clues seem to suggest alternatively that the world we attend is sometimes similar to ours and sometimes obeys an alien logic. Too well-structured to be simply oneiric, too realistic to accept a mythic framework, the nature of the fictional surroundings remains elusive" (1986, 93). Archetypal progressions alternate with, complement, and contradict equally insistent naturalistic sequences. In contemporary Latin American "magic realism," these antinomies are likewise blurred and problematized. In the major novels of Alejo Carpentier, Gabriel García Marquez, and Joao Guimares Rosa, no single incident is particularly implausible, yet the regular succession of mythopoetic episodes is utterly unlikely.

In the theater of the absurd, as in Kafka's *Metamorphosis*, one or more constants of naturalistic causation is suppressed or transformed, as the resulting action follows ruthlessly from the original impossible premises. Our fascination with such works stems in part from our recognition of the logically impeccable development of a fundamentally outrageous set of postulates. Related constructions inform the expressionistic fiction of Knut Hamsun, Charles Williams, Djuna Barnes, and Ralph Ellison.[19] Some of these figures tend to be marginalized or ignored in many accounts of modernism; the term I use to describe their work, expressionism, comes from art history rather than literary criticism. Like the high modernists, they too manipulate causal progressions. But whereas Joyce, Proust, and Woolf subtly defer or attenuate causal ties, expressionistic authors speed up the machinery of causality, as unlikely events infallibly engender a dangerous succession of still more improbable happenings, as often happens in our worst nightmares. It is to be hoped that an emphasis on cause can draw deserved attention to these relatively neglected writers.

Radically unreliable narrators can make it impossible to determine the causal laws of the world distorted by their narratives. Something like this occurs in *Pale Fire* or Pynchon's *V*, where the motives and desires of each successive narrator are much more determinate than the "facts" they claim to interpret. The progressive revelation of actions is retarded by an equally insistent obfuscation of the narrative's events. Another extreme version of epistemological impasse is Bioy Casares' *A Plan For Escape*, a work in which every putative action is ambiguous, all narrations are suspect or spurious, and each attempt to comprehend what happens is equally inadequate. *A Plan for Escape* is both a narrative and a labyrinth, an infinity of possible plots and contradictory readings. While immersed in these novels, the reader is invited to assume that some consistent causal setting governs the fictional world and to construct various hypothetical orders to explain obvious anomalies. But our constructions are always provisional and inadequate; we can never conclusively differentiate the operations of fabrication, coincidence, and the narrator's mental instability. These worlds certainly do not appear to obey naturalistic laws, though just how far they diverge from this norm is inherently indeterminable. The causal order in these novels can be located halfway between that of *Absalom, Absalom!*, in which ambiguous events unfold within a naturalistic causal system, and the impenetrable, fragmentary "settings" of the later Beckett, which will be discussed below.

RADICAL FORMS OF CHANCE

More extreme forms of "chance" or contingent ontologies can even transcend the notion of chance itself, as we move from the statistically unlikely to the logically impossible. The difficulty of naming this odd relation between events is manifested in a curious description in Todorov's *Introduction to Poetics*. Discussing the work of Kafka and Gombrowicz, Todorov states: "[A] literature of initially fantastic inspiration has replaced the causality of common sense by a so to speak irrational causality; here we are in the realm of anti-causality, but this is still causality's realm" (1981, 45). This apparent conceptual paradox is more playfully expressed by Gertrude Stein:

> What is the difference between accident and coincidence.
> An accident is when a thing happens. A coincidence is when a thing is going to happen and does. (1971, 83)

Both mild and extreme forms of chance are best understood as the proliferation of unlikely causal sequences that defy naturalistic systems and are incapable of any supernatural recuperation. Furthermore, we may note an additional corollary that applies equally well to the entire spectrum of chance worlds: the more unlikely the succession of events, the more the author's guiding hand becomes evident and a second-order, metafictional dimension is at work.

One of the most celebrated types of "radical chance" is the surrealist notion of *le hasard objectif*, which Breton defends in the following terms: "The attention that on every occasion I have, for my part, attempted to call to certain disturbing facts, to certain overwhelming coincidences in works such as *Nadja*, *Les Vases communiquants*, and in other later reports has raised, with an acuteness that is completely new, the problem of *objective chance*, or in other words that sort of chance that shows man, in a way that is still very mysterious, a necessity that escapes him, even though he experiences it as a vital necessity" (1969, 268). Despite its quasi-mystical rhetoric, this concept is as equally opposed to spiritualism as to naturalism; it implies design but denies teleology. It is unnecessary to dwell on the contradictions or deliberate paradoxes of such a position; its importance lies in the explicit theoretical claim of the hidden powers of chance and the desire for its embodiment within fictional worlds.

Less strident but equally pervasive deployments of coincidence are prominent in novels of Gombrowicz, Céline, and Nabokov. The narrator of *Cosmos*, a certain Witold, finds himself in a universe in which there are too many connections: implausible events, like a series of objects hanging from strings or ropes, imply a teleology even as they continue to defy explanation: "[T]hese curious coincidences were more frequent than one would have expected, things kept popping up and sticking together as if they were glued, events and happenings were like those magnetized particles that sought each other out and joined up with one another as soon as they got close, never mind how" (1978, 130). This leads to large, metaphysical doubts, since "everything was always possible, and among the thousands of millions of possible reasons for everything you could always find one to explain anything" (143).

Wherever Bardamu is driven in *Journey to the End of the Night*, whether a European battlefield, an African outpost, or an American honky-tonk, he keeps running into his sordid acquaintance, Robinson. These encounters serve to parody coincidence, and yet are perfectly appropriate in the dubious world Céline depicts. In *Lolita*, Humbert Humbert tries to separate clusters of fortunate accidents ("those dazzling coincidences that logicians loathe and poets love" [1970, 33]) from the calculated designs of his nemesis and double, Clare Quilty. He first attributes the vicissitudes of his lot to fate, "that synchronizing phantom" (105), though he soon learns that the author of his destiny is far more devious than Humbert can conceive.

Nabokov, who believes in the "essential spirality of all things in their relation to time" (1971, xxvi), has a metaphysical counterpart in Jorge Luis Borges, who has formally attempted to refute time. This artificer has invented a number of fabulous worlds that distort chronology and violate causality. One of the more intriguing is Tlön, a fictional realm within a fictional universe where the inhabitants "do not conceive that the spatial persists in time. The perception of a cloud of smoke on the horizon and then of the burning field and then of the half-extinguished cigarette that produced the blaze is considered an example of the association of ideas" (1964, 9). The philosophers of Tlön have nevertheless produced several theories of time, one of which declares (with unmistakable metafictional resonances) that the history of the universe is the scripture produced by a subordinate god in order to communicate with a demon. In several other tales, Borges fabricates exquisite and curious causal laws, and the same is true of Italo Calvino's cosmologies, particularly the ones mapped out in *t zero*.[20]

By contrast, the fictional worlds of Maurice Blanchot are more claustrophobic, obsessive, and contradictory. To open one of his books is to enter a symmetrical nightmare. Space shrinks and time folds back on itself; concerning *Death Sentence*, Derrida in his study of this piece (1979) has suggested that the text is designed to tempt the reader into insanity. Despite the desperate attempts of narrator and characters to escape, they are repeatedly returned to the same cramped, dark threshold where the same experience of transgressing human boundaries is restaged. Chronology is deformed as a number of events designated to have taken place "later" all lead back to earlier episodes, and new characters become ever more transparent versions of those who have previously appeared. The narrator and the reader are forced continually to reexperience the same primal scene, as temporality is collapsed and causality implodes.[21]

Perhaps the most radical distortion of causality occurs in *Daniel Deronda*, where the ordinary progression from cause to effect is inverted and the reader is presented with a kind of "*post hoc* causality." As Cynthia Chase has ingeniously explained, Deronda comes to act as if he were Jewish, though he is presented in the text as non-Jewish. Much later, it turns out that he was actually born a Jew, but the beliefs he has come to hold are not a result of any genetic sympathy or racial memory (Morde-cai's protestations to the contrary), but because of rational, tolerant observation. In this respect his actual Jewishness is epiphenomenal; in the terms of the fictional world it is, as Chase remarks, "the effect of the account of his vocation; his origin is the effect of its effects" (1978, 218). Here is the ultimate coincidence, the retroactive cause that, coming *after* the effect it should produce, is not a cause at all.[22] George Eliot has created a fictional world in which the deconstruction of causality appears—the same deconstruction, it will be noted, that de Man and Culler unsuccessfully sought to find inherent in the principle of cause and the experience of everyday existence. It may also be observed that a comic treatment of an analogous progression is present in Wilde's *The Importance of Being Earnest*.

We arrive now at the characteristic works of Stein, Robbe-Grillet, and the later Beckett, in which a tale's causal laws, like its precise temporal and spatial setting, are fundamentally indeterminable. These narratives are regularly fragmentary and disjointed; the reader is made to invent a possible setting for the narrative's events and discover the system through which the work is presented. One fragment will invite a reading that is then contradicted by a subsequent section, while the following portion may suggest yet another interpretive trajectory. As the text unfolds, the narrative world—insofar as there is a single, consistent narrative world—is regularly altered, displaced or collapsed. Playing along the borders of representation, narrativity, and disorder, novels like *Jealousy*, *Company*, Brooke-Rose's *Between*, and Sollers's *H* consistently present a fictional world the causal system of which is repeatedly problematized or undermined by the arrangement of the composition, as the unfolding of the story is displaced by the generation of the text.

The last step is a move into the aleatory. In certain dada exercises and pieces by authors like John Cage, random assemblages take the place of any narrative. There are no causal systems to be discerned because there is no setting—causal, spatial, or temporal. Contingency shifts from being an attribute of the story's setting to that of the text's composition, or rather, conglomeration. And when this point is reached, it is probably fair to say that we are no longer discussing narrative.

With few exceptions, the contingent universes of modern fiction and drama negate naturalism without invoking supernatural orders. Though randomness, coincidence, and the oneiric can be found throughout literary history, the conscious creation of insistently unlikely and

causally inexplicable worlds is found only in modern narratives. Until
the end of the eighteenth century, the supernatural and the naturalistic
alone vied for explanatory supremacy. C. C. Barfoot, quoting the classical Greek scholar William Chase Greene, is able to assert that the basic
division of Greek thinkers into

> those who conceive "of Nature as the product of necessity, without
> plan or purpose" and those "who believe that the universe is the
> product not of blind, mechanical necessity but of law or destiny which
> is rational and good, whether it be called the will of Zeus or Provi-
> dence or Fate" seems to describe the two basic attitudes of mankind,
> which is as applicable to the characters in a novel by Jane Austen as
> it is to Plato's philosophical world. (1982, 190)

Modern literature offers us a third alternative, chance, which by
its novelty as well as its ambiguous nature has played a major role in
revitalizing narrative with original settings, compelling themes, and
experimental forms. Perhaps most importantly, it helped add a new
dimension to the act of reading: confronted by the play of chance, the
audience can no longer comfortably rely on its own ideological system
but is forced to make and test decisions about the nature and proximity
of the fictional world.

Metafictional Orderings

One author describes a man's desperate attempt to flee his pursu-
ers in the following language: "He was moving again almost before he
had stopped, with that lean, swift, blind obedience to whatever Player
moved him on the Board. . . . He seemed indefatigable, not flesh and
blood, as if the Player who moved him for pawn likewise found him
breath" (1972, 437). These lines, that both convey a sense of fatality and,
by personifying it, refer back to the creator of the fictional events, are
the kind we normally associate with Nabokov, Queneau, or Flann
O'Brien, self-conscious artificers who regularly draw attention to the
fictionality of their narratives. It may surprise some readers that the
moving figure is Joe Christmas, and that the Player (at least at some
level) is William Faulkner, thinly disguised as Fate. Whenever a man or
woman makes a fictional narrative, inventing episodes, coordinating
plots, and killing off characters, the author functions as destiny, or in
Nabokov's phrase, "An anthropomorphic deity impersonated by me"

(1971, 245). Not even the most resolutely naturalistic novelist ever loses sight of this relation. Anthony Trollope once happened to overhear a conversation in which two clergymen were vigorously condemning characters he had created:

> Then one of them fell foul of Mrs. Proudie. It was impossible for me not to hear their words, and almost impossible to hear them and be quiet. I got up, and standing between them, I acknowledged myself to be the culprit. "As to Mrs. Proudie," I said, "I will go home and kill her before the week is over." And so I did. The two gentlemen were utterly confounded, and one of them begged me to forget his frivolous observations. (Cited in Allen 1948, 195)

Authorial excursions into a fictional world have always been common, though they have varied considerably in function, extent, and explicitness. A novelist like Fielding continually reminds us that he is the artificer of *Tom Jones*; he not only tells us when we should particularly admire his skill in plotting, but also warns that "for a little reptile of a critic to presume to find fault with any of its parts, without knowing the manner in which the whole is connected . . . is a most presumptuous absurdity" (*Tom Jones* , bk. 10, chap. 1). Similar demonstrations of authorial control can be found in the drama. Within his own comedies, Aristophanes regularly criticizes other playwrights' constructions, and even depicts Agathon in the act of piecing together a play in the *Thesmophoriazusae*. In other works he speaks to the audience directly to point out his own compositional excellence:

> 'Twere proper and right for the Ushers to smite, if
> ever bard we confess,
> Were to fill with the praise of himself and his plays
> our own anapaestic address.
> But if ever, O daughter of Zeus, it were fit with honor
>   to praise and adorn
> A Chorus Instructor, the ablest of men, the noblest
> that ever was born,
> Our Poet is free to acknowledge that he is deserving of
>   high commendation. . . .
>
> (*The Peace*, 734–38)

Other authors employ less direct but equally stark methods to remind the audience just who is the governing intelligence of the world of the narrative. Shakespeare's Talbot, lamenting the abrupt killing of

Salisbury by a French sniper, utters the following imprecation: "Accursed tower! Accursed fatal hand / That hath contrived this woeful tragedy!" (*1 Henry VI*, 1.4.76–77). At the end of *Bend Sinister*, the protagonist Krug, about to meet his maker, vaguely realizes that "death is but a question of style, a mere literary device, a musical resolution" (1971, 246). Beckett's narrators are troubled by the notion that they "exist" (qua narrators) only insofar as they continue to produce their own narrative. In Fielding's *The Author's Farce* and *The Grub Street Opera*, playwrights come on stage to alter the course of events of plays within larger frame plays; in works of Pirandello and O'Brien, the opposite occurs as characters wrest control from their putative creators, challenge their authority, and even threaten the authors' lives. And in Cortázar's "Continuity of Parks," a man is killed by a character in the novel that he is reading.

A fictional world, as long as it is fictional, is always susceptible to authorial intervention, although such intrusions can impair the integrity of the created universe. Fiction making comes with two antithetical temptations: the need for convincing representation and the desire to acknowledge its fictionality. Or in the terms of this study, there is a drive to construct a consistent, all-embracing causal system and an equal but opposite urge to alter the orders one has established. Naturally enough, different authors foreground opposite stances. When asked to comment on E. M. Forster's claim that characters sometimes take power and dictate the course of events, Vladimir Nabokov archly responded:

> My knowledge of Mr. Forster's works is limited to one novel which I dislike; and anyway it was not he who fathered that trite little whimsy about characters getting out of hand; it is as old as the quills, although of course one sympathizes with *his* people if they try to wriggle out of that trip to India or wherever he takes them. My characters are galley slaves. (1973, 95)

Forster's stress is on the autonomy and integrity of the created world, while Nabokov centers on the suzerainty of the world's inventor. Some version of this debate has gone on for centuries. Walter Scott was deeply annoyed by Fielding's auctorial forays,[23] and Henry James in a frequently cited passage severely castigates Trollope for similar interpolations:

> In a digression, a parenthesis or an aside, he concedes to the reader that he and his trusting friend are only "making believe." He admits

that the events he narrates have not really happened, and that he
can give the narrative any turn the reader may like best. Such a be-
trayal of a sacred office seems to me, I confess, a terrible crime; it . . .
shocks me every whit as much in Trollope as it would have shocked
me in Gibbon or Macaulay. (1972, 31–21)

This may seem an exceedingly strange claim for James to make.
For one thing, James is clearly the more metafictional writer of the two:
if "The Figure in the Carpet" is not self-referential, then no text is; the
same can hardly be said of *Barchester Towers*.[24] More importantly, James
is always talking about form, composition, art, and selection; his prefaces are a series of accounts of the patterning of his raw material, including his characters' destinies. What he objects to in the passage just
cited is not so much that Trollope made such an admission, as that he
did it within the fiction rather than in a preface. It is curious that James
takes Scott's position in opposition to that of the odd trio of Fielding,
Trollope, and Nabokov. Literary theory can engender strange alliances.
James's allusion to historians is both revelatory and something of a red
herring. The conventions of fictional representation generally demand
that an author present his fiction as factual. Nevertheless the fact remains that fiction is fiction. As Samuel Johnson cogently observes: "The
delight of tragedy proceeds from our consciousness of fiction; if we
thought murders and treasons real, they would please no more" (1960,
39). And since playing with conventions is virtually a convention of the
novel, one should come to expect, rather than attempt to suppress, various forms of frame-breaking and reflexivity.

One must wonder how the prejudice against metafiction could ever
arise (and in some form, it has been around since Aristotle, who decreed: "The poet should speak as little as possible in his own person,
for it is not this that makes him an imitator" [cited in Hazard Adams
1971, 63]). The answer, or at least part of it, is I believe closely related to
causal systems. While metafiction can easily coexist with other types of
causation, its explicit forms necessarily undermine the internal consistency of a naturalistic world. Unlike the authorial commentary of an
Eliot, Tolstoy, or Wharton, which ultimately enhances the verisimilitude of the tale, more radical interjections create a rupture in the foundations of naturalism. At one point Thackeray writes: "If Rawdon
Crawley had been then and there present, instead of being at the club
nervously drinking claret, the pair might have gone down on their knees
before the old spinster, avowed all, and have been forgiven in a twin-
kling. But that good chance was denied to the young couple, doubtless

in order that this story might be written. . . ." (*Vanity Fair*, chap. 16). This aside problematizes the enterprise of narrative representation by implying that the events appear not because they are depictions of genuine affairs or even the ineluctable consequences of earlier actions, but because the author invented them in order to conform to an independent trajectory, thus violating the work's realistic premises. A critic like James—and there are many of them—is right to object when the pretense of factuality is admitted to be mere "making believe"; Thackeray, like Trollope and Fielding, is of course doing just that, but to admit it is to impair the integrity of the naturalistic causation he has worked so diligently to establish. On the other hand, a metafictional transgression of the naturalistic provides a work with a new dialectic that can operate like the interpretive tension between the supernatural and the naturalistic in a tale of the fantastic.

In this respect allegory may be considered as a cousin of metafiction. Here too an alternative ordering (the development of an ideological thesis) is superimposed on a narrative progression and can tamper with the work's causal system. In the more interesting allegories, these two modes complement, problematize, and enrich each other; in tiresome ones the narrative world never fully attains autonomy. An example from Camões should illustrate the proximity of allegory and metafiction as related interventions of more basic systems of causation. In the scandalous ninth canto of *The Lusiad*, Venus causes the Nereides to be overwhelmed with desire and placed on a paradisiacal island in the path of Vasco da Gama's ship. After an extensive account of the ensuing amorous delights and voluptuous riot, Camões shifts gears and reduces the entire scene to a parable of fame:

> For these fair daughters of the ocean,
> Thetys and the angelic pencilled isle,
> Are nothing but sweet honor, which these won,
> With whatsoever makes a life not vile.
> The privileges of the martial man,
> The palm, the laurelled triumph, the rich spoil,
> > The admiration purchased by his sword,
> > These are the joys the island doth afford.
> > > (Stanza 89, Fawnshawe trans.)

In this passage, the causal laws governing the fictional world are temporarily suspended and the authorial allegoresis is as complete an intervention as the metafictional frame-breaking of Shakespeare, Thackeray, or Nabokov noted above.[25] A comparable interpenetration of the allegorical and the metafictional in *The Scarlet Letter* has been analyzed by Maureen Quilligan (1979, 51–58); a contemporary fusion of these modes appears in Günter Grass's satire of Brecht, *The Plebeians Rehearse the Uprising*.

It is important to observe that the four possible causal systems are all in close proximity to each other. The naturalistic and supernatural interpretations have found it difficult to dislodge each other; there is enough apparent design in nature to make the teleological argument for the existence of God perennially popular, though after Kant's critique it has lost its respectability among the philosophically minded: even Cardinal Newman had to concede that he believed in design because he believed in God, not in a God because he saw design. Since the end of the eighteenth century, it was generally accepted that some amount of chance was compatible with a naturalistic worldview; certain realist authors placed a few unlikely events in their narratives to make them appear more realistic. Both supernatural and chance universes are fundamentally opposed to naturalism, the former asserting there is more extensive and directed causal connection than the naturalist standpoint allows, while the latter assumes there is much less. Furthermore, truly chance worlds—that is, those that thoroughly defy or ignore probability—can only exist in fiction. The trope of nature as the book of God is of venerable antiquity, and so is the corollary idea of the author as the god of his own creation.[26] It should not be surprising that metaliterary appropriations of fate have survived any belief in the divine teleologies they had formerly mirrored.[27]

While supernatural and metafictive constructions of fate are always analogues of each other, the opposite is true concerning chance. Chance events are common enough in diurnal experience but can only be found in a narrative if first planted there by the author. This is probably why too many coincidences in a novel may annoy its readers. Even when plausible enough within the fictional world, excessively fortuitous encounters clearly show the author's hand. Where a character sees coincidence, a reader will discern contrivance. For this reason, explicit thematizations of chance in modernist literature are frequently accompanied by metafictional developments. Because of this interrelation, Philippe Sollers, in an essay articulating fiction's duty to contest the officially sanctioned stories of society, praises the novelist who "in passing made these two apparently contradictory assertions: 'to write is to impose one's will.' 'To write is to pursue chance.' To passivity and resignation, we must therefore oppose will and chance, will as chance, which is what is effectively disclosed by the writing of Georges Bataille" (1983, 205).[28]

As interpretations of the structure of the nonfictional world, each causal system precludes the others. In a naturalistic interpretation, the supernatural has no place and the improbable, by definition, must be relatively rare. A thorough supernatural teleology, on the other hand, goes far beyond the mechanical explanations of naturalism, and precludes the possibility of chance since, to recall Hamlet's paraphrase of the biblical verse, "There is a special providence in the fall of a sparrow" (5.2.220–21). If every event is ordered, then chance cannot exist. Similarly, a universe ruled by accident and coincidence is necessarily devoid of an all-encompassing supernatural order and subverts the idea of universal regularities that it is the purpose of natural laws to reveal. The three systems, as explanations of the world, are autonomous and mutually exclusive. Because of this fundamental incompatibility they are always as it were in a state of ideological war. The significance of Todorov's analysis of the literature of the fantastic lies partially in his identification of incompatible causal systems and his explanation of the way the reader is made to experience this antinomy.

When an event occurs that cannot be explained by the laws of our world, the person

> who experiences the event must opt for one of two possible solutions: either he is the victim of an illusion of the senses, of a product of the imagination—and laws of the world then remain what they are; or else the event has indeed taken place, it is an integral part of reality—but then this reality is controlled by laws unknown to us. (1975, 25)

Todorov goes on to state that the fantastic "occupies the duration of this uncertainty," and that it inhabits "that hesitation experienced by a person who knows only the laws of nature, confronting an apparently supernatural event" (25). The fundamental ambiguity that Todorov isolates is located more in the reader than in any character. Don Quixote occasionally is torn between naturalistic and supernatural interpretations of events, but this does not make Cervantes's novel a specimen of the fantastic. "The Turn of the Screw," however, does belong to the genre since the reader is made to choose between rival and incompatible explanations of events.[29] As we have seen, a hermeneutical conflict also exists between naturalistic and coincidental causal systems (as in "A Problem"), and even between supernatural and contingent universes (in *Oedipus Rex*, fate triumphs over chance). The metafictive can also be placed in opposition to each causal model. Todorov finds Hoffmann's "The Golden Pot" problematic for his account of the fantastic (103–4); I would suggest instead that the tale's conclusion, which invites us to view the strange events as an allegory of art, replaces the original natural/supernatural tension with a new opposition between the supernatural and the metafictional. Narrative fiction also allows for the possibility that several different, incompatible causal systems may all emerge, at the end of a text, to appear equally able to explain the events of the story (Achim von Arnim's *The Madman of Fort Ratonneau*, Pushkin's "Queen of Spades," perhaps Hawthorne's *The House of the Seven Gables*).

Going far beyond the parameters of Todorov's project, one may also identify the interpretive struggles engaged in by characters within a particular causal system, and note as well the epistemological skirmishing that goes on between differing versions of the same causal model. We can identify the causal systems that ultimately govern a fictional world, as well as designate unresolvable ambiguities or overdeterminations that go far beyond the natural/supernatural opposition. Causation is a basic feature of the setting of any narrative, and the determination of the extent and nature of a fiction's causal order is a crucial function of the act of reading. Beginning with Homer, authors have staged interpretive battles between characters over the teleological significance of events; since Chaucer, if not earlier, the audience has also been implicated, presented with the same ontological dilemmas that try the protagonists. It is essential to identify these issues to appreciate the destinies of characters, the complexities of the worlds they inhabit, and the appropriate critical response to such creations.

We may now summarize and further refine the distinctions set forth above. Every work has a causal setting—a canon of probabilities that govern the events of the fictional world. The supernatural may be totally predetermined, as it is in *Oedipus Rex*, or it may yield to the operation of free will, divine grace, or Christian providence, as occurs in *Life Is a Dream*. The naturalistic system may also be rigorously deterministic (the novels of Zola or Gorki), tightly connected (the plays of Corneille or the novels of Austen), or loosely conjoined *(Lazarillo de Tormes, Roderick Random)*. Chance worlds may defer or dilute causal connection *(Remembrance of Things Past)* or valorize coincidence *(Ulysses)*. Expressionistic authors (Kafka, Rhys, Céline) stress rigorous causal ties between dubious antecedents and unlikely consequences. Extreme deployments of chance can collapse the notion of cause (Blanchot) or show it moving backwards in time (Eliot). When the established causal setting is tampered with by an author or narrator, metafictional causal play results. This can occur within any of the other causal settings. In addition, some recent narratives contain inherently unknowable causal laws (Robbe-Grillet's *La Maison de Rendezvous*, Beckett's *Worstward Ho*). And, as will be discussed in greater detail in the last chapter, postmodern works that conflate different ontological levels can thereby vitiate the significance of any attributions of cause. Like many narratives centered on the embodiment of chance, these works are closely aligned to metafictional modes.

It is important to remember that many of the most interesting deployments of cause include interpretive battles between characters struggling to understand the causal laws of the world they inhabit, as well as hermeneutic challenges between the author and the reader who tries to make sense of the fictional world. Finally, it will be observed that the causal systems outlined tend to suggest at least a partial or intermittent historical pattern (which is not unconnected to the ideological issues discussed in my introduction): supernatural systems begin to vanish toward the end of the eighteenth century, naturalistic systems dominate the later nineteenth century, the fictional universes based on chance are preponderant in the past hundred years or so, and the flamboyantly metafictional orderings typical of postmodern texts flourish in every decade of the twentieth century. As interest in chance proliferated, fragmentation of linear narrative sequences and conventional teleological progressions became more pronounced, as novelists and playwrights tested the limits of randomness, disjunction, and disorder. This led to an interrogation of the nature and limits of narrative itself, an interrogation that will be described in the following chapter.

3

Temporal Sequence, Causal Connection, and the Nature of Narrative: Disjunction and Convergence in *Mrs. Dalloway* and Pinter's *Landscape*

Since Aristotle, literary theorists have tried to define and distinguish the forms of narrative. Today, the quest for differentiation between epic and drama or novel and romance has largely been displaced by the more basic questions concerning what is and what is not a narrative. The search for a working definition goes beyond the normal desire of students of narrative to be able to explain just what it is they study. (This desire, it might be observed, becomes a demand as the study of narrative extends still further into disciplines like history and philosophy whose methodological considerations are much less indulgent than those typical of contemporary critical theory.)

A number of novels and dramas have appeared in the last forty years that seem to challenge or transgress the boundaries of narrative. This has occasioned a note of urgency in the speculation concerning the nature of narrative—we are impelled as never before to clarify the frontiers of narrative if only to be able to articulate just what limits are being violated or transcended. At the same time, the proliferation of "limit texts" has driven many theorists to despair of ever articulating a category able to encompass a literary practice that thrives on conflating different categories. Noting that the novel is a kind of antigenre, "a type of literature suspicious of its own literariness" (1977, 64) that regularly cannibalizes various adjacent types of writing, Walter Reed argues against the theoretical possibility of a poetics of the novel. And when the subject is the more capacious one of narrative—drama, film, narrative poetry and painting, etc.—the task of conceptualizing this entity seems even more arduous.

However much we may want to throw our hands in the air and affirm that everything (or nothing) is a narrative, the fact remains that the work of numerous creative writers continues to force us to take a stand on the question of narrativity as we are repeatedly challenged and provoked by daring as well as dubious experiments. By defying accustomed expectations, the polyphonic fragments that open *The Waves* or the odd assemblages that generate the later novels of Simon or Robbe-Grillet taunt the reader into finding the principle that allows these works to be called novels. In analyzing other innovative works, it becomes not only meaningful but essential to determine whether a narrative can consist of a batch of transcribed conversations, two tales bound together in one book, intricately ordered scraps of description, speculation, and information, or repeated and contradictory versions of the "same" events.

In many cases, the answer is negative. For every such provocative text, the practicing critic is obligated to do some narrative theory, and poeticians can find their most abstruse pronouncements immediately challenged by a tangible counterexample. Andy Warhol's *a* is a transcription of actual conversations collected by a friend of the author. Robert Scholes is unambiguous about its narrative status: "His book is not a 'novel,' and it is not by Andy Warhol. He has neither edited nor written it; he has merely marketed it" (1979, 125). Scholes's primary concern is that the book is a transcription of talk rather than a representation of events, and that it is boring, trivial, and vacuous talk, at that. Even if these issues were obviated, it still might not be a narrative. Seymour Chatman discusses this as a theoretical possibility: "If we were to extract randomly from cocktail chatter a set of events that happened at different times and different places to different persons, we would clearly not have a narrative. . . ." (1978, 21). This is the case, he argues, because narratives presuppose some kind of cohesion: "The events in a true narrative, on the other band, 'come on the scene as already ordered,' in Piaget's phrase. Unlike a random agglomerate of events, they manifest a discernible organization" (21). This position, though it contradicts many earlier writers' statements, seems difficult to deny.

Other works pose harder questions. Whether Faulkner's "double novel" *The Wild Palms* is one or two narratives has been debated since its publication, and texts like *Go Down, Moses, The Unvanquished,* and *Light in August* have engendered similar controversies. Butor's "stereophonic constructions" are hard to designate with precision; it may be significant that their author, himself no mean theorist of fiction, chooses not to call them novels. Roland Barthes was delighted to observe that Butor's "*Mobile* offended the very idea of the Book" (1972, 171). Jacques Derrida, speculating on Blanchot's tale "La folie du jour" (originally entitled "Un récit?"), is impelled to ask: "What is a narrative—this thing we call a narrative? Does it take place? Where and when? What might the taking-place or the event of a narrative be?" (1979, 87).[1]

Robbe-Grillet's work is some of the most vexing for narratologists; often it seems constructed to defy any possible theory of fiction. Structuralists in particular have trouble placing his work within their typologies, and at times describe his works in unusual ways in order to fit them into a universal model. Gerald Prince offers one of the more ingenious methods of cutting this Gordian knot; referring to *Jealousy* he claims: "Though it may, to a certain extent, function as a narrative because it adopts many of the trappings associated with narrative art, it is not a narrative since no satisfactory chronology of its events can be established. . . . *La Jalousie* is a novel, of course, but a pseudo-narrative one" (1982, 65). One wonders what sort of theory of fiction is being invoked. That a text can be a "novel, of course" and yet not be a narrative may be a stranger fiction than any Robbe-Grillet ever devised. On the other hand, Prince's statement, implying that the text mimics but does not possess the quality of narrativity, impels us yet again to reflect on just what that quality might be.

These examples should reveal that the understanding of modern fiction is intimately linked to the interpretation of what constitutes narrativity. Here, reading, writing, practical criticism, critical theory, and narrative poetics are inextricably interwoven. It virtually becomes necessary to postulate a theory of narrative in order to discuss texts like those described above.

Numerous definitions of narrative have recently been set forth. Robert L. Caserio states that "A story is . . . a relating of an intelligence of relations in such a way that further relational thought is incited" (1979, 6). However, as Thomas B. Leitch remarks, this formulation "offers no way of distinguishing between narrative and non-narrative relations" (1986, 203). Leitch's own rhetorical, transactional analysis of the ways that words are recognized as stories is itself open to an analogous critique; laying too much stress on how any text could be read as a narrative, Leitch minimizes the importance of what Ross Chambers calls the interpretive "self-situating" of the literary work. Robert Scholes suggests that once a process of enactment or recounting is "sufficiently coherent and developed to detach itself from the flux of cultural exchange, we perceive it as a *narrative*" (1982, 60); this position seems both needlessly vague and overly subjective. Barbara Herrnstein Smith's casual and commonsensical claim that narrative discourse is "someone telling someone else that something happened" (1981, 228) is altogether too casual, leaving unexamined the obvious follow-up question of precisely what then characterizes that "something." This can be seen as an attempt to dissolve, rather than resolve, the question of narrativity.

Among most other narrative theorists, two rival conceptions are prominent, one of which stresses temporal succession while the other insists on causal connection.[2] Gerald Prince (1982), Shlomith Rimmon-Kenan (1983, 18–19), and Jean-Michel Adam (1984, 12) argue for the former position. Prince states that "narrative is the representation of *at least two* real or fictive events in a time sequence, neither of which presupposes or entails the other"(4). Roland Barthes also inclines to this position, since he affirms that any causal attribution is inherently suspect (1977, 94). Tzvetan Todorov tries to find a middle ground, and suggests that some narrative literature may be devoid of chronology and that other, equally rare forms may lack causality (1981, 41–46).[3]

Boris Tomashevsky, on the other hand, argues that "a story [*fabula*] requires not only indications of time, but also indications of cause," and opposes story to non-narrative works such as "descriptive and didactic poems, lyrics, and travel books" (1965, 66). It should be noted that Tomashevsky avoids much of the confusion or overgeneralization by using the phrase "indications of cause." It is this move that allows him not only to define story—and, implicitly, narrative—but also to establish the approximate point of demarcation between narrative and other forms. An account of a journey may be either a story proper or a record of successive descriptions: "[I]f the account is only about the sights and not about the personal adventures of the travelers, we have exposition without story. The weaker the causal connection, the stronger the purely chronological connection" (66). In this statement, Tomashevsky carefully isolates a fundamental factor: human interaction and mediation, however multiform. A similar emphasis is also stressed by Mieke Bal, who defines a *fabula* as "a series of logically and chronologically related events that are caused or experienced by actors [i.e., agents]" (1985, 5), and J. Arthur Honeywell (1968, 46), Peter Rabinowitz (1987, 104–9), and Jon-K. Adams (1989) seem to incline toward a comparable position.

The most compelling argument for a causal definition of narrative comes from film theory. This should not be surprising since, like a poem though unlike a novel, narrative may be present or absent in a film. To distinguish narrative from non-narrative cinema, David Bordwell and Kristin Thompson offer the following example: "A man tosses and turns, unable to sleep. A mirror breaks. A telephone rings." This is a non-narrative sequence of events. If on the other hand "[a] man has a fight with his boss; he tosses and turns that night, unable to sleep. In the morning he is still so angry that he smashes the mirror while shaving. Then his telephone rings, his boss has called to apologize" (1979, 51). This series of nearly identical events clearly forms a narrative. Bordwell and Thompson thus affirm that a cinematic narrative presents *a chain of events in cause-effect relationship occurring in time*" (50).

It should also be observed that Hayden White's work with narrative and non-narrative types of historical representation reaches similar conclusions. In language that rather approximates Seymour Chatman's, White explains that the events in narrative history must be "revealed as possessing a structure, an order of meaning, which they do *not* possess as mere sequence" (1981, 5). By contrast, White continues, the annals form "completely lacks this narrative component, consisting only of a list of events ordered in chronological sequence" (5). Here again, a powerful counterexample militates against a merely sequential definition of narrative.

It is necessary now to address two questions provoked by these rival conceptions of narrative: the view that emphasizes temporal succession will have to accept a number of highly dubious concatenations of events as legitimate narratives, while the stance based on causal connection flies in the face of accepted critical distinctions first noted by Aristotle and subsequently reformulated by E. M. Forster as the difference between "story" and "plot"—a differentiation also accepted by Todorov (1981, 41–45), Meir Sternberg (1978, 10–17), Gerald Prince (1982, 66–67), and Shlomith Rimmon-Kenan (1983, 17–19). To begin with the juxtaposition of unconnected occurrences, consider the temporal conjunction of any two events: say, "A young boy examines ice, decades later he is shot," or "A man in Paris nodded; some time later a man in China died." It seems quite evident that these sentences are not narratives, however minimal, even though they fit Prince's criteria of temporal succession. Cut two or three sentences of reported action from a newspaper, paste them together, and they will not, even if presented in a chronological sequence, necessarily constitute a narrative.[4] More is needed: specifically, some kind of causal connection, however oblique or indirect. In fact, what may intrigue us most about the sentences just adduced when considered as possible narratives is speculation over the kind of cause that could connect such unrelated elements, thereby providing the preconditions of narrativity. And connections can be made that will form miniature narratives out of otherwise unrelated events. The first can become, "Many years later, as he faced the firing squad, Colonel Aureliano Buendia was to remember that distant afternoon when his father took him to discover ice" (1970, 11), as it does at the beginning of *One Hundred Years of Solitude*. The two incidents are not in a direct causal order; viewing the ice did not cause Buendia to be shot years later, but they are part of a larger causal matrix so that one event can occasion the memory of the other. If there is a causal connection between the young Frenchman's assent and the death of the Chinese, as there is in Rastignac's hypothetical version of Vautrin's proposal in *Père Goriot*, then we are in the presence of a narrative.

Shlomith Rimmon-Kenan is the only advocate of the temporal succession position to face squarely the curious implications of this stance. After affirming Prince's definition, she speculates:

> Does this mean then any two events, arranged in chronological order would constitute a story? Theoretically speaking, the answer must be Yes. . . . There would indeed be something very odd about the following bit of story: "Little Red Riding-Hood strays into the forest and then Pip aids the runaway convict." But if we accept this as the possible paraphrase of *some* text (perhaps a narrative pastiche by Robert Coover or Donald Barthelme), then the temporal conjunction requires us to imagine some world where these events can co-exist." (1983, 19)

This bit of argumentation, once it has been scrutinized, may turn out to be almost as odd as the example it considers. By accepting the bit of story as a narrative text and then imagining the possible world in which such elements could be conjoined begs the question: to prove that this is a story, just assume that it is a story. The absence of causal connection makes it appear non-narrative, if not nonsense, as the author is ready enough to admit. However, to imagine a world where such events can coexist is not a requirement of "the temporal conjunction," but surely a way to conceive of a possible causal interaction.[5]

If mere temporal succession fails to provide a necessary condition of narrativity, what is to be made of the traditional critical distinction

between unconnected, episodic events and causally conjoined succes-
sions? This distinction, first articulated by Aristotle (1971, 53–54), has
been reformulated by E. M. Forster in his widely accepted differentiation between what he calls "story" and "plot."[6] One response is suggested by Seymour Chatman's careful scrutiny of Forster's now classic
examples. Unless instructed otherwise, readers will generally assume
that even the statement "The king died and the queen died" contains
some causal link,

> that the king's death has something to do with the queen's. . . . "The
> king died and then the queen died" and "The king died and then the
> queen died of grief" differ narratively only in degrees of explicitness
> at the surface level; at the deeper structural level the causal element
> is present in both. . . . "Because" is inferred through ordinary pre-
> sumptions about the world, including the purposive character of
> speech. (1978, 46)

And, one may add, by the nature of narrative itself; if the protagonists
were the first king of Ireland and the last queen of Hawaii, there could
be no causal connection, and no narrative, either. Chatman's claim may
be somewhat overstated, though his general position, I believe, is largely
accurate. "The king died and then the queen died" does not exactly
present an inferable causal link between the two deaths, but it does
imply participation within the same general causal matrix.[7] The citi-
zenry may well feel the effects caused by this double demise, and it
certainly indicates that the throne's heir apparent will be greatly affected.

At this point, it will be useful to indicate the different types of causal
connection that can appear in a narrative. There is direct entailment,
where consecutive events follow inexorably from each other, as in the
plays of Corneille or the novels of Austen. There are also intersecting
causal chains when the events of two or more largely independent stories fuse together (*King Lear*). In episodic tales, the successive events do
not always follow from each other, though their cumulative effects ultimately cause some transformation of the protagonist: as one critic
observes, Lazarillo de Tormes "is a character who is modified and
molded psychologically by his adventures and his ambience. The innocent child who has his head smashed against the bull is quite different from the vengeful child who makes his blind master smash his head
against the pillar" (Fiore 1984, 84). We may also recognize deferred causation, where a number of apparently unrelated incidents are finally

brought into a causal skein (Proust's *Recherche*). In addition, successive events may be part of an allegorical pattern *(Pilgrim's Progress)*, parallel construction *(Mrs. Dalloway)*, or the exfoliation of generative metaphors (the later novels of Robbe-Grillet); in these cases, the causal connection between events is minimal (though central) and complemented by other ideological or aesthetic modes of connection.[8] In each case, the principle of causation is firmly intact, but the locus of connection and the ultimate causal agencies differ and shift. The position of Prince, Rimmon-Kenan, and Adam in the last analysis distinguishes between different types of narratives, rather than between narrative and the non-narrative.

From the perspective offered by literary theory, it seems fair to conclude that some causal connection is a necessary precondition of narrativity. Such a conclusion needs to be tested by literary practice, however. Two examples immediately suggest themselves: Woolf's *Mrs. Dalloway*, which often seems to dispense with connection at several levels of the text, and Pinter's *Landscape*, which roughly juxtaposes the monologues of apparently unrelated speakers. Both works foreground and problematize issues of disjunction and convergence to the point where each can be seen as a kind of metanarrative of causal connection. And by suspending or deferring any union between significant parts (or, in the case of Pinter, the audience's knowledge of such a union), each work produces an interpretive instability.

Mrs. Dalloway invokes questions of causality at almost every level of the text. Many descriptive sequences of phrases can seem randomly assembled: "Bond Street early in the morning in the season; its flags flying; its shops; no splash; no glitter; one roll of tweed in the shop where her father had bought his suits for fifty years; a few pearls; salmon on an iceblock" (n.d., 15). The progression of thoughts of the protagonist is, at the very least, highly idiosyncratic, while that of Septimus Smith presents even more unusual conjunctions. As Lucio Ruotolo notes, "Like some foreign visitor, Septimus the outsider sees familiar objects as if for the first time" (103). In the tradition of other causally bewildered characters in modern fiction (the narrator of *Hunger*, Faulkner's Benjy and Vardaman, Beckett's Molloy), Smith fails to perceive ordinary connections and imagines outlandish ones.

The relations between the novel's characters are frequently confused, disjointed, and unknowingly at cross-purposes; we find numerous conversations but very little communication. The sequencing of the narrative often appears rather arbitrary: within a fairly strict linear chronology, we move back and forth between the minds of Clarissa Dalloway, Peter Walsh, Septimus Smith, and several other figures, though the precise motivation for the shift of focalizers is often unclear and the reasons for the varying durations of the forays into the different minds are not always immediately evident. This picture of disjunction, fragmentation, and chaos is an important aspect of the novel and one that is frequently thematized and inscribed within the work. The most extreme specimen of disorder might well be contained in Smith's curious papers:

> Diagrams, designs, little men and women brandishing sticks for arms, with wings—were they?—on their backs; circles traced round shillings and sixpences—the suns and stars; zigzagging precipices with mountaineers ascending roped together, exactly like knives and forks; sea pieces with little faces laughing out of what might perhaps be waves: the map of the world. Burn them! he cried. (223–24)

As the novel progresses, the numerous disparate narrative strands coalesce into two independent though occasionally contiguous stories, that of Mrs. Dalloway's party and that of Septimus Smith's suicide, and some unifying link between the two story lines seems imminent. In an early conception of the novel's ending, Woolf resolved to have Mrs. Dalloway kill herself upon hearing of Smith's death, thus fusing all the varied strands of the action (cf. Daiches 1942, 75). Instead, she chose to unite the story lines in a more subtle and tenuous manner.

Fragmentation and disjunction however are only half of the novel's business. The text also contains an equal though opposite urge to create, unite, and interconnect; the Dalloway story line comes with a centrifugal force that is opposed to the centripetal movement of the Smith narrative. As Clarissa exudes, "Heaven only knows why one loves it so, making it up, building it round one, tumbling it, creating it every moment afresh" (5). Not untypically, the specific pronominal referent is unimportant, if not abandoned, as the motif of connection increases in force. Peter Walsh also experiences an almost motiveless feeling of the unitary convergence of unusual events: as the ambulance bearing Smith's mangled body rushes past, Walsh feels something like an epiphany, "a moment, in which things came together; this ambulance; and life and death" (230). As we will see, this moment is both a foreshadowing and a *mise en abyme* of the novel's final causal deployment. In the meantime, we may note that it is just this oscillation between order and anarchy, symmetry and dissolution, beauty and madness that is dramatically embodied throughout the text.

Numerous critics have drawn attention to some facet of this basic antinomy; Alice van Buren Kelley has noted the numerous binary oppositions in which this dichotomy has been expressed: permanence and change, individual and society, male and female, subjective thought and objective reality, etc. (1973, 251–54), and goes on to oppose these to her own dyad, fact and vision.[9] The problem with all of these oppositions is that they tend to remain at the level of concept and characterization, and leave the composition of this unusual text as a kind of afterthought, when in fact the work's thesis, theme, and architecture embody the more basic opposition of order and fragmentation. A merely thematic analysis all too often mutes or glosses over the extreme and extensive conflicts of the text; the threat of disorder is much more powerful than is usually acknowledged and the resulting moments of interpenetration are therefore achieved with greater difficulty, invested with more significance, and imply a more profound synthesis than has generally been perceived.[10]

The disjunction that concerns us most here is the deferral of connection between the two main story lines. Of its significance to the author there can be little doubt. In the preface to the American edition, Woolf states that in a first version, "Septimus, who is later intended to be [Clarissa's] double, had no existence" (cited in Daiches 1942, 75). The second plot is a compositional afterthought, but one which gives Woolf a great feeling of accomplishment. She notes in her diary: "The design is so queer and so masterful. I'm always having to wrench my substance to fit it. The design is certainly original and interests me hugely" (1973, 57). One of the most striking features of this queer yet masterful design is, I believe, the suspension of connection between the two major narrative strands and the establishment of a series of analogical correspondences between the thoughts of Mrs. Dalloway and the consciousness of Mr. Smith. The number and extent of the elaborate parallels in theme, situation, imagery, and language has been carefully observed, as the studies of Daiches (1942, 75ff.), Guiguet (1965, 232–37), J. Hillis Miller (1982, 184–85, 196–201), and Harper (1982, 126–30) amply demonstrate. The larger implications of this strategy for narrative theory are nevertheless still to be fully articulated.

Woolf is not simply adding a new technique to the novelist's repertoire but is radically challenging the nature of narrative. By juxtaposing the two story lines, she necessarily invokes the causal principle she suspends—if there were no connection whatsoever, there would be no novel, but merely two unrelated tales gratuitously glued together within the same binding. Consequently, a kind of aesthetic tension mounts as long as the two strands resist unification. Woolf plays with the reader concerning this issue, as the idea of curious connections between distant individuals frequently appears in a variety of guises. For example, Mrs. Dalloway feels that she and Peter "lived in each other" ([1925b] n.d., 12); later she thinks that to know "anyone, one must seek out the people who completed them" (231). This in turn echoes Lady Burton's thoughts about her departing guests:

> And they went further and further from her, being attached to her by a thin thread (since they had lunched with her) which would stretch and stretch, get thinner and thinner as they walked across London; as if one's friends were attached to one's body, after lunching with them, by a thin thread, which (as she dozed there) became hazy with the sound of bells, striking the hour or ringing to service, as a single spider's thread is blotted with raindrops, and, burdened, sags down. So she slept. (170)

Passages like these invite us to look for analogical correspondences to supplement or take the place of absent causal ties, or even to imagine different possible causal agencies that could actually provide the connections here described in figurative language.[11]

By the end of the novel, an elaborate series of architectural parallels connects Smith to Mrs. Dalloway, even though their worlds have hardly touched, and, until the final pages, neither is even aware of the existence of the other. By this point, the two story lines have become antithetical versions of the same basic narrative. Direct connection from event to event is replaced by analogical relations between events, as the governing causal agency shifts from the actions of characters to the arrangement of the text.

Parallelism alone is not enough; like the authors of earlier such experiments—Middleton and Rowley's *The Changeling*, Eliot's *Daniel Deronda*—Woolf is impelled to weave the symmetrical strands together. In the final pages, Clarissa learns of Smith's suicide, the death affects her deeply, and she even identifies herself with him: "She felt somehow very like him—the young man who had killed himself. She felt glad he had done it" (283). Once he is dead, he can enter her life; plotlines and thematic concerns are brought together as Clarissa reflects that "[d]eath was an attempt to communicate. . . . There was an embrace in death" (280–81). Ultimately, the forces of connection and interanimation triumph over disorder and death, and a causally complete narrative emerges out of the fragments of isolated events. Having toyed with mere temporal sequence throughout most of the text, Woolf finally provides a slight though distinct causal nexus.

While Woolf defers the moment of connection between independent narrative strands, Pinter retards the audience's knowledge of the relation between his characters' narrations and thereby draws attention to the role of causal connection in *Landscape* more forcefully. The play is set in the kitchen of a country home with the characters Beth and Duff seated at a table. The drama begins as Beth says:

> I would like to stand by the sea. It is there.
> *Pause*
> I have. Many times. It's something I cared for. I've done it.
> *Pause*
> I'll stand on the beach. On the beach. Well . . . it was very fresh. But it was hot, in the dunes. But it was so fresh, on the shore. I loved it very much.
> *Pause*
>
> (1978, 177; Pinter's ellipsis)

The precise status of Beth's speech is ambiguous. First, she expresses a desire for the future, then she indicates that that scene is present, presumably in her mind—or at least present as narrative. She then delves into the past, revealing that she has often been by the sea, in some sense or another. Next we move from what Genette calls the iterative to the historical past proper: "it was very fresh." In this opening section, one feels a tension between memory and invention, personal experience and wish-fulfillment, the past tense and the subjunctive. As her monologue continues, it becomes more precise, concrete, and descriptive: "I walked from the dune to the shore. My man slept in the dune. He turned over as I stood. . . . Would you like a baby? I said. Children? Babies? Of our own? Would be nice" (177). Despite a couple of incursions into what may be the present (e.g., "I am beautiful"), the past tense predominates and a narrative starts to emerge.

At this point Duff's speech begins. He recounts events from the immediate past in a tone and vocabulary totally different from Beth's:

> The dog's gone. I didn't tell you.
> *Pause*

I had to shelter under a tree for twenty minutes yesterday. Because of the rain. I meant to tell you. With some youngsters. I didn't know them.

(178)

The most striking feature of Duff's speech is its complete irrelevance to the lines spoken by Beth. The two narrations have nothing in common; any audience would be hard-pressed to imagine a possible context that could frame such disparate locutions. The interpretive situation is further complicated by the fact that (as the stage directions indicate) Duff refers normally to Beth though he does not appear to hear her voice, while Beth never looks at Duff and does not appear to hear his words, even though both characters sit in chairs at opposite ends of the same table.[12] As the play progresses, the two stories narrated by the protagonists remain autonomous and unconnected, even as the personalities of the characters appear increasingly antithetical. Beth is romantic and imaginative; her monologue is a series of arabesques that embellish and re-create her primal experience with the man on the beach. Duff's speech is terse, stark, direct, and crude; his narrative is relentlessly linear, obviously motivated, and addressed to a familiar auditor.

The question provoked by Beth's unheard monologue and Duff's semidialogue goes to the very basis of poetics: in what sense can these independent accounts be considered parts of a single narrative? Or are we being presented with two narratives disguised as one? Considered this way, Aristotle's animadversion toward episodic plots and Elizabethan playwrights' recklessness with subplots tend to pale into insignificance.[13] Here we are forced to decide what is and what is not a story (fabula).

To be sure, Pinter plants numerous hints—and perhaps a few red herrings as well. The naturalistic setting of the drama (the conventional country house) invites us to find a naturalistic explanation for the strikingly disjoined speeches. One may simply assert, as some critics do, that two people are engaged in ordinary conversation, though they consistently ignore each other's words.[14] It is equally possible that Beth is verbally articulating her stream-of-consciousness while Duff is telling her his story. The problem with either of these readings is that there is no indication, verbal or semiotic, that Beth ever hears a word spoken by Duff. Consider the following exchange:

Duff: I should have had some bread with me. I could have fed the birds.

Beth: Sand on his arms.
Duff: They were hopping about. Making a racket.
Beth: I lay down by him, not touching.
Duff: There wasn't anyone else in the shelter. There was a man and woman, under the trees, on the other side of the pond. I didn't feel like getting wet. I stayed where I was.
Pause
Yes, I've forgotten something. The dog was with me.

(179)

Neither narration has a discernible effect on the speech of the other. If anything, Duff's admission that he had "forgotten something" suggests he may be responding to a comment that he alone is able to perceive. To maintain a "naturalistic" thesis it may well be necessary to imagine that Beth is in fact conversing with Duff, offering questions and promptings that only he can hear; or, alternatively, that Duff is mentally rehearsing a story he will tell Beth, complete with responses to her anticipated comments. But at this point the possible naturalistic recuperation becomes so byzantine that one is virtually forced to reject it altogether.

At the same time, it is equally difficult to write the play off as two juxtaposed but independent narratives. The counterpoint between the birds' vigor ("They were hopping about. Making a racket") and Beth's demureness ("I lay down by him, not touching") is too weak for causal connection, though too strong for mere coincidence. The same might be said of the parallel settings of the two narrations. Duff sees a man and a woman on the other side of the pond; Beth and her man at the beach can be seen by another fellow at a distance (181). The symmetry teases our understanding of narrativity such that we may be tempted to reinterpret the speeches as the same event viewed from two perspectives (in which case Duff would be the observer) or as two versions of the same event (in which Duff perhaps displaces himself from participant to observer in his own "recounting"). On the other hand, radical differences in the time frame and season work against this kind of identification.

As the play develops, another discrepancy arises. The man in Beth's monologue is one who notes that she looks grave while she waters and arranges flowers. It is hard to imagine that this lover, in any avatar however romantically reconstructed, can be the figure Duff, who says "Mind you, there was a lot of shit all over the place, all along the paths, by the pond. Dogshit, duckshit . . . all kinds of shit . . . all over the paths" (180; Pinter's ellipses). Throughout most of the play, disjunction reigns. But just at the points where the speeches seem most unconnected, new parallels and symmetries emerge, depriving the audience of even the dubious consolation that the two narratives are in fact independent ones. Shortly after the last lines cited, Duff muses on the nature of fish, concluding that they are very shy creatures who need to be wooed (182), a thought that just might have been shared by Beth's consort on the beach. A further twist in this plot of connection and disjunction appears when Duff narrates his trip to a local pub, followed immediately by Beth's decision within her own narrative to visit the hotel bar with her friend (183). Once again the repetition is too obvious to be devoid of significance, but just what the significance might be is at this point indeterminable.

By juxtaposing apparently unrelated series of events, Pinter seems to be challenging the very preconditions of narrativity. And this, I believe, can illuminate the controversy over what constitutes a narrative. Up to this point, what we have are represented events in a temporal sequence. In fact, we have two forms of representation that occupy several periods of time. Beth's monologue recounts events in a remote past, while Duff narrates what happened "yesterday." Actors portraying the two characters take turns relating those events in sequence. Here, it seems, the criterion for narrativity set forth by Prince, Adam, and Rimmon-Kenan is scrupulously adhered to, and yet we cannot say we are in the presence of a single narrative. In fact, the opposite seems to be the case; at some level, the drama is about the suspension, deferral, or transgression of narrative. Temporal succession alone is inadequate; some causal connection is essential if the piece is in fact one drama, rather than two disparate ones forcibly yoked together. And it is just this ambiguity that Pinter exacerbates by hinting at and then denying causal connection between the two characters' accounts.

Roughly halfway through the play, the first real evidence for connection appears. Duff states vaguely "I was thinking . . . when you were young . . . you didn't laugh much. You were . . . grave" (186; Pinter's ellipses). He also mentions having planted flowers she might like (184), and still later observes, "I was very gentle to you. I was kind to you, that day. I knew you'd had a shock, so I was gentle with you" (190). These lines confirm the possibility that Duff just might have been the subject of Beth's narration, though this is by no means certain, particularly since her shock and Duff's gentleness are caused by his admission of infidelity.

A stronger case for connection is occasioned by the following metadiscursive commentary that Duff addresses to Beth:

> Do you like me to talk to you?
> *Pause*
> Do you like me to tell you about all the things I've been doing?
> *Pause*
> About all the things I've been thinking?
> *Pause*
> Mmmnn?
> *Pause*
> I think you do.
>
> (189)

Instead of reciting events to a person who does not seem to hear his words, Duff is now drawing attention to his act of narration, suggesting that he is partially aware of the monological nature of his discourse, and that it is not as utterly unnatural as the audience might understandably perceive it to be. Duff's questions are rhetorical, demanding no response; consequently, Beth's silence during the pauses takes on an aura of naturalness, as some submerged form of connection between the two speakers grows increasingly plausible.

Some minutes later, Beth narrates another scene, this time in a different landscape. Now she works as a housekeeper exactly as Duff's wife does. She refers to a dog that could be Duff's dog. The day she describes is sunny but wet. "Wet, I mean wetness, all over the ground" (193). At this point the two narratives begin to converge. She talks about stroking the dog silently while looking through a window. Duff now says:

> I never saw your face. You were standing by the windows. One of those black nights. A downfall. . . . You knew I'd come in but you didn't move. . . . What were you looking at? . . . I stood close to you. Perhaps you were just thinking, in a dream . . . (195)

This passage also tends to "naturalize" the odd dialogical relationships between the two characters, making it possible that the representation just might consist of Duff's actual speech juxtaposed to Beth's internal monologue—though if this were the case, Beth's ability to block out all of Duff's words is genuinely preternatural. Nevertheless, some such connection is further reinforced by Beth's admission that when she asked "him" to look at her, "he turned to look at me but I couldn't see his look" (197). This statement simultaneously refers to the hero of her private narrative, symbolically depicts her emotional estrangement from Duff (assuming that she is the wife addressed by Duff's speech), and also articulates the position of the characters on stage—from where she is sitting, Beth cannot see Duff's eyes.

The forces of connection finally defeat the pattern of disjunction in the final speeches of the play. In a virtually fugal counterpoint, Duff narrates his sudden copulation with his wife as Beth reiterates details of her memory-fantasy encounter with the man on the beach. Here, the balancing of past and present, romance and carnality, "he" and "you" form a perfect architecture, and some interpretive fusion seems to be demanded. The final line of the play, Beth's "Oh my true love I said" (198), contrasting so starkly with Duff's robust vulgarity, leaves the audience with the perception that they have seen opposite perspectives of the same marriage. Although the play's precise temporal and spatial coordinates will always remain dubious (can they really be in the same room at the same time?), the causal connection, however vague or oblique, seems firmly in place. And for this reason, the two accounts form in the end a single narrative, albeit an ambiguous one. It is unfortunate that so many of Pinter's critics, sensing the connection implied by the ending, tend to downplay or ignore the "drama of disjunction" that precedes the moment of intersection.[15]

Pinter's achievement in *Landscape* is perhaps best appreciated when contrasted to similar experiments in story construction. Both *King Lear* and *Ulysses* contain two main coplots that begin to affect each other toward the middle of each narrative and are fused together at the end of each work (though the fusion is more tenuous and deferred longer in Joyce's novel). *Light in August* employs several story lines of varying complexity that touch one another without ever merging in a direct causal chain. In *The Changeling* and *Mrs. Dalloway*, the main plot is almost entirely independent of the subplot until the ending of each work, although numerous thematic parallels abound. Beckett's *Molloy* juxtaposes a pair of suspiciously similar narratives, one purportedly by Molloy, the other about Moran's quest for Molloy (or perhaps Mollose; Moran is not entirely sure). There is no question *that* these two narrations are connected; just how they are conjoined, however, has vexed critics for decades. Still more tenuous is the series of largely independent but occasionally interpenetrating chapters of Calvino's *If on a winter's night a traveler*; here, the framing device of frequent authorial addresses to the reader provides additional cohesion, though perhaps not enough for the book to be a narrative.[16] Finally, in Faulkner's *The Wild Palms*, two completely distinct narratives are juxtaposed chapter by chapter as different characters in different locations confront analogous dilemmas.

On this spectrum of works with increasingly divergent story lines, *Landscape* might be placed somewhere between *Molloy* and *If on a winter's night*. While the Molloy and the Moran sections of Beckett's novel must be related in some way, Pinter leaves open the possibility that Beth and Duff might just be unknown to each other, though most of the rather scanty evidence does point to the opposite conclusion. For this reason, there is a greater epistemological tension inherent in this work than is present in *The Wild Palms*, the stories of which do not and cannot affect each other.[17] Pinter takes us to the limit of possible causal connection, which is also the boundary of narrative.

Pinter's lesson makes it apparent that causality is in fact a necessary condition of narrativity, as Tomashevsky, Bal, and Bordwell and Thompson have averred. This in turn leads to the definition of narrative as the representation of a causally related series of events. I use "causally related" instead of "directly entailing" to include the numerous works that defer, interrupt, or otherwise play with direct causal connection from event to event. Indeed, this suspension of apparent causal ties usually results in a productive narrative tension. It will also be observed that "causal relation" is employed instead of, rather than in addition to, the more customary "temporal succession" since, as I trust has already been demonstrated, a genuinely unconnected sequence is inadequate to define our subject.

On the other hand, it is not clear that temporal succession is a necessary condition of any possible narrative; one may imagine four or five utterly simultaneous though causally connected events that would constitute a narrative, and Borges and Robbe-Grillet may have actually composed them in the short stories "The Aleph" and "The Secret Room." In any event, it seems to be a theoretical possibility. The criterion of representation is necessary, otherwise we are dealing not with fiction but its double, life. There is perhaps no need to restrict this conception to sentient agents since, for example, a geological account of the movements of a glacier may plausibly be considered a narrative. Finally, I use the term "series" because two events, though necessary to constitute a minimal narrative, are not in themselves sufficient conditions of narrativity. "John looked hard at Mary; she returned his stare . . ." does not strike me as being a narrative, even though the events are causally connected and contain a temporal progression. Something more is certainly needed.

It is my hope that this definition will help clarify what it is we refer to when we speak of narrative. To attempt to identify a notoriously indefinable entity is an especially difficult challenge, yet it is one we neglect at our peril for both theoretical and practical reasons: (1) not every group of words constitutes a narrative; some (like *War and Peace*) do, while others (a telephone directory) certainly don't. It is our responsibility to clarify this distinction, to observe its significance, and to examine possible counterexamples and borderline cases. (2) Although many critics and theorists wisely hesitate to offer pronouncements that can be construed as essentialist or prescriptive, the fact remains that a large number of interesting creative writers attempt to toy with, problematize, or transgress the boundaries of narrative. Without some sense of what these boundaries might be, we will be unable to appreciate or articulate the precise achievements of such peculiar works. A flexible definition of narrative is essential if we are to comprehend fully the audacious experiments of Beckett, Robbe-Grillet, or Pinter, as I hope this chapter has disclosed. The history of critical theory has been filled with overzealous and overly restrictive definitions; this should not drive us into silence and "know-nothing" postures, but rather impel us to more comprehensive, dynamic, and sophisticated theoretical positions.

Part Two

Fabricating Destiny in Modern and Postmodern Narrative

4

Modernism's Unlikely Stories: Necessity, Chance, and Death in *Nostromo, Light in August,* and *Invisible Man*

The three texts selected for analysis here are characteristic of three central moments of modernism, each of which can be depicted in causal terms. *Nostromo* exemplifies the early-modern move away from naturalistic causal sequences, as chance plays an unusually powerful role in the unfolding and interaction of events. In *Light in August*, a classic of "high modernism," the play of coincidence is sufficiently great as to destabilize naturalistic claims; unlikely progressions and seemingly unmotivated shifts in narration frequently call attention to the artificer of the fictional world. *Invisible Man* challenges the ordering myths of both Christian providentialism and a narrow version of historical materialism as history is revealed to be permeated by chance events, and realism is superseded by expressionism. These choices, though perhaps somewhat arbitrary, are by no means random. The proliferation of chance events within a largely naturalistic framework can also be found in the late-Victorian and Edwardian novels of Hardy, Ford, and Forster; the high-modernist valorization of chance can be traced very nicely in *Ulysses* and *To the Lighthouse*; and equally compelling expressionist works have been written by Kafka, Céline, and Blanchot, though none of these authors deals as directly with issues of chance, cause, and fate as Ellison does. For these reasons, I feel there is something both representative and insistent about the three modernist authors I have selected. In addition, these works trace a pattern within the history of the modern novel (to be sure, one of many patterns that might be traced, but a significant one nonetheless) of the gradual increase of the presence and powers of chance within fictional worlds. Such a narrative of literary history can help explain not only the transformation but the mechanism of change in the transition from naturalism to postmodernism, as the ever more pervasive role of chance problematizes naturalistic foundations, postulates the parallel though self-contained worlds of modernism and expressionism, and ends in the flagrantly and self-consciously artificial worlds of postmodernism.

Throughout his career, Conrad explores the often curious relation between causes and effects. The early work frequently embodies what Marlow in *Heart of Darkness*, musing on the idea of destiny, calls "a mysterious arrangement of merciless logic for a futile purpose" (1989, 86). In these tales, Conrad dramatizes the conflict between a confused idealism and an intractable reality ("Youth," *Lord Jim*). In the later works, a series of increasingly improbable events plays a major role in the development of the story ("A Smile of Fortune," *Chance*). In *The Shadow Line*, Conrad's last novella, the proliferation of unlikely events has led many readers to suspect that some supernatural causal agency is at work; Conrad, in the preface to the volume, takes pains to explain his disbelief in the supernatural, noting that the "world of the living contains enough marvels and mysteries as it is." In addition, most of Conrad's fictions contain a general, almost Shakespearean concern with the unintended consequences of carefully plotted intrigues and dubiously motivated actions. *Nostromo* can be situated near the turning point of Conrad's growing fascination with the role of coincidence, as he fleshes out Marlow's observation in *Lord Jim* that "It's always the unexpected that happens."[1]

In *Nostromo*, a number of mutually incompatible causal systems are evoked by the characters and tested in the story. The causal master narrative of official turn-of-the-century ideology is embodied in the shadowy figure of Holroyd, the San Francisco-based millionaire entrepreneur. For him, international capitalism, historical progress, and Christian providence form a happy marriage—or at least a comfortable ménage à trois—and combine to produce "vast conceptions of destiny" (1960, 76). As the local intellectual, Martin Decoud, observes, "[A]s long as the treasure flowed north, that utter sentimentalist, Holroyd, would not drop his idea of introducing, not only justice, industry, peace, to the benighted continents, but also that pet dream of his of a purer form of Christianity" (197). For the characters who actually inhabit Sulaco, the situation is not nearly so simple; most are forced to alter or abandon some aspect of Holroyd's happy trinity. It is here that interpretive clashes over the agencies of effective causation emerge and become embattled. For Charles Gould, proprietor of the silver mine, divine teleology is irrelevant. Holroyd had advised to hold on like grim death and trust in God; to this, Gould can only observe that Holroyd "is very far away, you know, and, as they say in this country, God is very high above" (172); elsewhere, Gould equates Holroyd's "voice of destiny" (a term with manifest imperialist overtones) with "a bit of claptrap eloquence" (79). For Giorgio Viola, the Italian republican, the wounding and imprisonment of Garibaldi was "a catastrophe that had instilled into him a gloomy doubt of ever being able to understand the ways of Divine justice" (38).

Other personages, from the fatuous Captain Mitchell to Gould's wife, Emilia, adhere to a quasi-secular teleology, that of the myth of universal progress. The skeptical Decoud, while doubting all cosmological orderings, nevertheless enjoys employing the rhetoric of fate: "I came here on a fool's errand, and perhaps impelled by some treason of fate lurking behind the unaccountable turns of a man's life" (181). Then there are those like Father Roman, who is acutely aware of powerful retrograde motions in the trajectory of providence:

> He had no illusions as to [the Indian mine workers'] fate, not from penetration, but from long experience of political atrocities, which seemed to him fatal and unavoidable in the life of a state. The workings of the usual public institutions presented itself to him most distinctly as a series of calamities overtaking private individuals and flowing logically from one another through hate, revenge, folly, and rapacity, as though they had been part of a divine dispensation. (320)

The novel's characters frequently turn to such confused or conflicting interpretations to understand the events that surround and engulf them. As the series of accidental causes, ruthless intentions, and unexpected consequences proliferate, all principles of order are strongly challenged or decisively refuted. The cruel irony permeating each turn of events mocks all notions of general or special providence. As the indigenous inhabitants occasionally aver with "grim profanity," the "eye of God Himself" cannot "find out what work a man's hand is doing in there" (22). In this world, there can be neither providence nor divinity.

Illusions of the progressive force of history and civilization are also articulated and exposed. In a passage often cited, one of the characters sums up the community's experience in the following words: "There is no peace and no rest in the development of material interests. They have their own law, and their justice. But it is founded on expediency, and it is inhuman; it is without rectitude, without the continuity and force that can be found only in a moral principle" (406). As William W. Bonney has observed, "[T]his novel conclusively exhibits Conrad's opposition to nearly all redemptive efforts that maintain a sense of cosmic purpose, whether their scope is personal or international" (1980, 109)—or, we might add, metaphysical. The various causal agencies evoked by the characters seem ultimately epiphenomenal of the brutal, impersonal forces of the demands of capital. The silver-rich San Tomé mountain is in the end "more soulless than any tyrant, more pitiless and autocratic than the worst government, ready to crush innumerable lives in the expansion of its greatness" (414), and no one can escape its influence.

Edward Said notes that "Nostromo and Decoud are irrevocably tied to this devotion, even though each thinks that he is acting for his own reasons. In the same way that Gould is 'run' by Holroyd, Nostromo and Decoud are 'run' by Gould. None of the three has any freedom" (1985, 132). The chains of origins and influence extend still further: most of the populace of Sulaco is controlled to some degree by actions of Gould; the desire to rule him and the mine is a primary cause of the Monteros' rebellion, and the dominant motives driving Nostromo (to be well spoken of) and Decoud (the love of Antonia) can only be achieved in the terms dictated by the overriding material interests of the region. At this point, we are left with an extremely cynical version of historical materialism—one that, unlike Marx's variety, does not come with a happy ending to the narrative of history, but remains confused, without any significant progress, and devoid of both teleology and closure.[2]

But the story of causal relations does not end in an inhuman, machinelike naturalism. The logical series of individual calamities perceived by Father Roman defies all modes of prediction, whether based on necessity, probability, fatalism, or providence. As many of the characters come to learn, there is a consistent and almost uncanny infusion of chance events and unfathomable coincidences throughout the narrative's turns; the barest plot summary of this novel discloses the strangest concatenations of unlikely events. Nostromo, the incorruptible man of the people, is perpetually confronted by the wildest improbabilities. To note only the most compelling sets of coincidences,

one might enumerate the curious circumstances surrounding Nostromo's transport of the cargo of silver ingots. That the silver lay in the
port just as the rebel force approached was, as Decoud himself affirms,
"only an accident" (201). As chance would have it, the night was inscrutably dark and virtually windless. As the lighter carrying the silver
drifts through the gulf, Nostromo and Decoud discover that someone
is hiding in the boat. Decoud remarks on the improbability of this "bi-
zarre event" (224), and Nostromo finds it "most amazing" that a person could have concealed himself on board while the lighter was being
loaded (221), concluding that "[h]is being here is a miracle of fear" (224).
Unfortunately, the stowaway just happens to be the miserable hide
merchant Hirsch—the one man in the area who could not be trusted to
maintain silence on board. This becomes an important issue since, as
chance would have it, the steamer bearing Sotillo's invading force just
happens to run into the lighter in the middle of the gulf. Hirsch is ab-
surdly carried away while holding onto the anchor of the enemy
steamer; Nostromo and Decoud head for the nearby island of the Great
Isabel, where no one "is ever likely to come" (240).

    Later, after the silver is believed to be lost, Dr. Monygham tells
Nostromo that he will lie when interrogated and state that the treasure
is buried on the Great Isabel—which is, in fact, the truth. Nostromo
quickly suggests that the doctor say instead the ingots are sunk in the
gulf, to which, with exquisite irony, the mistaken Monygham responds,
"'This has the merit of being the truth. . . . He will not believe it'" (367).
Nostromo soon persuades him otherwise, and the silver remains untouched. Still later, Nostromo receives a greater shock when he learns
that a lighthouse is being built on the island. There, as he is about to
remove some more of the ingots, his identity is mistaken in the dark
and he is shot and killed by his friend and prospective father-in-law,
Viola.[3]

    In the world of this novel, the extraordinary is typical and the acci-
dental is the rule. The reader may well sympathize with Captain
Mitchell, who imagined that the events prior to Nostromo's departure
in the lighter "had exhausted every startling surprise the political life
of Costaguana could offer. He used to confess afterwards that the events
which followed surpassed his imagination" (261). The ubiquitous determinism emanating from the silver of the mine is tempered, challenged,
and interrupted by interjections of chance, as the force of material necessity is jostled by the play of coincidence. The major role chance holds
in Conrad's works, which is frequently remarked on by the characters,

has begun to enter critical discourse thanks to critics like William Bonney, Robert Siegle, and Leland Monk, who have drawn noteworthy attention to Conrad's problematization of conventional, naturalistic binary oppositions. Some of these critics, however, tend to affirm and retain those oppositions while simply shifting the valorization from one pole to the other.[4]

Conrad's poetics of causation is, I believe, considerably more elusive. It is important to recognize the interactions and permutations between the antithetical agencies of determinism and chance. Each collides with, interanimates, and is incorporated by the other: chance events that interrupt causal skeins become the sources of new causal progressions as determinism is alternately routed by and made master of an unusual series of unexpected coincidences. This can be read as Conrad's attack on the narrow causalism that informs earlier mechanistic programs of literary realism and naturalism. Insofar as Austen, Balzac, and Zola fail to include the play of chance, their novels may be faulted as unrealistic; Conrad would no doubt strongly assent to the position Aristotle attributes to Agathon: "[I]t is probable . . . that many things should happen contrary to probability" (1971, 59). For this reason Conrad found it useful to toy frequently with the genre of romance, even to the point of composing what might be termed antiromantic romances in which chance and determinism continuously modify the role of each other in unpredictable though consistent ways.[5]

There is one other significant causal agency present in *Nostromo*: the power of language. One may even go so far as to say that the novel is to a large degree a drama of the use and abuse of language. It contains numerous conflicting acts of narration, discloses the mechanics of propaganda, reveals the motives and limitations of its historians, and charts the fates of the names that men make for themselves. Characters accuse each other of behaving as if life were a "moral romance" (181); at the same time they find it essential to narrativize their aspirations in order to achieve their ends. Decoud remarks of Gould: "He could not believe his own motives if he did not make them first a part of some fairy tale" (178). As Jeremy Hawthorn explains, "Decoud understands that such fairy tales are not just a by-product of material interest, but are the very means whereby these interests effect their goals" (1979, 61). At the opposite extreme, fanciful historical chronicles engender actual political maneuvers: Pedrito Montero, leader of the rebellion, had in Paris been "devouring the lighter sort of historical works in the French language" and imagining himself as another Duc de Morny.

"Nobody could have guessed that. And yet this was one of the immediate causes of the Monterist revolution" (311).

Because of the confusions over the real motivations of individuals' behavior and because of the frequent causal gaps or coincidental ties between disparate events, the act of narration, with its implicit causal connection, teleology, and closure, becomes an inescapable activity for all of the major characters. As Said has noted, nearly everyone seems anxious about keeping and leaving a personal "record" of his thoughts and action (1985, 100), and he also points out that, in their "recollection of the past, the characters of *Nostromo* are also affected by their idealism, which to judge by its force, borders on vanity" (106). Idealism is invariably equated with illusion by Conrad, as several commentators have observed.[6] What needs to be stressed is that many of these narratives are conscious falsehoods intended to engender the very situation they pretend to describe.

Decoud's role is typical. His involvement in his homeland's politics is caused by a letter sent by his beloved Antonia (1960, 131). His letter to his sister in Paris is the only account we have of the revolt in Sulaco—and it is a limited account; conversing with European journalists, he tries to engender favorable if inaccurate news: "My friends, you had better write up Señor Ribiera all you can in kindness to your own bondholders. Really, if what I am told in my letters is true, there is some chance for them at last" (130); in Sulaco, he becomes the principal propagandist for the Ribierists, and his published satires on the Monteros make him the most wanted man in Costaguana. In the end, the poet-journalist literally dies by silence. Alone on the Great Isabel, "he could look at the silence like a still cord stretched to the breaking point, with his life, his vain life, suspended to it like a weight" (307). The absence of speech proves unendurable; the glib intellectual commits suicide to break the silence.[7] He is a man who lives and dies by language.

Every politician in the novel, whether in pursuit of money, power, or prestige, is nourished on fictions: the mind of Pedro Montero, we are told, was wrapped in "the futilities of historical anecdote" (323); and each in turn fabricates lies of his own, which the narrator never fails to expose. Conrad's deployment of a cynical omniscient narrator is a key tactic in the subversion of his characters' fictitious accounts of the same events. The same might be said of the deployment of narrative time: events are noted; then various accounts of those events are given; the narrator's version, whether it comes before or after the characters' narratives, always exposes them as self-interested distortions—in fact, many characters are partially defined by the kinds of fabrications they offer.[8] The fictions they generate are always tainted by the illusions they live by; they are either mythic versions of sordid facts or rationalizations of a system of domination.

It is also the case that extreme situations in life can resemble or imitate the most stylized fictional genres, including opera, farce, and fairy tale. This is hinted at in many places in the text. Decoud's plan of secession, the chief engineer tells Monygham, "sounds like a comic fairy tale—and behold, it may come off, because it is true to the very spirit of this country" (256). It does. Ironically, this is the very plan Monygham originally ridiculed as wildly impractical, saying, "Life is not for me a moral romance derived from the tradition of a pretty fairy tale" (181). But life at times can be just that. Conrad's moral seems to be that as long as men continue to mythologize rapacity and idealize material forces, they are doomed to live a stylized farce, a parody of a myth. At the same time, he suggests that reality cannot be contained within the probabilistic logic of conventional realism and that the chance encounters foregrounded in nonrealist genres are derived from lived experience.

In *Nostromo*, Conrad exfoliates the idealization of material forces, the arbitrary play of chance, and the material effects of linguistic acts. The more misunderstood, inexplicable, or absurd a sequence of events is, the greater its potential to be forcibly narrativized into a self-serving, fictional totality. The most highly stylized kind of comic opera is at once an obscurely accurate image of the world, a conceptual model characters use to influence each other, the literal background music to diatribes of pseudopatriotic lies (86), and an emblem of all the narratives that are used to attempt to explain the merciless logic and absurd contingencies governing human existence. Conrad not only documents the way unlikely events and determining forces are fabricated into totalizing narratives but also enacts this process by creating subtle, virtually hidden dramas of names, words, and silences within the text. Perry Meisel, tracing the "recession of centers" in *Heart of Darkness*, suggests that apparently grounded reality finally becomes mere "representation of itself" (1978, 24). Analogously, it would be fair to conclude that *Nostromo* is a narrative of the forces and pressures of narrativization, a kind of realistic romance about the melodramatic imagination. Throughout, chance is the element that counters and resists narrative totality, even as its presence provokes ever more insistent narratives that deny its effects. Paradoxically, Conrad finally presents us with an avowed fiction that accurately discloses the fabrications inherent in every historical representation of events.

We are now in a position to understand why Conrad in a letter once claimed that the historical part of *Nostromo* "seems to me much more true than any history I ever learned" (cited in Karl 1979, 812n). *Nostromo*'s narrative insists on including the irruptions of chance that traditional historical narrative regularly suppresses.[9] As David F. Bell observes: "History, continually in the process of revealing itself, seems to have a motor all its own which drives it, despite and beyond the individual participants. It thus appears eminently rational and explicable through causal reasoning (but only after the fact)" (1993, 3). It is just this easy explicability that Conrad interrogates and dismisses as he reveals the actual mechanics of (and the social forces behind) the dubious goal of a causally seamless narrative.

William Faulkner is regularly considered to be a fatalistic author, and to be sure the rhetoric of fatalism is frequently employed by his characters.[10] In *Light in August*, Faulkner—like Conrad—undercuts the supernatural and mechanistic notions of necessity invoked by the characters and replaces these systemic forms of causalism with both the play of coincidence and a subtle though pervasive account of the powers of language, in particular the language of narrative representation.[11] Unlike Conrad, whose repeated versions of the same unlikely events reveal the ideological forces that inform and deform the act of narration, Faulkner manipulates sequencing in a different way by juxtaposing apparently unconnected series of happenings. The multiple plot lines, notoriously lacking in causal connection, may however be read as different versions of the same story of the paradox of teleology and the promises and dangers of narrative.

The world the characters inhabit simultaneously demands and defies interpretation. As Joseph Reed observes, "Accidental triggers rouse the past, chance encounters rule the present" (1973, 115). Reed goes on to conclude that these chance events "become by the end a web of inevitability" (116); we will find, on the contrary, that chance is not so easily subsumed into this pattern. Consider one of the novel's most crucial clusters of accidents: Lena Grove comes to Jefferson in search of Lucas Burch, the man who impregnated her. Once there, she asks after him (incredibly, he is in the town, using the name "Joe Brown"). The man she questions, Byron Bunch, responds curiously, "I don't recall none named Burch except me, and my name is Bunch" (1972, 56). By the end of the novel, Byron is attached to her, having assumed the function of the name he conflated with his own. As Arnold Weinstein observes: "Verbally, Bunch and Burch are so alike as to be taken for one another, and indeed Lena Grove is, at the outset, misled by this similarity, coming to Byron Bunch, thinking he is Lucas Burch. Yet, the poetic logic of this novel is such that this initial confusion will become a fusion" (1986, 12), as the sign becomes—or, indeed, generates—its referent.

Given the series of unlikely events in this novel, it is not surprising that the characters regularly evoke a number of disparate causal stances in order to interpret the events around them. Many are obsessed by some variety of determinism. Doc Hines sees "God's wrathful purpose" behind every event, and Gavin Stevens suavely offers crude theories of racial motivation (although it is not clear how literally he means them to be understood). Nathaniel Burden blames the death of his father and his son on "the curse which God put on a whole race before your grandfather or your brother or me or you were even thought of" and adds to Joanna, "None can escape it. . . . Least of all, you" (1972, 278). She of course does not escape, but carefully constructs the scenario of her own demise, fueled by the Calvinist rhetoric of her grandfather. When she asks Joe to pray and then points a gun at him, she precipitates her own death by the same cycle of fanaticism that destroyed her progenitors. Hightower is the character whose life is most obviously patterned on a previous death: the fate of his grandfather dominates his actions and obscures his judgment.

The actions of Christmas have the greatest aura of inevitability. Faulkner ensures this effect by employing numerous strategies such as the extended flashback of Joe's earlier life, the protracted hunt for him, and the pressure of allegorical patterns. He also uses suggestive rhetorical strokes. We find sentences like, "He was saying to himself *I had to do it* already in the past tense; *I had to do it. She said so herself*" (307); this statement is made a few pages before the killing is depicted, but several chapters after its occurrence has been mentioned.

All the types of determinism noted above have two interesting features in common. In every case, the characters' actions are not fated, but only believed to be; each finally chooses to be subject to his or her own doom. Furthermore, each of these "fates" is based on a fiction. The tale Hightower orders his life around is probably spurious: "Now this is what Cinthy told me. And I believe. I know. It's too fine to doubt. . . . A negro might have invented it. And if Cinthy did, I still believe.

Because even fact cannot stand with it" (534). Memory does indeed believe before knowing remembers, because often there are no facts to be known.

There is even less epistemological support for the fatalism of the Burdens—the curse of a Calvinist god interpreted by a fanatic is hardly a solid ground for certainty. Hines's maniacal exegeses of the events around him are worse fabrications. Finally, Joe's racial status is inherently indeterminable, based solely on his grandfather's obscure hunch. When asked by Joanna how he knows he is part black, he responds, "I don't know it. . . . If I'm not, damned if I haven't wasted a lot of time" (280).

Trapped by the designation "Negro," Joe does waste time and is horribly damned. He uncritically accepts a name, instead of challenging its interpretation, and thus acquiesces to playing his role in a larger social fiction. Colonel Sartoris had justified his killing of Joanna's brother and grandfather by a fabrication: he claimed these men's goal was "stirring up the negroes to murder and rape" (274). After Joanna's death, this is precisely the context in which Joe's actions are placed; those who gathered at the burning cabin "believed aloud that it was an anonymous negro crime committed not by a negro but by Negro and who knew, believed, and hoped that she had been ravished too: at least once before her throat was cut and at least once afterward" (315–16). The political consequences of these struggles for control of interpretation exemplify Foucault's thesis that speech is no mere verbalization of conflicts and systems of domination, but is the very object of man's conflicts.

For this reason, linguistic constructs are of paramount importance, and Faulkner takes pains to document the inventive power of words, names, texts, and, above all, fictions.[12] We find that the power of language to engender events ends in an equation of fiction and death. More precisely, the characters who insist on living out earlier narratives will die by them; or, in Hightower's final revealing words, "How false the most profound book turns out to be when applied to life" (531). This "tragedy of metafiction" has plagued Joe all along. He finds Joanna's behavior inexplicable: "It was as if she had invented the whole thing deliberately, for the purpose of playing it out like a play" (284). It is a very dangerous play, however, as the text makes clear once Joe takes up her last note: "He should have seen that he was bound just as tightly by that small square of still undivulging paper as though it were a lock and chain" (299). On this point, Gavin Stevens is as adamant as the narrator: Joe was sent "against all reason and all reality, into the embrace of a chimera, a blind faith in something read in a printed Book" (495).

That claim has several intriguing implications. To live by a fiction of the past, whether private, social, or mythic, is to doom oneself to recurrent patterns of thought and action that are at best stultifying and at worst deadly. Such a thesis has additional implications at the level of metafiction. During his flight, Christmas wonders why he has not been apprehended: "Any of them could have captured me, if that's what they want. Since that's what they all want: for me to be captured. But they all run first. . . . Like there is a rule to catch me by, and to capture me that way would not be like the rule says" (371). Within the world of the fiction, this statement expresses Joe's determined fatalism about his own actions. In the context of self-referentiality, however, it indicates he has not yet completed the author's pattern for him. Like Oedipus, he must return to his birthplace; like Christ, he must be jeered at by a multitude before his "crucifixion" can occur. A metafictional narrative thus emerges to parallel, complement, and occasionally eclipse the hitherto naturalistic account.

The same paradoxical nemesis drives other characters just as ruthlessly. Grimm pursues Christmas "with that lean, swift, blind obedience to whatever Player moved him on the Board" (510); Hightower admits, "I am in turn the instrument of someone outside myself" (542); and Joe Brown is driven to employ ludic tropes to comprehend the action around him: "It seemed to him now that they were all just shapes like chessmen—the negro, the sheriff, the money, all—unpredictable and without reason moved here and there by an Opponent who could read his moves before he made them and who created spontaneous rules which he and not the Opponent, must follow" (483).

Brown's confusion ironically anticipates the puzzlement that many of the book's readers, confronted by the same series of inscrutably ordered events, cannot help but experience. It underscores Brown's sense of fatalism while alluding to the inventor of that destiny—the novelist, thinly disguised as fate. The metafictional development does problematize the work's naturalistic pretensions by pointing to the fictionality of the fiction. At the same time, the central thesis of the linguistic nature of destiny, evident in the lives of the characters, is reinscribed at the larger level of textual production. By hinting that he is free to give the tale any twist he chooses, the author (or "Player") becomes a kind of prototype of the characters who take the direction of their lives into their own hands. This in turn draws attention to the paradoxical status of causality in fiction: any coincidence, determinism, or teleology within a fictional world is present because it has been placed there by the author. At some level, destiny is always a fabrication.

Two characters do escape the novel's cycle of violent repetitions. Lena Grove and—ultimately—Byron resist the various narratives surrounding them to create instead new lives in a different state.[13] They become authors of their own destinies, instead of agents of someone else's. Lena's tranquil naïveté saves her from entrapment in the myths that damn the more clever folk around her. For Byron, the case is more difficult, but he too finally rejects Hightower's (and the community's) designation of Lena as "bad" and a "lost" woman (402) as thoroughly if not as effortlessly as Lena ignores the word "whore" (6). At last, the world triumphs over a book.

We may now summarize the construction and disclosure of the causal laws that govern the universe of *Light in August*. The characters' consistent rhetoric of fate and doom evokes a supernatural ordering that close analysis shows to be illusory. The great majority of the book's events can be squarely placed within the framework of a nondeterministic naturalism. There are also, however, a number of curious "linguistic coincidences" and self-reflexive statements that point to an additional metafictional ordering that parallels, complements, and occasionally destabilizes the naturalistic system. Faulkner rejects supernatural teleologies and tampers with naturalistic laws of probability. In doing so, he emends the ancient trope of nature being the book of God; in this fictional universe, the author is the sole divinity. Faulkner thus goes beyond Conrad's narrative of the subtle ubiquity of chance and looks ahead to the more sustained metafictional interventions of Beckett and Nabokov.

In *Light in August* fate is ultimately a verbal construct, a preexistent name, tale, or text; as its etymology reveals, it is nothing more than that which is spoken. A character trapped in the nexus of repeated narratives can expect to share the ontological vertigo of Christmas, who "believed with calm paradox that he was the volitionless servant of the fatality in which he believed he did not believe" (307). On the other hand, psychological and allegorical identifications notwithstanding, Lena's child is not destined to be another Joe Christmas. Unlike Joe's mother, Lena will not acquiesce in the social interpretation of her natural act; she will ignore the mad allegoresis of men like Hines (or her brother-in-law). Faced with the same dilemma as Christmas, she leaves

her home, but not to return; she refutes its epithet by inventing another—not, like Joe, to die for a word that is probably false.

Ralph Ellison's *Invisible Man* also contains extended meditations
on and dramatizations of the power of language, the fate of names, and
the material effects of written documents and oral narratives.[14] It too
enacts a systematic causal drama that interrogates the competing forces
of destiny, possibility, chance, and the teleology of history. This drama
is conducted on a more philosophical plane than Faulkner's and has
not yet been fully demarcated in the critical literature on Ellison. The
theme of destiny is first explicitly broached by Mr. Norton, a major
benefactor of the black college that the narrator attends. Mr. Norton
tells the narrator he believes that "your people were somehow connected with my destiny. That what happened to you was connected
with what happened to me" (1972a, 41). In the face of the narrator's
incomprehension, the white philanthropist becomes more blunt, though
he remains obscure: "[Y]ou are my fate" (41). Norton goes on to explain that he wishes to see the consequences of his endowment, to learn
to what extent his money, time and hopes have been fruitfully invested
(45), and he insists that the narrator write to him later in life and thereby,
in Norton's words "tell me my fate" (44). This oracular colloquy is suc-
ceeded by an accidental encounter with a poor Southern black who has
unwittingly committed incest. Norton, incredulous, questions the ironically named Trueblood, employing Calvinist rhetoric and oedipal imagery that prove to be singularly inappropriate:

> "You have looked upon chaos and are not destroyed!"
> "No suh! I feels all right."
> "You do? You feel no inner turmoil, no need to cast out the offending
> eye?"
> "*Suh?*"
> "Answer me!"
> "I'm all right suh," Trueblood said uneasily.
> "My eyes is all right too. And when I feels po'ly in my gut I takes a
> little soda and it goes away."
>
> (51)

In addition to being "a witty 'puttin' on massa' performance," as Bernard
W. Bell dubs it (1987, 202), this exchange can be read as a demystifi-
cation of the supposed inevitability of necessitarian claims, as a sanguine rebuke to deterministic schemes.

This reading is underscored when the dialogue on destiny is resumed in a nearby honky-tonk and fate is denounced as both a fabrication and a mask for other interests. A shell-shocked black veteran tells Mr. Norton: "You cannot see or hear or smell the truth of what you see—and you, looking for destiny! It's classic! And this boy, this automaton. . . . To you he is a mark on the score-card of your achievement, a thing and not a man" (93). Later, after the narrator has been expelled from college, he runs into the vet at the train station. The narrator finds this to be an unpleasant coincidence, but the vet urges him to look beneath the surface of events and discern the actual force that orchestrated the apparent coincidence, namely "the white folks, authority, the gods, fate, circumstances—the force that pulls your strings until you refuse to be pulled any more" (152). Supernatural orderings and aleatory sequences are shown to be illusory; there is a power that does propel events, but that power is white supremacy, not fate or chance.

This lesson is reenacted when the narrator, now in New York, falls in with The Brotherhood, a fictionalized version of the Communist Party. Once again, dubious claims of teleology are accompanied by a rigorous script imposed on the narrator's actions. This time the necessity of history is claimed to be the hidden force that drives events; only by working with it can one understand the structure of society, invest individual life with meaning, and keep from falling "outside of history." At the same time, the members of The Brotherhood carefully choreograph all of his actions and statements, and act as if they know intimately the role he is to play.[15] For the credulous narrator, this produces the uncanny feeling that he had somehow been through it all before, as if he had viewed the scene he was now enacting in the movies, or read it in a book, or experienced it in a "recurrent but deeply buried dream" (293).

There are of course excellent reasons for this sense of déjà vu: The Brotherhood's grand narrative of the structure of events, complete with its carefully scripted roles for all involved, is a reverse image of Mr. Norton's liberal tale of providential design. In a key passage, the ontological dimensions of The Brotherhood's stance are set forth:

> Thus for one lone stretch of time I lived with the intensity displayed by those chronic numbers players who see clues to their fortune in the most minute and insignificant phenomena: in clouds, on passing trucks and subway cars, in dreams, comic strips, the shape of dog-luck fouled on the pavements. I was dominated by the all-embracing

idea of Brotherhood. The organization had given the world a new shape, and me a vital role. We recognized no loose ends, everything could be controlled by our science. Life was all pattern and discipline. . . . (373)

It is significant that the deterministic version of historical materialism set forth (what we would now refer to as "vulgar Marxism") is compared to the hoped-for auguries of deluded gamblers. Both parties seek to find a hidden network of correspondences that pattern the phenomenal world and empower those who perceive it. As the novel continues, the narrator discovers an ever widening gap between the world and The Brotherhood's model of it, as an increasing number of "loose ends" threaten to unravel the party's hermeneutical paradigm. In a moment of illumination he wonders, "What if history was a gambler, instead of a force in a laboratory experiment . . . ? What if history was not a reasonable citizen, but a madman full of paranoid guile . . . ?" (431). Here the image of the gambler does not point to chance so much as to an antideterminist conception of possibility, including the possibility to form and re-form one's self. In a key passage that emends the famous Hegelian (and Marxist) adage, Ellison writes: "You could actually make yourself anew. The notion was frightening, for now the world seemed to flow before my eyes. All boundaries down, freedom was not only the recognition of necessity, it was the recognition of possibility" (488).

With this insight, the narrator is finally able to elude the series of inaccurate and debilitating social narratives that have been thrust upon him, and he quickly realizes the need for a counternarrative that can more accurately describe the world he experiences and help him attain an authentic self-definition.[16] As Ellison remarked in an interview, before the narrator "could have some voice in his own destiny he had to discard these old identities and illusions; his enlightenment couldn't come until then" (1972b, 177). He must, in short, reject the destinies invented for him by others before he can begin to forge his own. In one of the novel's most brilliant and bitter ironies, the narrator happens to run into Mr. Norton once more. Norton does not recognize him; when the narrator states "I'm your destiny," Norton hurries off, thinking that his interlocutor must be insane (564). This is the final scene in the narrative proper; the narrator, living underground, now resolves to write down his life, trying "to give pattern to the chaos which lives within the pattern of your certainties" (567), empowered by the knowledge that, until "some gang succeeds in putting the world in a strait jacket, its definition is possibility" (563). Like Lena Grove, he must reject society's existing master narratives (both liberal and radical) in order to create an original life story, free of the enforced closure of others' constricting teleologies. Like Byron Bunch, he ceases to be an actor in a debilitating social drama once he resolves to author his own life story.

Looking back at the worlds presented in *Nostromo* and *Light in August* from the vantage point of *Invisible Man*, we see an increasing contamination of the naturalistic system as the play of chance (or chaos) grows more disruptive and ostentatious, and the metafictional component progressively more evident. In Ellison's novel, the rapid acceleration and abrupt disjunction of causal skeins is reinscribed in the expressionistic sequences that not only represent the emotionally charged perceptions of the narrator but further demarcate an underlying ontological instability. The next major step toward the abyss will be taken by Beckett who, I will suggest, constructs roughly parallel universes that fail to intersect—either with each other or with the world that we inhabit. Furthermore, it is just this incongruity that situates Beckett precisely at the fault line separating modernism from postmodernism.

5

Molloy and the Limits of Causality: Ontological Skepticism, Narrative Transgression, and Metafictional Paradox

The works of Samuel Beckett are filled with unexpected conjunctions, dubious origins, and implausible consequences.[1] *Molloy*, however, represents Beckett's most exhaustive interrogation of causal issues and consequently deserves a sustained analysis. In this novel, there are conspicuous gaps between intention and result, cause and effect, and word and object. The connection between events within each of the novel's two sections is suspicious at best, the relation of the narrators to the events they recount is avowedly skewed, and the conjunction (or disjunction) between the two halves of the book has been the subject of debate since its publication.

The idea of cause first appears in the opening lines of the text as Molloy observes he is in his mother's room though he does not know how he got there—despite the fact that the ostensible goal that directed his actions during the previous several years was the desire to reach his mother. The significance of causality is further highlighted by numerous allusions to philosophical theories of cause. By following out the variations on this theme, I will attempt to disclose some unexamined aspects of *Molloy*, including the important role of Humean skepticism in the text, and explore Beckett's play with the conventions of representation.

Two philosophical systems collide in the novel. Humean skepticism informs the Molloy section while the Moran narrative can be read as a parody of Cartesian rationalism. Molloy is unable to discern genuine causal ties, while Moran frequently postulates connections that do not in fact exist. The governing metaphysics of each section—and, in particular, the causal theory of each metaphysics—has far-reaching consequences for the narrative construction, interpretive dilemmas, and metafictional play of its narration.

The presence of the ideas of Descartes and later rationalists in the work of Beckett has been exhaustively documented.[2] This research has been so extensive, in fact, that its very bulk can occasion some confusion.[3] Consequently, by foregrounding references to formally articulated theories of causation, we can attain a useful focus on Beckett's practice. It is important to recall that the medieval "axiom of causality" that presupposes an equality between causes and their effects underlay Descartes's metaphysical reasonings. He also postulated simple, mechanistic causal connections to explain all events in the physical world, and he assumed an unproblematic interaction between the disparate and incommensurable realms of mind and matter. Subsequent Cartesians, while acknowledging this ontological dualism, pushed harder to explain how minds and bodies, being so dissimilar, can possibly affect one another. In most cases, their answer was that no such causal union is possible. In *Molloy*, three of these systems are alluded to. Molloy's claim that "all things hang together, by the operation of the Holy Ghost, as the saying is" (1965, 41) in the context of his decision to start his journey points to Malebranche's theory of occasionalism—that God miraculously intervenes into the natural order to arrange the otherwise impossible interaction of mind and matter. The "image of old Geulincx" (51) may well refer to the Belgian philosopher's famous model—two clocks that tell exactly the same time—to explain the regular correspondences between the physical and spiritual realms. This example was later developed by Leibnitz in his doctrine of "pre-established harmony," a phrase that significantly occurs twice in *Molloy* (12, 62). In these long-abandoned philosophical accounts designed to explain the appearance of causation while denying its reality, one may find an analogue of the apparent though evanescent causal connection between the two parts of *Molloy*.

It is easy to see Moran as a modern embodiment of the seventeenth-century Continental philosophers' aspirations. Moran is constantly cogitating, his perceptions are annoyingly clear and distinct, and each of his actions is carefully reasoned, hierarchically ordered, and directed toward a fixed goal. He is a willing component of that well-ordered system that is an integral part of a larger (though ultimately irrational) totality.[4] When narrating he displays an almost neurotic obsession with probabilistic thinking and causal explanation as he seeks to fit every

element into a cohesive teleological order in which each cause unprob-
lematically produces its intended and appropriate effect. In the writing
of his account there is a frantic urge to eliminate the random and deprecate the inexplicable. Moran's frenzied compulsion to connect finally
infects his act of narration; desperate to achieve closure, to force the
end of the tale up to the moment of its telling, he is reduced to avowed
fabrication: "Then I went back into the house and wrote, It is midnight.
The rain is beating on the windows. It was not midnight. It was not
raining" (176). In his narrative we see the social world fail to conform
to his teleological imperative; his insistence on order, obedience, and
causal explanation are ultimately refuted by his experience in the world.
Beckett's allusive parody of rationalism is materially embodied in
Moran's failures, as the recalcitrant disorder of events and the abrupt
turns of neatly planned causal chains lead to confusion and collapse.

Molloy, on the other hand, is a personification of Humean skepticism. Tongue in cheek, Hume had warned that if his critique of metaphysics were ever to gain popular acceptance, "All discourse, all action
would immediately cease; and men remain in a total lethargy, till the
necessities of nature, unsatisfied, put an end to their miserable existence" (1902, 160). Molloy would feel quite at home in such a state. He
finds no connection between the successive episodes of his life, he frequently points out causal gaps in his narration, and he can no more
derive "ought" from "is" than Hume could. Molloy puts into practice
Hume's critique of the classical concept of the self. For the Scottish philosopher, there is no such thing as personal identity, but only a bundle
or collection of different perceptions; Molloy cannot remember his name,
says that if he keeps on telling the story of his life he'll end up believing
it (53), and pointedly notes "even my sense of identity was wrapped in
a namelessness often hard to penetrate" (31).

In his monograph on Proust, Beckett praises what he calls Proust's
"skepticism before causality" (1957, 61). By creating Molloy, Beckett
moves one step further. This protagonist fails to perceive genuine causal
relations—when the policeman requests his papers, Molloy produces
not identification but the bits of newspaper he uses to wipe himself. At
other times, he acts on impossible causal progressions, as when he "com-
municates" with his mother by giving her one to four blows on the head,
despite the fact that she could only count to two—and that Molloy himself often confused the code of knocks (18). In other situations, he doesn't
know his motives: wondering why he began his labyrinthine journey
to visit his mother he says, "My reasons? I had forgotten them" (27).

What is most unsettling or amusing about Molloy is his adamant refusal to believe that any sequence of events is causally connected. Hume, in his well-known critique of causality, denied that we can ever observe any force or power that binds one event to another; at best we can only perceive repeated conjunctions of sequential events and then assume that some causal tie connects them: "We then call the one object, *Cause*; the other *Effect*. We suppose that there is some connection between them; some power in the one, by which it infallibly produces the other, and operates with the greatest certainty and strongest necessity" (1902, 75). But such an inference is a habit of the mind, rather than a law of nature.

What Molloy does is not only to hold such beliefs but to act on them as well—a practice never ventured on by Hume who, in the conclusion to his *Enquiry Concerning the Human Understanding*, wisely observes that action, employment, and "the occupations of common life" are the great subverters of Pyrrhonism; outside of the academy, principles of skepticism "vanish like smoke, and leave the most determined skeptic in the same condition as other mortals" (159). Molloy approaches all human experience rather like Hume's hypothetical person, "endowed with the strongest faculties of reason and reflection . . . brought on a sudden into this world; he would, indeed, immediately observe a continual succession of objects, and one event following another; but he would not be able to reach the idea of cause and effect" (42). Molloy carries this agnosticism to ludicrous extremes. When staying with Lousse, the room he inhabits seems to change and shift at every fresh inspection. "But that there were natural causes to all these things I am willing to concede, for the resources of nature are infinite apparently," Molloy reasons. "It was I who was not natural enough to enter into that order of things, and appreciate its niceties" (44). The protagonist cannot determine whether he misunderstands the laws of nature, whether those laws have changed, or whether he has simply made some blunder. In this particular case, the reader may safely choose the last explanation, since the evidence for Molloy's disorientation is the configuration of boughs outside the window (presumably shifted by the wind) and the changing images reflected in the pane (altered by different vantage points).

Other dilemmas of perception are more difficult to explain and may well defy the idea of causality. During his sojourn with Lousse, Molloy is astounded by the sight of the full moon, since the night before (or perhaps two nights before) it was "all young and slender, on her back, a shaving" (41). In an attempt to come to grips with this anomaly, Molloy adumbrates the following explanation, wondering whether, between the two nights, there had in fact elapsed a full fourteen days; and if so, where had they gone? Where would there be a place for the missing days, "in the so rigorous chain of events I had just undergone?," he wonders (41). Speculating further, he muses:

> Was it not wiser to suppose either that the moon seen two nights before, far from being new as I had thought, was on the eve of being full, or else that the moon seen from Lousse's house, far from being full, as it had appeared to me, was in fact merely entering on its first quarter, or else finally that here I had to do with two moons, as far from the new as from the full and so alike in outline that the naked eye could hardly tell between them, and that whatever was at variance with these hypotheses was so much smoke and delusion. (41–42)

Here the protagonist is thrust into a position comparable to that of Hume's hypothetical person who observes conjoined events for the first time. Molloy does his share of speculation about this unique succession of events, but finally refrains from attributing causal connection; he is left to merely note an unexpected conjunction. Most readers, confronted by this passage, probably assume that the world described by Newtonian physics is firmly intact and that the apparent oddity can be easily explained away by Molloy's hopelessly fallible memory, his ineptitude as a narrator, or simply as an optical illusion—one more of "nature's pranks" (42). In his famous essay on sense and reference, Gottlob Frege remarked that the discovery that "the morning star" and "the evening star" referred to the same object was an advance in knowledge; however, by positing the existence of two moons, Molloy seems to be speeding in the opposite direction toward irremediable ignorance. But this judgment too presumes a set of naturalistic conventions that are by no means firmly in place.

Faulkner's *The Sound and the Fury* and *As I Lay Dying* are set in a recognizable extension of the historical world, and the canons of probability that operate in Yoknapatawpha County are basically the same ones that govern the reader's own world. A character who has problems with causality in these texts (such as Benjy or Vardaman) is unable to perceive the genuine causal chains that do in fact occur. But we cannot assume that the strange region haunted by Molloy follows what we know as the laws of nature: it is much closer to Kafka's oneiric landscapes than to, say, Joyce's Dublin or Proust's Combray.[5] In Molloy's universe, it may well be that there are two moons, or at least that the lunar phases do not correspond to those tabulated in any known almanac. Such a theory is of course no more plausible than the alternative explanation that Molloy misperceives the laws of our world; the point is that there can be no way to determine whether Molloy is wrong or that nature, in his world, is skewed.

In his study of Proust, Beckett observes that the French novelist "is aware of the many concessions required of the literary artist by the shortcomings of the literary convention. As a writer he is not altogether at liberty to detach effect from cause" (1957, 1). Nevertheless, Proust receives Beckett's praise for having stretched, attenuated, and circumvented familiar types of causal progression. In *Molloy*, Beckett goes much further. Both protagonists are confused about their motives and misperceive causal ties and disjunctions. The precise causal laws of the fictional world of the text are inherently indeterminable, and the relation of each narration to the events it purports to recount is avowedly unreliable: Molloy repeatedly calls attention to his fallibility as a chronicler, while Moran admits that part of his account is false.[6]

Beckett's attack on causality does not stop here. The "concessions required of the literary artist by the shortcomings of the literary convention" no doubt include traditional demands for causal connection between discrete narrative units. In *Remembrance of Things Past*, Proust continually defers the causal nexus between his book's heterogeneous incidents, and thereby transgresses the expectations of the reader: for hundreds of pages we seem to be offered a mere collocation of fragmentary episodes; at the same time, knowing that the work is a narrative, we correctly sense that some interlocking causal pattern will ultimately weave the disparate elements together. Beckett's project is more radical; as H. Porter Abbott explains, the problem for the reader "is that *Molloy* is divided into two parts that appear at once to be intimately related and to have no relation. The parts are distinct, yet they abound in parallels and cross-references" (1973, 99). What is at stake is both the interpretation of *Molloy* and, regarding the issues discussed earlier in chapter 3, the definition of narrative. Are these merely two unconnected similar tales, or do they form a single novel—and on what grounds does a critic or theorist make such a determination? Abbott's comparison of the text to Faulkner's *The Wild Palms* is quite illuminating. The echoes between the two parts of *Molloy* take on importance because "they are the only clues we have—in our obsession with unity—to go on in finding the connection." This tension is exacerbated by the very abundance of parallels. Faulkner's novel is essentially two narratives that alternate chapter by chapter, though "its narratives are so different and the parallels so few the reader accepts the fact that he is reading two different stories that, at most, provide an effective contrast to each other. But Moran is seeking Molloy (or Mollose, he is not sure). This is enough to lodge the hook. The parallels in turn force their way on the reader's consciousness." (99)

It is not our "obsession with unity" so much as the very concept of narrative that is most profoundly challenged: if the parts are causally connected—if Moran finds Molloy, or if he becomes Molloy—then the work is a novel. If on the other hand the Moran section is distinct, merely another version of the Molloy tale in the same general way that *Malone Dies* is another version, analogically related but logically independent, then the text contains two narratives disguised as one. By playing on the notion of causal connection and disjunction at yet another level, Beckett succeeds in challenging the very concept of narrativity. Moran's quest for Molloy (or Mollose) tempts us to make connections without ever providing sufficient evidence to go beyond mere conjunction.

Several hypotheses concerning the relation between the problematic segments have been set forth; one of the most ingenious is David Hayman's belief that "Molloy's mother, Molloy, Moran, and Moran's son all inhabit the same body; further, the events described in the two narratives are simultaneous and identical though viewed from different angles and differently ordered" (1970, 135–36).[7] Hayman's hypothesis, though rather elegant, is ultimately inadequate. The text defies any single critical recuperation. Numerous hints abound; one may form any number of plausible interpretations of the various actions. But the work is so constructed as to defy any one reading; the evidence is simply inadequate. As Steven Connor observes, "[E]ach possible reading of the novel . . . leaves important material unaccounted for. The problem is not so much that the novel doesn't give us enough material as that it gives us too much" (1988, 57). It is easy to share Molloy's hunch that "all things run together, in the body's long madness, I feel it" (56), but in the end the reader, like Molloy, like Hume, is left with tantalizing promises of causality that upon analysis turn out to be fabrications generated by force of habit.[8] The text remains suspended in a kind of theoretical no-man's land, both a narrative and, simultaneously, more than a single narrative.[9]

Fabrication is of course one of the novel's central tropes. As Molloy is the first to admit: "And when I say I said, etc., all I mean is that I knew confusedly things were so, without knowing exactly what it was all about. And every time I say, I said this, or I said that . . . I am merely complying with the convention that demands you either lie or hold your peace. For what really happened was quite different" (88). Such a confession of falsehood problematizes the notion of representation by positing antecedent events that cannot or will not be disclosed. Molloy's fusion of recounting and invention ensures that we will never know what actually transpired and points to the tenuous foundations of any purported representation of events: it presupposes a causal connection between past actions and present narration that, as we see in this text, can be easily disrupted. Traditional mimesis entails a narrative chronology that can be reconstructed; this too presupposes a connection between the tale and its telling that is strikingly absent in *Molloy*: "But perhaps I am merging two times in one, and two women, one coming towards me, shyly, urged on by the cries and laughter of her companions, and the other going away from me, unhesitatingly" (75). Without causality, there can be no fidelity of representation; in the terminology of narrative poetics, the *fabula (histoire)* is unknowable in principle, and we can never go beyond or behind the *sjuzhet (récit)* that is presented.

Neither tale in *Molloy* purports to depict actual events. They are fictions in the fullest sense of the word. This fact helps explain the subtle obsession with reflexivity that permeates the text. It is self-conscious to a high degree, containing numerous statements like "it is useless to drag out this chapter of my, how shall I say, my existence" (56) and "She had a somewhat hairy face, or am I imagining it, in the interests of the narrative?" (56). These are not gratuitous panaches or stolid reminders that the book before us is "only pretend," but rather signs that direct us to a deeper level of metafiction—in this book, there is no reference but self-reference.

The text is grounded in profuse and varied forms of reflexivity.[10] When Molloy notes, "If I go on long enough calling that my life I'll end up by believing it" (53), he is alluding both to the fictitious nature of his narrative, and to the fact that his life qua character is identical to the words written about him. Moran makes a similar though more explicit observation: "For in describing this day I am once more he who suffered it, who crammed it full of futile anxious life" (122). Again, as an autobiographical narrator, Moran's sole existence is in his narrative.

He lives by writing himself, and his "life" is ended when his narrative ceases. (This will become the central trope of *Malone Dies*, as that narrator struggles to "finish dying"—i.e., stop writing.)

There is a metaphysical twist to Beckett's self-referentiality: not only are his characters' words solely about themselves, this appears to be the case for all human discourse: "Yes, even then, when already all was fading, waves and particles, there could be no things but nameless things, no names but thingless names. I say that now, but after all what do I know now about then, now when the icy words hail down upon me, the icy meanings, and the world dies too, foully named" (31). Here, in similar passages (23, 176), and in the possible allusion to Frege already mentioned we are invited to reflect on the failure of all referential language, and not just that of *Molloy's* narrators. For Beckett, all language is fabrication.

This is the dilemma Beckett talks around in the dialogues with George Duthuit and had emphatically expressed in *Proust*:

> And art is the apotheosis of solitude. There is no communication because there are no vehicles of communication. . . . Either we speak and act for ourselves—in which case speech and action are distorted and emptied of their meaning by an intelligence that is not ours, or else we speak and act for others—in which case we speak and act a lie. (1957, 47)

In Beckett's maelstrom of fictionality, every thought and word is necessarily a fabrication. This is even true of the sun and the night. A glance at the tropes of light and dark can reveal the scope of Beckett's linguistic crucible. Both Molloy and Moran strongly prefer the dark to the light (1965, 67, 110, 174), and the former even feels "poisoned" by the sun (19). Moran describes his attempts at writing as "a kind of clawing towards a light and countenance I could not name" (148), and Molloy explicitly desires "to blacken a few more pages" (68). Their nocturnal predilection is mirrored by their narrative compulsion; they must pursue black on white.[11] As Mallarmé states in "Quant au livre," "Tu remarquas, on n'écrit pas, lumineusement, sur champ obscur, l'alphabet des astres, seul, ainsi s'indique, ébauché ou interrompu; l'homme poursuit noir sur blanc" [You observed, one does not write luminously, on a dark field; the alphabet of stars is thus indicated, traced or interrupted; man pursues black on white] (1945, 370). This passage seems to be parodied in Molloy's lament: "And don't come talking to me of the stars, they all look the same to me, yes, I cannot read the stars, in spite of my astronomical studies" (1965, 60). Everything in the world exists to end up in this book. Even the personages are depicted as black marks on a white field. On the pale seashore, people at a distance are called "black specks" (75), and Molloy refers to the "black speck I was" at that time (74) before going on to darken more pages. Such characters only exist by writing and as writing.

Five distinct though interpenetrating varieties of reflexivity (most of which we have already encountered in Conrad, Faulkner, and Ellison) may be now be distinguished: the subtle, almost hidden dialectic of black on white; the narrators' self-conscious reflections on the progress of their compositions; the frame-breaking that occurs once the narrators reveal the fictionality of their accounts; the sound, Humean critique of vague notions like the self, which are shown to be largely fabrication; and the more speculative, protodeconstructionist theory of language that laments the referential failures of human speech.[12] But even this last position is not without its own ironies. To state, "Saying is inventing" (32), is to flirt with the paradox of the Cretan liar: if this statement is true, then it is also false, and some statements are therefore accurate.[13] Such a contradiction, it may be presumed, would only delight the author of *Molloy*, and it certainly is an integral facet of the overall structure of the text.

At this point we arrive at the metafictional paradox that permeates this work. The reflexivity, so insistent and pervasive, functioning in a multiplicity of ways, convincingly expresses and compulsively documents the causal breakdown between self and other, intention and action, and word and object. The fictionality of discourse has perhaps never been more effectively presented in a fictional discourse. But such metafictional overdetermination is self-consuming: an eloquently articulated series of ineffective narrative acts can be read as a magisterial narrative of self-referentiality. The more the characters fail to express their perceptions, the more compellingly the author demonstrates his mastery as he meticulously orders the narrators' disorders. This exemplification of the absence of communication expresses its message in a remarkably clear and direct manner, as denotative failures within the fictional world form a compelling pattern in the novel: on this subject, there is a virtual "mania for symmetry" (85). In the end, every causal disjunction points to a first cause—Beckett's strategies of composition—that must always remain hidden from characters compelled to "obey

my master and his designs" (132). The very causal disjunctions that
frustrate the characters, problematize the fictional world, confound each
narrator, and challenge the nature of the novel are at the same time the
master tropes that inform the elaborate, elusive architecture of *Molloy*.

6

Forgotten Causes: Non-Western Beliefs and Metaphysical Contestation in Modern Asian, Postcolonial, and U.S. Ethnic Narratives

One might reasonably expect that the cultural confrontations that animate so much of the emergent ethnic and world literatures would also embrace questions of causal agency, and that traditional non-Western metaphysics would engage and frequently discredit specifically Western notions of (Christian) providence and naturalism. However, the scenario I have just described rarely occurs, even in works that attack standard European and North American value systems, ideas of progress, political agendas, and cultural practices. The causal contestations that arise usually pit supernatural forces against naturalistic ones; in general, it is the traditional supernatural beliefs that are revealed to be inadequate. This ontological struggle is nevertheless considerably more complex and nuanced than the ostensibly similar naturalistic refutations of Christian philosophies carried out by Flaubert and Zola; the authors we are about to examine often employ a variety of techniques to do homage to or recapture the metaphorical force of older beliefs that can no longer be professed literally. The familiar dyads Western/non-Western, modern/traditional, and naturalistic/supernatural, though often homologous are by no means identical; the modern writer with a non-Western heritage must make a number of hard choices between these alternatives, abandoning some oppositions and eluding, defying, or conflating others.

In this chapter, I will focus on the topos of prophecy (with occasional forays into the related areas of conjuration and shamanism) as it is deployed by a wide range of non-European and U.S. ethnic authors:

Tawfik al-Hakim (Egypt), Attia Hosain and R. K. Narayan (India), Lu Hsun (China), Chinua Achebe and Wole Soyinka (Nigeria), Njabulo Ndebele (South Africa), Olive Senior (Jamaica), Charles W. Chesnutt and Charles Johnson (African American), Maxine Hong Kingston (Chinese American), and Leslie Marmon Silko (Native American). I do not by any means intend to suggest that the disparate societies and beliefs described by these authors are in any sense interchangeable or even homologous; indeed, they are largely incommensurable. There is virtually nothing in common between the cosmologies of a Pueblo culture in transition, philosophically-informed Islam, traditional Chinese peasant society, and the fusion of Christianity and Obeah in Jamaica. The focus of this analysis is more abstract, more ontological than sociological, and should not be construed as denying the significant historical and social differences that lie beyond the scope of this study. Each of the texts discussed below does, nevertheless, attempt to interrogate the pressing claims of an indigenous supernaturalism. One need not assume that all third-world and minority cultures are basically the same in order to perceive that each of them must inevitably confront, in its own way, the various challenges raised by Western metaphysics. It is also noteworthy that even at this very general level of analysis certain suggestive correspondences do emerge, for example in the legacy of "conjuring" in the work of the six authors of the African continuum, in the counterhegemonic discourse of the four U.S. ethnic writers, and of course in the shared interest in the consequences of the idea of divining the future.

As we have seen in works ranging from the *Iliad* and *Oedipus Rex* to *Macbeth* and *Life is a Dream*, prophecy is a key site for the staging of metaphysical contestations. If a given supernatural agency is valid, its oracles will be corroborated; if false, divination will prove fruitless. And, given the notorious ambiguity of vatic pronouncements, authors usually find the subject of prophecy rich in possibilities for linguistic play and ironic reversals. Perhaps most important for non-Western authors is the social relevance of the issue: while the European and much of the American reading public has been largely skeptical of the efficacy of any supernatural mode of prognostication for the past two centuries, in many non-Western societies it continues to play a major role in official ideology and popular belief. Writers drawing on such a heritage face stark choices, and must affirm, repudiate, or somehow negotiate this central and often problematic facet of their culture; their situation can rapidly become complicated when they wish to oppose the ideological hegemony of the West and legitimize alternative cultural expression, even as they feel uneasy over aspects of their cultures' supernatural claims. Thus we find a fascination with prophecy and an intriguing set of guarded, nostalgic, critical, and self-reflexive responses to its function and import. In the following account, I will begin with texts that affirm a supernatural causal system, move on to those that provide sympathetic critiques of traditional beliefs, discuss works that feature naturalistic attacks on the supernatural, and conclude with narratives that employ metafictional stances.

It should prove helpful to preface the following analyses with an example of a relatively unproblematic account of the power of divinely ordained fate from a non-Western tradition: Attia Hosain's story, "Time is Unredeemable" (1953), a story that will also provide a useful background for subsequent discussions of the work of Tawfik al-Hakim and Bharati Mukherjee. It is perhaps appropriate that the story is set in a fairly remote Indian village during the thirties and forties; it is here that Indian beliefs and customs remained the most traditional—Anita Desai, in her preface to the volume of stories, refers to this society as feudal. Though not mentioning prophecy per se, the tale chronicles the ways that individuals vainly attempt to chart and direct a future that clashes with their kismet. Kismet, as Desai explains, is the Indian (both Hindu and Muslim) equivalent of fate, "the overruling belief that what is written into the palm of the hand, spelt out by the stars in the sky, cannot be altered or escaped and it is the test of a human being how he or she carries that burden, honourably or with shame" (1953, xviii).

"Time is Unredeemable" opens with a young bride, Bano, awaiting the return of her husband from England. She hardy knows him; an arranged marriage was quickly engineered nine years earlier in order to keep him from the temptations of foreign women. As his parents discuss his arrival, his mother makes plans for immediate celebrations, while his father worries about the son's future. Here the theme of fate is explicitly mentioned, as the mother shrugs off her husband's concerns: "Whatever is in his Kismet and hers must happen. Their life is beginning, and, for all I care, mine can end" (58). Their kismet, it turns out, holds some cruel surprises. Bano goes to the city to buy a sari in the current urban fashion, purchases Western makeup, and under the direction of old Mrs. Ram even acquires what she is told is a fashionable, English-style coat to wear instead of the customary Indian shawl. When she finally sees her husband, he tells her they must separate. As he leaves, he accidentally spills oil on the dowdy coat. He says he dislikes the old coat, since it reminds him of his former landlady and of Mrs. Ram. All of the forces, individual and communal, that work to keep the couple together are powerless before the kismet that sunders them; its power is inalterable even though its course is unknown.

An ostensibly similar opposition is present in Leslie Marmon Silko's *Ceremony* as the traditional Laguna Pueblo *Weltanschauung* is pitted against modern Euro-American ideology—a conflict well documented in the critical literature on the text. And yet there is a great difference in the tone and sense of urgency in these two works: Hosain meticulously chronicles the culture of an age that has passed, dispassionately observing its strengths and limitations. In Silko's narrative the stakes are much higher; her people's history, identity, well-being, and even survival seem to be implicated in the novel's desire to articulate and justify the primordial tribal narratives. Not only are the stakes high, but the metaphysical contestation is arduous and bitter. Tayo, the protagonist, had once believed that on certain nights, a person standing on a mesa could reach the moon. Distances and days were not barriers; they all had a story:

> If a person wanted to get to the moon, there was a way; it all depended . . . on whether you knew the story of how others before you had gone. He had believed in the stories for a long time, until the teachers at Indian school taught him not to believe in that kind of "nonsense". But they had been wrong. (1978, 19)

Elsewhere, this epistemic struggle is expressed in causal terms: "He knew what white people thought about the stories. In school the science teacher had explained what superstition was, and then held the science textbook up for the class to see the true source of explanations. . . . The science books explained the causes and effects" (99).

Throughout the novel these two belief systems struggle against each other for explanatory supremacy; often it seems that the ancestral Native American worldview is on the defensive. Rocky, the brightest young man on the reservation, is exasperated by the ignorance of the others; "That's the trouble with the way people around here have always done things—they never knew what they were doing" (79). But the white man's knowledge fails the crucial test of pragmatism. It brings only destruction, dissolution, and death. Tayo, a World War II veteran suffering terribly from battle fatigue, is wracked by anguish until he goes to a medicine man, is reintegrated into the ancient tribal narrative, and is finally healed through his encounters with Ts'eh, a Native American woman who seems to be an incarnation of the deity, Thought-Woman, "the Grandmother Spider," who created the world. The medicine man's divination—that the lost cattle would be found in the north—is shown to be correct, and the book's message, as Alan R. Velie states, "is that Indians are best off when they remain within their traditional culture (even though that is constantly changing) and the old gods still have power" (1982, 114).[1] Throughout, this is an arduous struggle; Tayo, even as he reaps the benefits of the ancestral beliefs, wonders whether they are not in fact mere "old-time superstition" (1978, 203). The supernatural world is ultimately vindicated, even as it is constantly called into question.[2]

Tawfik al-Hakim's *King Oedipus* is an equally fascinating document, a suave reworking of Sophocles' play by a brilliant modern dramatist and Muslim intellectual. One of his major goals is to strip Oedipus of his legendary greatness in order to restore him to human greatness; another is to replace the tragedy of cruel, unalterable fate with the tragedy of man's will pitted against God's will. To this end, the drama's first act presents a very human Oedipus and an all too human Teiresias. All of the supernatural events of the Greek myth are subjected to a sustained naturalistic critique. As he approached Thebes, Oedipus killed an ordinary lion that had been attacking citizens who strayed beyond the town's walls. Teiresias then asserted that the beast also had the wings of an eagle, the face of a woman, and asked riddles, and Oedipus was at that time in no position to deny the mythmaking.

The status of the Delphic oracle is also subject to doubt. Oedipus strongly suspects that the priests generate oracles to suit their own purposes, and finds it hard to believe that the word of the gods can be so easily heard and interpreted. As the high priest complains, "Heavenly revelation is for you a subject for scrutiny and exploration" (1981, 86). He feels Teiresias fabricated the prophecy that Laius's son would kill his father, and he comes to think that Teiresias instigated the action of the band of robbers that slew the king. Oedipus's need to question every authority and speculate over all actions is paralleled by Teiresias's desire to continually change the course of events. Oedipus accuses him of being blinded by delusion; "You want . . . to be the fountainhead of events, the source of upheavals, the motive force changing and replacing human destinies and natural elements" (90). In short, Teiresias's unbridled will seeks to assume those powers ordinarily accorded to the divinity. He wishes to play the role of fate.

The second act by and large returns to the Sophoclean version of events, as the truth of the prophecy is gradually disclosed. There are, of course, numerous interesting twists and ironies. Al-Hakim's Jocasta, adducing the example of the divination concerning her son to show that prophets cannot foretell the future, does not conclude as in Sophocles' play that chance *(tyche)* governs all events, but offers instead a statement that many educated Muslims would agree with: "God's will has goals which man's mind is not able to grasp. Thus no person has complete sovereignty over the unknown or ability to prophesy" (104). In the third and final act, new variations emerge. Oedipus's discovery that his wife was also the woman who bore him does not particularly trouble him. His conjugal love for her stays constant, and he hopes they can move to another city and start life over. She, however, is horrified at the situation, and this response puzzles the unnaturally pragmatic Oedipus, who muses aloud on the social constructions that continue to shape his destiny: though called a hero for killing a beast they claimed had wings, and called a criminal for killing a man they showed to be his father, he is neither the one nor the other, "I am just another individual upon whom the people have cast their fictions and heaven its decrees" (117). He also points out the ironies of Teiresias's machinations—the man he intended to keep from the kingship is the same man he later brought to the throne. Teiresias's vaunted free will, Oedipus points out, "was always operating, without your knowing or sensing it, within the framework of heaven's will" (123).

These thoughts in turn lead to the play's final statement on fate: the design of God's system "is so straight a path that everyone who strays from it finds pits to fall into. You have a path you can proceed down according to your will, or you can stop. But you are not to challenge or deviate" (124). This assertion, with its emphasis on human choice within the larger parameters of divine order, undermines and contradicts the elements of predestination elsewhere in the plot. It affirms a supernatural teleology while denying the power of fate. In a postscript to the play, Al-Hakim acknowledges the conflict between his own beliefs and the fatalistic causal agency of the story he retells. As a Muslim, he cannot accept "the idea of God planning injuries for man in advance for no purpose or offense" (291). Yet even as he rejects this ancient pagan superstition, he knows one cannot write the "story of Oedipus without the superstition" (291). Hence the unusual causal disequilibrium in the text. Ironically, this tension which gives the play so much of its power and freshness has been misconstrued by Western commentators. Aloys de Marignac, in his note on the French translation of the drama, observed that the success of this version, unlike the twenty-nine adaptations made in French from 1614 to 1939, is due in part to the fact that its author, being a Muslim, is more comfortable with the idea of blind predestination. This Orientalist fiction, which remains widespread, was annoying to Al-Hakim, who in response explained the steps he took to recast the drama in more human terms and cited a long tradition of Islamic philosophical and juridical authors including ibn Rushd who have attacked the concept of determinism. Ironically, the very causal agency he attacks in the play is attributed to him by European exegesis.

Chinua Achebe's *Things Fall Apart* (1959) chronicles the life of Okonkwo, a prominent man in the Igbo village of Umofia, before and after European contact. The book is written largely though not exclusively from an Igbo perspective, and thus reveals the indigenous culture as a practical, rational totality while presenting the white Christian intruders as ridiculous, inscrutable, and destructive. The village's metaphysical tenets are generally treated as natural and accurate, though there is often a note of ambiguity, equivocation, or irony in the descriptions that allows a skeptical interpretation of every supernatural claim.[3] Umofia "was powerful in war and magic, and its priests and medicine men were feared in all the surrounding country" (1989, 9). Yet the village never went to war without the approval of its oracle, the "Oracle of the Hills and the Caves," which did on occasion forbid warfare. Since, as the *egwugwu* ritual reveals, supernatural presences are impersonated by members of the village, any reader who does not hold Igbo beliefs may reasonably conclude—not unlike Al-Hakim's Oedipus— that the oracle is merely another villager with a good feel for martial strategy and intravillage relations. Later, in the argument between Okonkwo and Obierika over the sacrifice of Ikemefuna, one has the distinct sense that the oracle can be ignored if necessary.

An epistemological dualism is thus created, as every event in the novel may be fully explained either by reference to Igbo supernaturalism or by an ironic naturalism. The village rainmaker, for example, is said to be equally unable to stop the rain in the middle of the rainy season or to make it fall in the heart of the dry season "without serious danger to his own health. The personal dynamism required to counter the forces of these extremes of weather would be far too great for the human frame" (24). That is, he is only able to "make" rain when it is more or less likely that showers will occur. Whether one finds a causal connection between the ritual invocation and the actual precipitation is, at this point in the text, left to the reader to determine. Similar ambiguities surround Okonkwo's *chi*, or personal daimon that directs one's destiny.[4] The protagonist attributes the disappointments in his life to the workings of his *chi*, contrary to the official beliefs of the community: "The saying of the elders was not true—that if a man said yea his *chi* also affirmed. Here was a man whose *chi* said nay despite his own affirmation" (92). Later, when events seem to be progressing more to his liking, Okonkwo believes that his *chi* is making amends for past disasters. The fluidity of this concept is such that any possible event can be attributed to its influence; it is equally plausible to interpret it as mysteriously inscrutable or simply nonexistent.

Toward the middle of the book the ontological weight shifts to the supernatural, as Chielo, the priestess of Agbala, addresses a prophecy to Okonkwo and heals the illness of his daughter. Similarly, a man said to have killed a sacred python dies suddenly, proving to the villagers that their gods are still powerful. The arrival of the Christian missionaries, however, discredits many of the local beliefs. The Christians live in the Evil Forest and yet are not destroyed by the malignant spirits there. A convert kills and eats a sacred python—but this time suffers no harmful consequences. The *egwugwu* ceremony is desecrated, but the gods do not avenge themselves. Once they are seriously contested, the tribal beliefs turn out to be hollow. The sympathetic portrayal of the indigenous cultural economy of the Igbo concludes with a disclosure of the fictionality and inadequacy of those beliefs.

The black South African writer, Njabulo Ndebele, offers a similarly sympathetic though ultimately more critical account of traditional African beliefs in his poignant story, "The Prophetess" (1983). The story recounts a boy's journey to a holy woman to have her bless the water he carries in order to relieve the suffering of his ailing mother. As he returns from his quest, he stumbles into a man on a bicycle; the bottle breaks and the holy water runs into the gutter. Outside his home, the boy carefully washes out a similar bottle and fills it with ordinary tap water. The boy, now extremely nervous, hands his mother the liquid; he is amazed and relieved when, after a sip of the "prophetess' water," she announces that she feels better already. The boy glows with happiness, knowing he has healed her. The reader, however, is implicitly invited to recall a similar scene, presented earlier in the story, in which characters on a bus speculate on the powers of the prophetess, in this case her reputed ability to charm the grapevine outside her house so that anyone touching it would be glued to it all night. In this discussion, a voice of skepticism is overwhelmed by credulous testimonies, until a well-dressed man interjects: "[I]s it any wonder that the white man is sitting on us: The mother there asked a very straightforward question, but she is answered vaguely about things happening. . . . The truth is you have no proof. None of you. Have you ever seen anybody caught by this prophetess? Never. It's all superstition" (1986, 35). The story's ending legitimates the well-dressed man's interpretation, debunking traditional supernatural accounts as mere superstition and suggesting the deleterious political consequences of such gullibility.[5]

The bewitched grapevine and the respected and feared puissance of the prophetess may well remind American readers of Charles W. Chesnutt's tales "The Goophered Grapevine," "The Conjurer's Revenge," and "Sis' Becky's Pickaninny" from *The Conjure Woman* (1899). In these stories, the act of supernatural fabrication is elevated to the status of an art form. Set in a North Carolina plantation during Reconstruction, each story begins with a casual meeting between the new Northern owner and an old black workman known as Uncle Julius. Julius invariably goes on to relate a fantastic tale involving conjuring that always obliquely reflects the situation between the two men, and the effects of the storytelling usually enhance Julius's position.

An especially interesting aspect of these interactions is the ironic vehemence with which Julius affirms the power of conjuring. In "Sis' Becky's Pickaninny," the owner, seeing Julius stroking a rabbit's foot for good luck, expostulates: "[Y]our people will never rise in the world until they throw off these childish superstitions and learn to live by the light of reason and common sense. How absurd to imagine that the fore-foot of a poor dead rabbit . . . can promote happiness or success, or ward off failure or misfortune!" (1969, 135). Julius, with exquisite and self-conscious irony, seems to agree: "Dat's w'at I tells dese niggers roun' heah. . . . De fo'-foot ain' got no power. It has ter be de hin'-foot, suh— de lef' hin'-foot er a grabeya'd rabbit, killt by a cross-eyed nigger on a da'k night in de full er de moon" (135). Julius undercuts the belief in such a talisman even as he insists on it, as the improbabilities of attaining such a specimen mount. He goes on to narrate a seemingly irrelevant tale of separated slaves, their transformation into a hummingbird and a mockingbird, and finally their reunion through conjuring. The landowner then praises the ingenuity of the "fairy tale" he has just heard, but his wife interrupts to state that "the story bears the stamp of truth, if ever a story did." When her husband objects to the supernatural events, she counters that "those are mere ornamental details and not at all essential. The story is true to nature" (159). With this, she articulates the method that lies behind Julius's canny narrative acts and Chesnutt's artistic deployment of the magical. These fictions are, in the words of Bernard W. Bell, "wry wonder tales that exploit the ignorance of whites about the ways of black folk while simultaneously affirming the humanity of both" (1987, 65). Here, the actual power of narration dwarfs the alleged power of the supernatural.

A comparable epistemic contest occurs in Olive Senior's novella, *Arrival of the Snake Woman* (1989). Set in late-nineteenth-century Jamaica, the two principal rival belief systems are the synthesis of Christianity and West African-derived Obeah, practiced by the recently freed slaves, and the orthodox Anglicanism espoused by the hard, hypocritical Pastor Bedlow. In addition, Hinduism and skepticism also appear as possible alternative systems of belief. Much respect is accorded to the local spiritualists, Mother Miracle and Papa Dias, who "could divine fate from throwing bisi the way his old Oyo grandfather had taught him, [and] some even said he could summon Shango God of Thunder" (15–16). These two were able to thrive even after the coming of Pastor Bedlow, who could cure "whooping cough, ringworm and running belly, taws and vomiting sickness," but was unable to "take away the effects of grudgefullness or cut-eye, counteract spitefulness, [or] cure love-fever" (22). In the end, as the narrator reflects on the unforeseen circumstances that shaped his own destiny, he admires the analytical sensibility of the Indian woman who provides the story with its title, observing that she had from the start a more cosmopolitan understanding of the world, and "a pragmatic drive that allowed her to dispassionately weigh alternatives, make her decisions and act, while we still floundered around in a confused tangle of emotions, family ties, custom and superstition" (43–44). By seeing beyond the faith that was structured on both "Mother Miracle's Holy water and Jesus' second coming" (44), the woman is able to introduce the spirit of a new age to the remote village, an age in which sentiment is replaced by pragmatism and "superstition by materialism" (44). In the end, both local and British forms of supernaturalism succumb to a naturalistic critique.

In Wole Soyinka's play *The Trials of Brother Jero* (1964), we find a more relentless and cynical exposure of popular belief in the supernatural. Brother Jeroboam is a more or less Christian prophet who wears a white velvet cape and carries a small divining rod along a beach on the coast of Nigeria. These days, he complains, the "trade" of prophecy is poor, its practitioners have fallen from respectability, the competition from rivals is intense, and "customers—I mean worshippers" (1974, 153) are few. Through monologues and asides, Brother Jero reveals both the standard tricks of the prophet's trade and the extraordinary measures that current diviners are forced to resort to: "Some prophets I could name gained their present beaches by getting women penitents to shake their bosoms in spiritual ecstasy" (145). And Jero himself, in order to enhance the popularity of the master prophet he was then apprenticed to, once inaugurated a proselytizing campaign by recruiting six dancing girls from the neighboring French territory, all dressed as Jehovah's Witnesses. But this, Jero admits, was ultimately a ploy to strengthen his own hand and enable him to displace the older prophet.

In the course of the play we observe the gulling of a particularly credulous character named Chume and learn some basic strategies of successful prophets:

> This one who comes earliest, I have prophesied that he will be made a chief in his home town. That is a very safe prophecy. As safe as our most popular prophecy, that a man will live to be eighty. If it doesn't come true, that man doesn't find out until he's on the other side. So everybody is quite happy. (157)

The mechanism of successful foretelling is revealed to be so simple— the enthusiastic corroboration of basic desires—that Chume himself stumbles into that role by accident. After Jero hands him the rod and chases after a woman, Chume begins to ask for the forgiveness of a follower who has gone into paroxysms of ecstasy. The assembled worshippers all chant "Amen!" and Chume goes on to ask forgiveness of all assembled there, again to thunderous cries of "Amen!" Soon he begins invocations, imploring that those who walk should receive bicycles and that those who have bicycles should receive cars. Just as he is getting a feel for this role, Brother Jero returns, his clothes torn and his face bleeding. He takes back the divining rod and dismisses the worshippers until the evening. As the evening services are getting underway, Chume returns, furious now that he realizes he has been duped by Brother Jero. In the meantime, however, Jero has been luring a much more intelligent, educated, and skeptical man, a backbencher of the federal parliament. At first, the legislator is contemptuous: "Go and practice your fraudulence on another person of greater gullibility" (168) he tells Jero. But the prophet soon begins to foresee a ministerial post for the legislator, and the man is soon caught by the prophet's artful rhetoric and what seems to be the divine sanction of his own vanity and ambition. In a concluding monologue, Jero brazenly informs the audience that, with the help of his newest conquest, he will have no problem in getting the troublesome Chume committed to a lunatic asylum for at least a year. His occupation remains secure.

Every supernatural prophecy in this play is shown to be bogus, and the mechanisms of prophetic trade are revealed and exposed. Even potential dramatic irony is sacrificed to social critique: Jero begins the day with a premonition that women will be his downfall, and he recalls the old curse of the prophet whose territory he had usurped. Neither one is fulfilled in any form—a rarity in drama, where what is foretold almost always occurs, if only in an ironic, unexpected, or metaphorical manner. In this play the only accurate predictions are those based on human greed, vanity, and gullibility.[6]

A similar perspective is present in R. K. Narayan's story, "An Astrologer's Day" (1964). Narayan's astrologer is, if possible, even more fraudulent than Soyinka's prophet. "His forehead was respondent with sacred ash and vermillion, and his eyes sparkled with a sharp abnormal gleam which was really an outcome of a continual searching for customers, but which his simple clients took to be a prophetic light and felt comforted" (1). This man, we soon learn, is a somewhat reluctant astrologer; he stumbled into the trade by chance. He holds no illusion concerning his powers of prediction:

> [H]e knew no more of what was going to happen to others than he knew what was going to happen to himself next minute. He was as much a stranger to the stars as were his innocent customers. Yet he said things that pleased and astonished everyone: that was more a matter of study, practice, and shrewd guesswork. (2)

His method was simple: he never opened his mouth until the customer had spoken for at least ten minutes, a tactic that usually would elicit all the information he needed to divine. He also used a number of foolproof lines: "In many ways you are not getting the fullest results for your efforts," "Most of your troubles are due to your nature" (3). Few would argue with these pronouncements. He had a good sense of mankind's major troubles—marriage, money, and social entanglement—and this enabled him to make accurate assessments and feel he had earned his money at the end of the day.

One night, as he is about to pack up his cowrie shells, mystic charts, and bundle of palmyra writing, he spots a potential customer. But this client is suspicious and demanding; he interrupts the astrologer's customary phrases and wagers that the seer cannot give him any useful information. As the man lights a cigar, the astrologer tells him that he had been attacked and left for dead; a knife had passed through his body. Surprised and impressed, the man pulls up his shirt and shows the scar. He demands to know what became of his attacker. The astrologer responds that the man died horribly four months earlier. The other man is pleased and is surprised once more when the astrologer tells him his own name. After a final pronouncement—go back to your village, and never come south again—the man pays his money and, satisfied, departs. That night the astrologer tells his wife that for many years he thought he had killed a man in a fight, but now he has learned that the man survived. He can finally sleep in peace. In this story knowledge comes only from experience, and all predictions are educated guesses or outright lies.[7]

Lu Hsun's story, "The New Year's Sacrifice" (1924), begins with a metaphysical conundrum. The narrator, a scholar, has returned to his native village in rural China just before the New Year. The townspeople are preparing chickens and geese to welcome the God of Fortune and solicit prosperity for the coming year. A former servant, now a beggar, meets him and asks whether or not ghosts and Hell exist. The narrator, who "had never given the least thought to the question of the existence of spirits" (1972, 127), but knowing that the village tradition favored such beliefs, responds in a way he thinks will please her and says he thinks they may. On further questioning, he admits instead he is not sure they do in fact exist. They part; the next day the woman is found dead. It is revealed that her life had been filled with misery, humiliation, and abuse. She had been particularly worried by the villagers' stories of the afterlife, especially the forecast that she, having had two husbands on earth, would be cut in two by the King of Hell so each man could possess half. The scholar's words, repudiating local myths, occasion her death; in a final irony, the unpropitiousness of her demise does nothing to detract from the village's optimism, and even the troubled narrator feels "that the saints of heaven and earth had accepted the sacrifice and incense and were . . . preparing to give the people of Luchen boundless good fortune" (143). This caustic tale points out the severe price exacted by the closed economy of ritual and folk belief, and hints at an underlying nihilism that enables the residents to ignore or deny any omen that might otherwise temper their collective optimism.

Maxine Hong Kingston's "No Name Woman" is a tale about the powers and consequences of storytelling. Shortly after Kingston has started menstruating, her mother relates the cautionary tale of Kingston's aunt, a woman who became pregnant by a man who was not her husband. This occurred in rural China in 1924 (the same year Lu's "New Year's Sacrifice" was published); because of the transgression, the villagers raided the family's house and slaughtered its livestock. After giving birth, the aunt killed herself and her infant. Her subsequent punishment was to be never mentioned again by her family—a terrible fate in a culture where ancestor worship is prominent. In telling this story, Kingston simultaneously discredits the villagers' literal beliefs and reinvests them with a deeper metaphorical significance. When the attackers arrive, they call the unfortunate woman "Pig" and "Ghost." Once dead, her being is far more shadowy than the ancestors that are celebrated and propitiated. The depiction of her gruesome existence in the legendary Chinese underworld functions as a parable of her neglect on earth: "Always hungry, always needing, she would have to beg food from other ghosts, snatch and steal it from those whose living descendants gave them gifts" (1977, 18). Finally, Kingston remarks that the ghost of her aunt still haunts her—not as a literal apparition, but as an instance of unrecorded injustice. Consequently, the author will "devote pages of paper to her, though not origamied into houses and clothes" (19). Her offering will be the long suppressed narrative rather than the traditional gifts to the dead. The various geometrical and figurative circles in the piece culminate in a narrative cycle that enables Kingston's tale to negate her mother's account, as she partially invents the biography that had been so long suppressed.[8]

In the reconstruction of the aunt's life, causal and predictive discourse is frequently invoked and critiqued. As in Lu Hsun's story, an assiduity to perform all the requisite acts that lead to "good fortune" underlies the course of events. Kingston imagines her aunt digging out a freckle on her chin at "a spot that the almanac said predestined her for unhappiness" (11), just as the village will later uproot her for opening up "a black hole, a maelstrom that pulled in the sky," since "[m]isallying couples snapped off the future" (14). For Kingston's mother, necessity is "a riverbank that guides her life" (6). The villagers, however, are less consistent; "People who refused fatalism because they could invent small resources insisted on culpability. Deny accidents and wrest fault from the stars" (15). Had they been thoroughly deterministic they would have concluded that the pregnancy could not have been avoided; instead, they try to punish and negate the event that they fear will alter their future. Kingston provides materialist reinterpretations of the origins of these rural beliefs—scarcity of resources, especially food, avoidance of endogamy, etc. And again, she provides a guiding metafictional thread that connects the life she invents to the life she lives. Assaying possible personalities for her aunt, she rejects one that would have her sexually wild: "I don't know any women like that, or men either. Unless I see her life branching into mine, she gives me no ancestral help" (10). In this story, Kingston strategically employs "myths to write a narrative that is deliberately anti-mythic," as Malini Schueller observes (1989, 431–32). In doing so, she exfoliates and extends the implicit metafictional premises of predicative statements when viewed from a more critical perspective (an implication also noted by many other authors discussed in this chapter): if a prophecy is false, it is just another fictional narrative, albeit one that attempts to disguise its own fictionality.

Charles Johnson's story, "The Sorcerer's Apprentice" (1983), is a postmodern exploration of the themes of conjuring, magic, and altering the future. The narrative's setting is "long ago, when many sorcerers lived in South Carolina, men not long from slavery who remembered the white magic of the Ekpe Cults and Cameroons" (1987, 149). The greatest of these wizards is a blacksmith named Rubin Bailey; as he advances in years he decides to take as an apprentice the son of a man he had once miraculously healed. After some time as an apprentice, the boy grows frustrated; he has learned a lot about being a blacksmith, but nothing at all about sorcery. The old man explains vaguely, "What I know has worked I will teach. There is no certainty these things can work for you, or even for me, a second time" (151). He confesses that white magic "comes and goes," and notes that even "after fifty years, I still can't foresee if an incantation will be magic or foolishness" (151). We have here an admittedly unreliable sorcerer who cannot look clearly into the future. Just as the reader is prepared for a by-now familiar debunking of claims of supernatural powers, a number of successful conjurations occur. Allan, the apprentice, learns how to drop birds dead by pointing at them; later, after more study, he is able to cure a broken hip. Now, it would seem, we are firmly in the realm of the supernatural. But Allan, like many similar pupils of the time, becomes suspicious of his own success and, despite his pride, is "as baffled as his audience and afraid for his future" (156). He grows to dread his first solo demonstration, which is quickly approaching. He practices by using the rainmaking charm, but it doesn't rain: "They're only words!" he laments (158). Later, he says the spell for good weather. A light rain falls. When he is then called to heal a sick child, he realizes his hour has come. Despite his most fervent incantations, the child gets worse. Once again, a naturalistic interpretation of the story seems to beckon. The sorcery "successes" must be wrong. Allan realizes that his talent is merely for pastiche: "He could imitate but never truly heal; impress but never conjure beauty; ape the good but never again give rise to a genuine spell" (164–65).

Despairing, he goes to the riverbank and conjures up several malignant spirits to help him end his life. These all appear, as various and ironic as those Faust encounters on Walpurgis Night. The most critical is Bazazath, the demon of the West. He explains that "to love the good, the beautiful is right, but to labor on and will the work when you are obviously *beneath* this service is to parody them. . . . Sorcery is relative, student—dialectical, if you like expensive speech" (167). Allan yields to a feeling of resignation, decides to keep on living, and embraces his father, who had appeared minutes earlier. The demon's speech, employing the idioms of Neoplatonism and literary criticism, dissolves the apparent causal laws of the fictional world. Naturalism is jettisoned and the supernatural can now be seen to function solely as a trope. Reading backwards, we can recover an allegory of aesthetic endeavor, as sorcery becomes an emblem of artistic creation, with the apprentice a kind of African American equivalent of Kafka's hunger artist or Shakespeare's Prospero. From this perspective, one may even divine a mild critique of African American attempts to ground an aesthetic on distant African origins: Allan acknowledges that he "had not been born among the Allmuseri Tribe in Africa, like Rubin, if this was necessary for magic. . . . He had only, it seemed, a vast and painfully acquired yet hollow repertoire of tricks" (159). It will be by embracing his real father, a former slave, that his social ties will be strengthened; similarly, for his art to flourish, he must not rely solely on "an armory of techniques, a thousand strategies" (157) in overly calculated attempts to force results, but instead be more spontaneous, personal, and, paradoxically, "anonymous, like a tool in which the spell sang itself, briefly borrowing his throat, then tossed him, Allan, aside when the miracle ended" (156). With this work, the causal drama centering on conjuration that appears in a great range of works within the African continuum reaches a new level of distinctively postmodern reflexivity.

In summary, we find a diverse but circumscribed series of literary responses to the claims of traditional supernatural metaphysics at the site of the key topos of prophecy. Hosein effortlessly dramatizes kismet; Silko makes an arduous affirmation of an indigenous otherworld; and Tafik al-Hakim asserts the power of the divinity while denying predestination and critiquing the prophecies he dramatizes. Achebe maintains an epistemological tension between competing Igbo and materialist interpretations; only at the end of the novel do we see the triumph of the latter. Ndebele and Senior produce compassionate, almost nostalgic accounts of beliefs they ultimately dismiss as superstition. Chesnutt, like Ndebele and Narayan, valorizes characters who successfully manipulate the unsophisticated credulity of their superiors and antagonists. Soyinka, Narayan, and Lu are unambiguous in their denunciations of the fraudulent claims of supernatural agents and diviners. Kingston, while demystifying popular rural Chinese beliefs, reinvests them with layers of metaphorical meaning and metafictional resonance. Charles Johnson invokes sorcery only to transform it into the central trope of a postmodern allegory. These writers taken together do provide a different focus on causal issues by centering on and reanimating the supernatural/naturalistic struggle that has tended to fade (though, as we will see, has by no means vanished) from more "standard" European and Euro-American texts. The different focus also yields unexpected results—in general, the valorization of skeptical responses to indigenous theocentric traditions. Another key difference is the repeated emphasis on the material conditions and material effects of the act of storytelling. The prophetic narratives of events that have not yet occurred demonstrate yet again, as we have seen in Conrad and Faulkner, the powers and dangers of the making of fictions; this is a kind of materialist reflexivity, far removed from the more facile metafictional gamesmanship that often appears in many Euro-American postmodern novels.

The reasons for the general absence of alternative supernatural causal agencies in modern non-Western narratives are not hard to find. First, narrative has largely been a secular affair since the 1840s; even Christian novelists and playwrights have rarely allowed God a significant role in the ordering of represented events. Each of the authors discussed is extremely erudite and fully aware of the forms and conventions of the Western literary tradition—so much so, in fact, that it is not certain that in many respects the distinction between modern Western and non-Western literature is as useful as the distinction between modernist and realist writing. The stories of Tagore and Hosain owe more to Chekhov than to the *Mahabharata*, and the plays of Soyinka, Cesaire, and Al-Hakim have closer affinities to Shakespeare, Brecht, and Ionesco than to traditional Yoruba drama or the Egyptian puppet theater under the caliphs. Though non-Western in origin and ideology, these artists are nevertheless significant presences in a literary modernism that has always been international.[9] It is also the case that the major or primary audience for many of these writers is an international one.

Advances in Western technology and medicine have also tended to legitimize the antitheological perspective that enabled their development. Witch doctors are no match for penicillin.[10] Another important reason for the discrediting of the supernatural is the influence of dialectical materialism. Western Europe is not the only corner of the globe where religion is the opium of the masses. Progressive writers, even as they struggle against political and cultural imperialism, do not usually wish to defend and restore ancient theocracies, however traditional. In this context it is intriguing to note that Christianity, whether in a hybrid or "purer" form, is never presented as a valuable option in any of the texts examined above. On the contrary, Christianity is seen more as the vessel of imperialism and domination that needs to be resisted even more assiduously than the indigenous metaphysics it seeks to supplant. Furthermore, the skepticism toward both native and foreign supernatural beliefs is generally presented as stemming from informed observation and self-reflection, and is not (except, at times, in Silko) thought of as an intellectual import from the West. In conclusion, we may observe that an analysis of causal systems in non-Western narratives reveals significant and unexpected areas of both difference and convergence with Western narrative traditions, which in turn suggests that neither monolithic universalist assumptions nor rigidly Manichaean notions of cultural alterity are adequate to comprehend the divergent yet familiar practices of the narratives of the world's emergent literatures.

7

Plotting against Probability: Tom Stoppard, Bharati Mukherjee, Angela Carter, and the Structure of Coincidence in Postmodern Narrative

Many recent authors have played with the ordering of events and have investigated the genesis, development, and consequences of causal progressions. All four types of causal systems outlined in chapter 2 are present in contemporary narrative, though one finds a pronounced shift away from the supernatural and naturalistic modes and a gravitation toward chance and metafictional worlds. An overview of some recent texts will show how some familiar causal dynamics continue to be played out and how the twentieth-century fascination with the role of chance transforms many of these in unexpected ways. We will find particularly interesting the extended symbiosis of naturalism and chance in Stanislaw Lem's *The Chain of Chance* and Iris Murdoch's *An Accidental Man*; the construction and subsequent defiance of probabilistic expectations in Bharati Mukherjee's *Jasmine*; and the ways in which Tom Stoppard and Angela Carter attempt to pattern the development of events after having removed all naturalistic constraints in *Rosencrantz and Guildenstern Are Dead* and *Wise Children*. In sequencing this chapter, I will proceed from the totalizing causal systems to the more fragmented and arbitrary ones.

Though supernatural causal systems have not entirely vanished, as the example of Silko's *Ceremony* shows, they are rapidly becoming a thing of the past. (Muriel Spark's *Not To Disturb*, which will be discussed later in this chapter, does however suggest a way by which supernatural concerns can be embodied within a metafictional framework, as does D. H. Thomas's *The White Hotel*.) Another interesting exception to this general pattern is the utilization of the supernatural by some contemporary African American writers such as Gloria Naylor, Toni Morrison, and, in *The Piano Lesson*, August Wilson.[1]

Naturalistic causal systems are still fairly common, and the by-now classic opposition between supernatural and naturalistic causal agencies appears in three recent novels: Anita Brookner's *Providence*, Richard Ford's *The Ultimate Good Luck*, and Gabriel García Marquez's *Chronicle of a Death Foretold*. In Brookner's novel the protagonist, originally skeptical of the notion of providence, is led to grant it some validity until, in the end, it is shown to be an illusion. The protagonist of Ford's book continuously speculates on the nature of luck and regularly tests its vagaries and limits; the work's conclusion, however, divests luck of any transcendent qualities. In García Marquez's novel we find that the death, though foretold, is hardly preordained: the perpetrators do all they can to allow their victim to escape. It is the communal belief in the inevitability of the act of revenge that finally goads the reluctant killers into performing their roles in the distasteful social script. Each of these works invokes a traditional supernatural causal agency— providence, luck, predestination—only to demystify it subsequently by a naturalistic critique.

Margaret Drabble's *The Ice Age* also explicitly thematizes and confronts providential claims as part of a larger investigation into causal agency. The character Anthony Keeting, for example, tries to uncover the laws that govern the world around him, seeking to find the "one common cause" that connects them (1977, 7). He rejects the notion of "the random malice of the fates, those three grey sisters" (294), convinces himself that providence must exist, and finally decides to write a book that will disclose the providential design. Elsewhere in the novel the concepts of luck, destiny, poetic justice, and even "a primitive causality" that claims that one's misfortunes are caused by one's state of mind (97)—a kind of "instant karma" effect—are set forth and critically scrutinized.[2] Finally, every teleological or supernatural system proffered within the text is shown to be inadequate; none can withstand the demands of realism and the vagaries of chance. As John Hannay states: "*The Ice Age* tests the Providential model by positing, but then subverting, various external orders. All patterns and explanations for the random disasters and fortunes fail; all models of reality are deceptive" (1986, 99).

Anne Tyler's *Celestial Navigation* is another work that employs a number of improbable events within a larger naturalistic framework,

though her focus is more personal than cosmic. The work's protagonist, the artistically successful but socially incompetent Jeremy Pauling,
has terrible problems with ordinary sequences of cause and effect. In
one memorable scene, he not only forgets to attend his own wedding
but forgets he was ever supposed to get married. All he notices is an
unusual stillness in the house: "Had he missed something? Had the
days carried everyone else on by and left him stranded in some vanished moment? Maybe his family had just gone to a movie. Maybe they
had abandoned him forever. Maybe they had grown up and moved
some thirty years before. . . . He couldn't prove that it wasn't so" (1984,
169).

Three philosophically minded novelists—Stanislaw Lem, Iris
Murdoch, and Geoffrey Wolff—produced novels in the seventies and
eighties that attempted to compile the greatest number of chance events
that could be plausibly located within a naturalistic perspective. Nineteenth-century materialism had generally deprecated the notion of
chance in favor of a mechanistic model of universal causation; Poincaré's
discovery that chance was compatible with a naturalistic worldview
was not widely appreciated until the twentieth century. Lem and
Murdoch in particular seek to display just how powerful and pervasive chance is in the nature of things.

In *The Chain of Chance*, Lem constructs an ontological detective story.
Eleven middle-aged men, all foreigners, have died mysteriously after
visits to a seaside spa in Naples. Many of the victims have common
characteristics: good health, partial baldness, substantial funds, susceptibility to allergies, and a proclivity for traveling alone. They all developed a paranoid schizophrenia and died in odd accidents or took
their own lives. Investigators suspect the work of a previously unknown
terrorist organization, while others involved in the case offer different
hypotheses. A certain Philippe Barth wonders whether causality is
present at all. The protagonist's assignment—to re-create exactly the
itinerary of one of the victims—is intended in part to determine whether
the deaths were crimes or coincidences. Barth cautions, "Naples is a
trap, there's no doubt about that. But one that operates like a lottery,
not like a machine" (1984, 93), and he also warns that the "element of
chance does not rule out the possibility of a crime" (93). A completely
random murder is still a murder. In the end, it turns out that all who
died were victims of repeated chance interactions of chemicals that are
harmless enough if taken alone. A chemical used in an ointment to reduce

balding, made volatile by exposure to sunlight, combined with a chemical in the decongestant, sulfur from the mineral baths, and a cyanate present in Neapolitan sugar-roasted almonds—all these taken together produced the lethal dementia. A sweet tooth was a prerequisite for sudden death.

The protagonist's discovery of the enigma's solution is equally filled with chance. As the protagonist states, "[T]he whole combination of fortuitous events leading up to the solving of the mystery now seemed to me more amazing than the mystery itself" (176). But another character, better versed in the theory of probability, suggests instead that both the deaths and their solution had to occur. He offers, for the second time in the book, the image of a marksman trying to hit a fly on a postage stamp from half a mile away. In such a scenario, no sharpshooter can succeed, because the target isn't even visible at that range. On the other hand, if you have hundreds of mediocre marksmen firing away for a long enough period of time, a perfect shot is not only possible but inevitable. There is nothing unusual about the man who hit the bull's-eye, since someone would have had to hit it. Similarly, the Naples mystery was solved by the same "random causality" that had caused it. Sooner or later, some investigator would have come upon and put together all the relevant elements. The book's conclusion states that "we now live in . . . a dense world of random chance, in a molecular and chaotic gas whose 'improbabilities' are amazing only to the individual atoms" (179).

In this novel, Lem has created an ontological thriller, a murder mystery without a murder. He has constructed a chain of related coincidences that not only can but must occur according to the remoter dictates of the theory of probability. A man struck by a bolt of lightning will (if he survives) regard his case as wildly unlikely, but the statistician knows that a substantial number of people suffer the same fate each year. Although the odds are more than a million to one that any specific individual will be hit, the odds are equally high that someone, somewhere, will be struck. Lem dramatizes both sides of this conundrum, as the wildly improbable is shown to be, within a scrupulously naturalistic framework, ultimately inevitable.

Geoffrey Wolff sets himself a somewhat different task in the rather cynically entitled novel, *Providence*. Its geographical setting is Providence, Rhode Island; its intellectual challenge is to follow out the many coincidences that necessarily happen "so often in so small a city" (1991, 1). Its method is revealed early in the book: when Dr. Asa Dwyer, just by chance, looks at his brother Adam's blood under a microscope, he learns that his brother probably has leukemia. Later, once the diagnosis is confirmed, Asa tries to discuss this cruel turn of fortune with his brother: "It's upside down. You're too young for this. Not medically, you're just the perfect age for leukemia medically, right on the money, mid-forties, the actuaries wouldn't bat an eye" (11). The cruelty of probability is here outlined and dissected.

Adam goes on to try "to open himself to chance" (19) but, as other characters who muse on the subject also learn (16, 56), the spectrum of chance in Providence is not very wide; their sense of unlimited possibility keeps getting pulled up short by coincidences that retrospectively seem inevitable. As the novel progresses, its multiple protagonists— attorney, policeman, burglar, judge, lounge singer, mobster, teacher— keep unwittingly brushing up against (and interfering with) each other, as their lives become increasingly intertwined. As the policeman accurately reflects, "Providence was a peewee metropolis, and the probability was high that whoever had wronged the attorney and sometime Public Defender was an ex-client" (38). This principle holds true throughout the novel and leads to a denouement that is simultaneously brutal and hilarious when chance, obsession, and predictable coincidences come together in unexpected but unsurprising ways. In *Providence*, Wolff constructs a modern kind of necessity that is informed by probability theory, as inevitability takes the shape of a coincidence that can no longer be deferred.

A different investigation into the limits of the unlikely is undertaken by Iris Murdoch in *An Accidental Man*, though here the setting is a reasonable facsimile of that of the traditional English novel of manners. The common practice—by now it may be described as a convention of narratives that investigate causal agency—of characters invoking disparate metaphysical orderings to explain the events around them is fully indulged; luck (1973, 19), destiny (84, 87), arbitrary determinism (61, 113), and fate (121) are alluded to by various characters. Most of these allusions are halfhearted, as few of the speakers seriously intend to call up the larger metaphysical implications of these words' archaic meanings. Most of the time, they function as synonyms for chance, and when they don't, the utterer is eventually disabused of his or her error. Charlotte Ledgard, for example, has witnessed her religious faith shrink into a bitter fatalism. "Usefulness" to the more fortunate members of her family "was her destiny. . . . She had no personal destiny and nothing extraordinary could ever happen to her now," she feels (100). Later, when she is contemplating suicide, she decides to let chance determine her lot: "[S]he had always been the slave of chance, let it kill her if it would by a random stroke" (310). But the power of coincidence is greater than she can imagine. Right after she swallows an entire bottle of sleeping pills, she is found by an acquaintance who breaks down the door and gets her to a hospital. There she finds herself in a bed next to another woman who had just attempted suicide over the father of the man who had rescued Charlotte. The two women then move to the country, get a house together, and become lovers.

This sequence of events illustrates a central preoccupation of the text—the far-reaching consequences of accidental events and arbitrary decisions. Indeed, every major turn of the plot is based on a chance action or whimsical choice. Austin Gibson Grey, who claims to be "an accidental man" (429) and who is said to be not only unlucky but contagious in his misfortunes (207), has suffered psychologically his entire adult life from an early accident that left one hand crippled. Mitzi Ricardo, the woman who eventually meets up and moves in with Charlotte Ledgard, had been a promising athlete until a freak accident on a tennis court ruined her ankle. Wondering why she had ever left the world of ballet for that of sport, she muses: "Any other path would not have led through a million entwining contingencies to that hideous tennis court moment when she sprang over the net, tripped, fell, and through some utterly improbable complex of injuries destroyed her ankle forever" (36). The "accidental man's" estranged wife, Dorina, is said to attract poltergeists. In her presence, uncanny things happened: "Pictures fell. Windows cracked. A noise like a grand piano falling down the stairs occurred once without visible cause" (61). When she dies from an accidental electrocution, another character, Ludwig Leferrier, thinks "[t]he thing was pure chance and yet weighed [on him] with a significance of horror which he could not bear to contemplate" (377); he suspects that her death might not be unrelated to the fact that hours earlier he had pretended not to notice her as he passed her in the street, knowing she was in distress. At that moment he too is about to make a decision that he knows will "affect his whole life, not only in its circumstances, but in its quality, in its very deepest texture. According to what he chose now he would become a totally different person later. Various forty-year-old, fifty-year-old Ludwigs regarded him from the shores of possibility with sad and perhaps cynical eyes" (378).

Ludwig's encountering Dorina, though a random happenstance, is not entirely gratuitous. As another man observes of another woman,

"[I]n the roulette of London social life, he would probably meet her somewhere or other eventually" (129). The chance events of the book can always be located within a larger naturalistic causal matrix. Invisible "networks of causes" are such that whenever "we do anything slightly bad it sets up a sort of wave which ends with someone committing suicide or murder or something" (387). The problem for the unwitting human agents and victims is that they cannot see, and therefore are not fully responsible for, the elusive, obscure, and skewed lines of causation. One of the more philosophical (and irresponsible) characters observes that, although individual acts may mean something in the largely unknowable "great web of cause and effect," they are for the most part insignificant—instead, "it's more like gambling, it's roulette" (275). Thus, there are moral absolutes "where calculation about causality comes up against a brick wall. . . . When you can't calculate, perhaps it doesn't matter so much how you act" (276).

Murdoch's novel traverses the vague terrain between apparently unrelated chance events and the larger though often unknowable causal ties that frame them. Ineluctable causal progressions generate multiple series of improbable conjunctions, arbitrary choices produce devastating effects, and ostensible accidents are often causally overdetermined. Dorina tells her husband that his vehicular homicide of a little girl "was brought about by chance and not by you" (183), but the reader—like the girl's blackmailing stepfather—knows it was caused by the driver's distraction, anger, and drinking. Whenever the sequence of chance events seems too unlikely to be probable, we find out that it was not chance at all, but part of a comprehensible causal pattern. As one character states:

> The point is it doesn't really matter very much what you do. What you do will be decided by causal factors in your nature which in a way are very deep, and in a way are utterly superficial. Deep because they're mechanical and old. Superficial because their significance is, in relation to the real you, trivial. (113)

This dynamic of the accidental and the unavoidable, here expressed in terms of personal choice, expresses the opposite poles between which the novel oscillates: the chance event and the causal chain. Murdoch's achievement is to reveal how thoroughly chance animates, interpenetrates, engenders, and is embraced within larger causal webs and chains. It is difficult to imagine a more thorough documentation of the range and force of chance within—and it does resolutely stay within—the naturalistic world of our experience. One simply never suspects that so much chance, accident, and coincidence can reside there.

Expressionistic fiction has been reinvigorated by new interrogations of cause and chance: Nicholas Mosley's *Accident* reflects on unlikely causal conjunctions that do occur, as well as the plausible sequences that never materialize, while Paul Auster in *The Music of Chance* speculates on the catastrophic consequences of arbitrary choices. Most interesting in this context is John Hawkes's *Second Skin*. In this work Skipper, a suspiciously sanguine narrator, recounts the "unlikely accidents, tabloid adventures, [and] shocking episodes" that constitute his life (1964, 5). Throughout, suggestions of different types of determinism and modes of destiny abound. Some are personal and seem sincere ("I always knew myself destined for this particular journey" [45]); others are more speculative ("I might have known from the copybook what I was destined for" [46]); still others suggest that "destiny" is adventitious and fails to conform, even retrospectively, to the narrative pattern demanded by the concept of fate. In a sentence that includes a touch of macabre comedy, Skipper writes, "I was off the porch and once more running after my destiny which always seemed to be racing ahead of me in black tires" (191).

This deployment and depletion of the term continues in the narrator's other statements. He describes eluding the end that his father's suicide had prepared for him—"I know it was meant for me, his deliberate shot. But it went wild" (3)—and instead partially causes the subsequent suicides of his mother and daughter. He imagines alternative existences, and even in these he believes he knows what his lot would be: had he been born a girl, he affirms, he would have grown not into another Clytemnestra but rather "a large and innocent Iphigenia betrayed on the beach" (1); and yet, he is somehow convinced that he should have been spared: "[T]o bleed but not to bleed to death would have been my fate" (2).[3] Even the numerous mythic and intertextual references (his daughter is named Cassandra, his mother Gertrude, his island lover Miranda) merely suggest but never complete an overarching system of correspondences—not even one of consistently ironic reversals. There is at most a series of partial and variable distortions. In short, the intermittently evoked concept of fate turns out to be nothing more than a name for the events that happen to occur; it does not reveal any pattern, order, or progression.

It is also the case that the narrator's self-indulgent projection of a moral order running through life ("how satisfying that virtue always wins" [98]) is equally incapable of comprehending the world it purports to describe. This simply does not happen except in his overly pleasant and obviously distorted reconstructions of events—events that invariably belie the ordering principle forced upon them. To use the terms of E. M. Forster, we may describe this work as a "story" of adventitious events that resist the narrator's assiduous efforts to shape them retrospectively into a discernible "plot." The novel is, in other words, a kind of undoing of Proust: whereas Marcel can transform his heterogenous experiences into a convincing artistic whole, Skipper can only delude himself into thinking he has done the same.

As Patrick O'Donnell states, "Skipper's history is a concatenation of seemingly random events which take on meaning as the history evolves" (1982, 86). This "meaning," however, is arbitrary, fallacious, and imposed, signifying not (as O'Donnell suggests) the triumph of an artistic imagination so much as the nearly limitless powers of self-delusion. Referring to his "naked history," Skipper confesses, "I will never be able to conceal myself completely in all those scenes which are even now on the tip of my tongue and crowding my eye" (99). In the end, the chaotic disorder of experience resists all conventional orders. This in turn results in a Beckett-like paradox, as the narrator's repeated failures are part of a larger authorial design.

We may also observe that the chance worlds of high modernism present in the later works of Conrad and in Forster can still be found in more recent novels by authors like Anthony Powell and Julio Cortázar, where the proliferation of random accidents and unlikely coincidences is sufficient to destabilize the represented world, edging it away from the superficially similar world of our experience where the laws of probability operate. It teases us with the gestures of mimesis, hovering between the reproduction and violation of the causal order of everyday existence before receding definitively into the realm of fabrication. The virtue of this approach is to challenge totalizing supernatural and naturalistic worldviews; the danger it risks is the establishment of idiosyncratic, arbitrary, and inconsequential private universes. This has proven to be a difficult balancing act; most contemporary authors who do not return to what Lem and Murdoch have shown to be the unexpectedly capacious fold of naturalism tend to impose conflicting and ostensibly gratuitous orderings of events (the stance I have termed metafictional, one characteristic of postmodernism). In texts like Vladimir Nabokov's *Lolita*, David Lodge's *Small World*, and Salman Rushdie's *Midnight's Children*, chance and coincidence become so conspicuous that they no longer destabilize a naturalistic order but rather point to authorial contrivance. The same is true of Muriel Spark's *Not to Disturb*, though here the metafictional intervention is presented as an analogue of a supernatural ordering of events. As Ruth Whitaker observes, "Both God and the novelist create a world which they then people with characters simultaneously free and limited. Sometimes in novels, as in real life, characters resent and fight back at authorial or divine omniscience, and the dynamic relationship between creator and character is integral to Mrs. Spark's plots" (1979, 162). A particularly interesting dialogue between chance and cause is present in Fay Weldon's *The Cloning of Joanna May*, as the book's antagonist, Carl May, obsessively attempts to refute the supernatural and eliminate chance, while its protagonist, Joanna, appeals to and is finally surrounded by an utterly improbable plethora of serendipitous accidents and coincidences.

This leads to the paradox of chance in fictional narratives: its absence indicates a specious causalism that posits a seamless and unreal chain of cause and effect; its presence, however, invariably reveals authorial intervention, since chance in fiction is never a chance occurrence.[4] As the narrator of Julian Barnes's *Flaubert's Parrot* observes, "[A]s for coincidences in books—there's something cheap and sentimental about the device; it can't help always seeming aesthetically gimcrack. That troubadour who passes by just in time to rescue the girl from a hedgerow scuffle; the sudden but convenient Dickensian benefactors; the neat shipwreck on a foreign shore which reunites siblings and lovers. . . . I'd ban coincidences, if I were a dictator of fiction" (1990, 67).

Coincidence, however startling in everyday life, can rapidly become tiresome in imaginative literature. An inverse correlation may be at work: the more unlikely a series of events is, the more compulsively narratable it becomes in everyday life, while the same events recounted in a fiction necessarily seem the most contrived.[5] In fiction, chance is a relation that always threatens to defy the conditions of its own representation. In small amounts, it can produce a "reality effect" in realistic narratives; in moderate amounts, it can destabilize totalizing supernatural and naturalistic settings; and in still larger amounts it destroys the integrity of the fictional world and eliminates any logical connection between successive events.

This effect can be seen by looking at *Macbett*, Ionesco's parodic reworking of one of Shakespeare's most devious investigations of causation. From the beginning, absurdist dialogue, obvious anachronisms, and systematic rhetorical deflections reveal that the world presented on stage is largely independent of either the world of our experience or the patterns of Shakespeare's text. The characters are barely distinguishable from each other, often speak the same lines, and are uniformly motivated by greed, suspicion, and treachery (if one may speak of motives when discussing such one-dimensional figures). In the course of the action, literally anything can happen. At one point Banco wonders how the witches can "explain the chain of cause and effect that will set my posterity on the throne" (1973, 47). Later, Banco, who states he has "no sons or daughters" (81), decides to get married and start a family: at precisely this point he is murdered by Macbett. In the play's final minutes Macbett, about to do battle with Macol, King Duncan's heir, expresses his indifference, affirming that no man of woman born can do him harm. But now it is suddenly revealed that Macol is in fact the son of Banco and a gazelle that a witch transformed into a woman. All the prophecies have, however ridiculously, come true, and Macbett feels that his is the "most cruelly ironic fate since Oedipus" (100).

Ionesco's satire is directed against autocrats, royal history plays, and the conventions of theatrical representation. He draws attention to Shakespeare's failure to mention the kingly status of Banquo's heirs (though the contemporary audience, which included King James, was well aware that the Stuarts claimed to have descended from the legendary Banquo), and he mocks the facility by which authors generally see to it that prophecies are fulfilled. But in doing so Ionesco avoids any recognizable ordering of events; what finally occurs is ultimately arbitrary and no particular causal principle (other than, perhaps, random repetition) connects the various episodes in any significant manner. The danger of such an approach, as Roy Jay Nelson has explained in a discussion of Robbe-Grillet's recent fiction, is that "[w]ithout reality-based causation, we obviously have no capacity for predicting what might or might not happen"; curiosity and suspense "must therefore also remain inoperative in such texts" (202). Furthermore, in the absence of any significant or recognizable causal connectives, "nothing can be of consequence" (1990, 203). Once anything can happen, nothing really matters.[6]

One of the most difficult challenges facing postmodern writers is to create a compelling narrative sequence that, eschewing traditional causal progressions and modernist formal symmetries, nevertheless is somehow significant, meaningful, or interesting. The postmodern author must choose between a largely gratuitous (and potentially inconsequential) arrangement of events and an original ordering that transcends the causal laws of each of the multiple worlds typically conflicted in postmodern narratives.

Three particularly ingenious responses to this dilemma have been set out by Tom Stoppard, Bharati Mukherjee, and Angela Carter. Stoppard's *Rosencrantz and Guildenstern Are Dead* begins in an ontological limbo, and the protagonists are able to recognize it as such precisely because of its violation of the canons of probability. In the opening coin-flipping scene, "heads" comes up ninety-two consecutive times. Guildenstern, who has bet and lost each time, speculates on possible explanations of this most unlikely series and proposes, among other alternatives, that he is somehow willing himself to lose, that divine intervention keeps interposing itself, and that "time has stopped dead, and the single experience of one coin being spun once has been repeated ninety times" (1968, 16). He concludes that, since "probability is a factor which operates within natural forces," he and Rosencrantz are now within "un- sub- or supernatural forces" (17). And indeed they do inhabit a kind of metaphysical no-man's land; they are literally characters between scenes, and as such they do not possess any conventional or recognizable mode of existence. When playing their scenes in *Hamlet*, they are part of the largely naturalistic world of that play. But between those appearances, they inhabit an alternate world with an indeterminate setting, devoid of clear or consistent spatial, temporal, or causal coordinates. This dichotomous existence is further reinforced by antithetical patterns of speech, style, and sensibility: when acting their roles in Shakespeare's drama, they speak the stylized Jacobean verse of that play; alone, Ros and Guil communicate in thoroughly modern prose filled with post-Renaissance terms and concepts. The two worlds soon clash, as the troupe of traveling players moves back and forth between them, providing a curiously unstable bridge—a bridge, that is, that dissolves into a palimpsest.

The epistemological drama that quickly emerges centers on which sets of rules govern the destinies of Rosencrantz and Guildenstern—the arbitrary, random, and lawless setting of their existence between scenes, or the tragic, overdetermined fate written out for them in Shakespeare's text.[7] This conflict is adumbrated in the confused dialogue on chance and fate between Guildenstern and the spokesman of the players, in which chance is rechristened fate (25). Guildenstern rapidly slides into a deterministic stance that resonates with metadramatic overtones: "We've been caught up. Your smallest action sets off another somewhere else, and is set off by it. . . . We'll be all right. . . . Till events have played themselves out. There's a logic at work" (39-40). Later in the play, he elaborates this position further: "Wheels have been set in motion, and they have their own pace, to which we are . . . condemned. Each move is dictated by the previous one—that is the meaning of order." But then he adds, "If we start being arbitrary it'll just be a shambles: at least let us hope so"; if they were to discover that their spontaneity was part of a larger order, then they would know they were lost, he concludes (60). Guildenstern is so seduced by the discourse of determinism that he can hardly imagine any kind of action outside its control, even as he is surrounded by apparent instances of indeterminate events. At this point in the text it is entirely possible that, like those of many of the characters in *Light in August*, his actions are fated only insofar as he believes them to be.

Many commentators uncritically accept Guildenstern's interpretation of the worlds he inhabits; as Susan Rusinko writes, "The small certainty of their deaths within the larger certainty of the inevitability of events is Guil's ultimate method of dealing with fate" (1986, 34). But it is precisely the "inevitability of events" that Stoppard continues to problematize, vitiate, interrupt, and deflect. There is no single logic of events at work in the play, but rather three separate though interactive orders—wheels within wheels that turn in opposite directions. The world of *Hamlet*, the play within this play, is causally determined, teleologically oriented, and governed by the authority of the antecedent text. Here events "must play themselves out to [their] aesthetic, moral and logical conclusion" (79), the figures "follow directions—there is no *choice* involved." (80). Causes produce specific events (111). In the shadow world between scenes, however, "anything could happen" (95), and does. In this realm, chance rules ("Life is a gamble, at terrible odds— if it was a bet you wouldn't take it" [114]); here too, choice is possible ("There must have been a moment, at the beginning, where we could have said—no" [125]). The productive tension of this text, as opposed to the less compelling *Macbett*, is that there are two realms in collision, each possessing its own integrity and each one threatening but never fully succeeding in subordinating the other. Each time Guil suspects that apparent freedom is merely ignorance of a larger, controlling design—"We can move, of course, change direction, rattle about, but our movement is contained within a larger one that carries us along as inexorably as the wind and current" (122)—a wildly improbable event ensues that mocks the notion of design. The play's curious framing technique enhances this ambiguity. The first third of the play takes place in the actors' limbo, and the scenes from *Hamlet* are embedded within it, while the play concludes with the final speeches of Shakespeare's tragedy, thus seeming to frame definitely the extra-Shakespearean material. It is the struggle between chance events and causal laws, choice and determinism, new scenes and the antecedent text, that gives the work its peculiar dynamism and precludes an easy interpretive solution.

As is evident from the citations already adduced, there is also a third ordering principle at work. Frequent metadramatic statements ("There's a design at work in all art" [79]) point to the governing intelligence that orders the unfolding drama, the literary demiurge who created (or borrowed) the two worlds placed in opposition. At this level, characters do not decide what they will do; instead, actors perform what "is written" (80), a possible allusion to a common Islamic notion of fate as "that which is written." The author thus personifies the fate that Guil perceives to be present and is the fabricator of the events attributed to chance. Here both the paradox of chance and the casuistry of necessity in works of fiction are exposed—the gaps of one and the machinery of the other are present only because the author has so ordered them.

Stoppard's metadramatic elements, though ubiquitous, are rarely interventional; the playwright impersonates general rather than special providence. Metadramatic causation occasionally jostles but never overthrows the other two causal systems; all three coexist in an uneasy equilibrium, enhancing the play's ontological drama while problematizing its critical recuperation. Stoppard has ingeniously conflated what, in the world of experience, are antithetical causal stances. It is impossible to finally determine what is chance, fate, or authorial decree. Until the end of the performance we do not know whether Ros and Guil will use their apparently boundless freedom "between the acts," whether the pressures of the intertext will bring them infallibly to their deaths, or whether Stoppard doesn't have an alternative ending up his sleeve and will change them, say, into the characters who speak the opening lines of *Cymbeline*, or will write beyond the ending of Shakespeare's *Hamlet*, or will return the play to its beginning (as Guil suggestively says, "[D]on't believe anything till it happens. And it *has* all happened. Hasn't it?" [108]). By forcibly juxtaposing a chance

world of limitless possibility to a closely regulated world of preestab-
lished fixity, Stoppard creates a compelling ontological drama of the
representation of the limitless and the circumscribing of the liminal.

In Bharati Mukherjee's *Jasmine,* an original and strangely compelling (though largely misunderstood) causal dynamic is at work. It is
one that successively embraces and contests the three types of causal
setting in a sequence that recapitulates the genealogy of fictional worlds
in narrative history, beginning with a supernatural framework, moving on to a naturalistic perspective, and concluding with chance interventions that cause the narrative to swerve away from the boundaries
of the probable. The novel starts with the account of a prophecy, that
central topos of emergent literatures. Here, however, the prophecy is
retrospectively stated to have been correct: when she is seven years old
and living in a rural area of Punjab, the village astrologer foretells
Jasmine's widowhood and exile . More skeptical than Jocasta and as
headstrong as Oedipus, Jasmine defies the seer, shouting: "You're a crazy
old man. You don't know what my future holds!" (1989, 3). The astrologer chucks her on the head and she falls down; as she falls, a stick is
embedded in her forehead, giving her a star-shaped scar. In northern
and eastern India, it is commonly believed that one's fate is written on
one's forehead; with this act, the fortuneteller seems to be reinscribing
his prophecy on Jasmine's body: "Bad times were on their way. I was
helpless, doomed. The star bled" (4).

Jasmine's animadversion toward prediction is not due to its inac-
curacy, but because of its denigration of human agency to influence
future events, its implication that she is powerless to create her own
destiny. As her friend Vimla, speaking for the community, reminds her,
"Just because you're clever in school doesn't mean you can ignore your
fate in the stars" (76). As long as she is in India the ancient Hindu cosmology appears to be adequate to explain the events around her: bad
luck is caused by the sins committed during an earlier existence; each
life has a specific though unknown assignment in God's master plan.
Worldviews based on the notion of fate are generally reactionary and
serve to perpetuate the status quo, since to try to alter one's position is
simultaneously futile and irreligious. Thus, the metaphysical oppres-
sion Jasmine feels is intimately tied to the social constraints of traditional Indian village life, here referred to as feudal: "I was the last to be
born to that kind of submission, that expectation of ignorance. When
the old astrologer swatted me under a banyan tree, we were both acting

out a final phase of a social order that had gone on untouched for thousands of years" (229). And the rigid village social codes are ruthlessly misogynistic: "If I had been a boy, my birth in a bountiful year would have marked me as lucky, a child with a special destiny to fulfill. But daughters were curses" (39).

Some contradictions begin however to appear in the putative supernatural order. Vimla's marriage, delayed out of concern for the dictates of the horoscope, later becomes stalled as her fiancé haggles for a new car as dowry. It becomes increasingly evident that the traditional metaphysics are not immutable truths, but inventions designed to legitimize existing social structures. What must be eluded is not a vague prophecy of distant events that are reasonably likely to happen anyway, but the master narrative of an oppressive social order, of which prophecy is ultimately merely a trope. Consequently, Jasmine is entirely correct in believing that if she and her husband "could just get away from India, then all fates would be cancelled. We'd start with new fates, new stars. We could say or be anything we wanted. We'd be on the other side of the earth, out of God's sight" (85).

At this point the supernatural presence begins to evaporate from the novel, leaving its powerful and gritty naturalistic order unalloyed as a general adherence to the laws of probability supersedes divine teleology. This transformation is concomitant with Jasmine's voyage to America and her escape from the patriarchal plot of rural India: after her husband is killed by Sikh terrorists, she travels to Florida (where she and her husband had planned to start a new life) in order to ritually burn his clothes and take her own life. This plan is interrupted when the American captain who had smuggled her into the United States then rapes her in a motel. In the motel bathroom, she prepares to cut her throat. Instead, she lacerates her tongue and thus becomes an image of Kali, the Hindu goddess of destruction and renewal whose red tongue hangs conspicuously from her dark mouth. Jasmine then stabs her attacker to death and resolves to go on living, makes her way to New York and then to Iowa, and takes on a new name and a new identity, becoming as it were an avatar of her former self.[8]

As the narrative progresses, though, unlikely events and numerous coincidences begin to proliferate. She happens to run into Sukhwinder, the man who had planted the bomb that killed her Indian husband, in New York City, where he is now selling hot dogs. The significant men in her life display a curious propensity to come to violent ends: her father is gored to death by a bull, her English teacher in India is killed by terrorists, her Indian husband is murdered by Sikh extremists, her Iowa husband is shot and paralyzed, her neighbor Darrel commits suicide. Numerous other seemingly unmotivated irruptions of chance and coincidence abound. Not surprisingly, several critics and reviewers have condemned these intrusions of the unlikely. To cite a mild though typical example, Liew-Geok Leong writes: "The picaresque, surrealistic, and no-holds-barred ethos of *Jasmine* more than occasionally strains reader credibility and recalls Mukherjee's resolution in her epilogue to *Days and Nights in Calcutta*: 'Even more than other writers, I must learn to astonish, to shock' (287). The voice of Jasmine, surprisingly articulate and assured, is not always believable" (1991, 494). Michiko Kakutani is more direct: "So rapidly does Jasmine's life change that the reader occasionally feels overwhelmed by the sheer amount of plot in Ms. Mukherjee's novel—much of it implausible" (1989, C18).

Such criticism mistakenly presumes that *Jasmine* is a realistic novel that unaccountably fails to adhere to the naturalistic laws of probability that ground the realist enterprise. I would suggest instead that the work is rather a particularly ingenious postmodern text, a pseudorealist one that interrogates and attacks naturalistic canons of probability as well as supernatural teleologies of destiny. Its causal dynamics invert the standard progression of conventional narratives. As Joanne S. Frye observes in her account of politics, literary form, and feminist poetics, "[T]he traditional plotting that moves from possibility to probability to necessity through the selection and structuring of events is closely tied to the available paradigms for reading women's lives" (1986, 39), and these paradigms, historically, have been limited to marriage, death, madness, or isolation. Jasmine is regularly tempted by these potential fates; at each juncture, however, she is always able to elude attempts—both Indian and American—to emplot her life within a conventional patriarchal cultural narrative. Jasmine's escape from the marriage plot is coextensive with Mukherjee's transcendence of probability. For her, as for Virginia Woolf, "the tyranny of convention—the expected, the accepted—and the tyranny of plot overlap," Susan Stanford Friedman has written (1989, 163). Here, the postmodern strategy of interpolating chance events merges with the long tradition of female writers' defiance of probabilistic constraints. Nancy K. Miller, in her justly celebrated article on plots and plausibilities in women's fiction, remarks that "the peculiar shape of a heroine's destiny in novels by women, the implausible twists of plot so common in these novels, is a form of insistence about the relation of women to writing" (1981, 44).

This insistence is most clearly exemplified in the final twist of the novel's plot. In Iowa, Jasmine is living with a paraplegic banker, pregnant with his child. She looks with envy at "the straight lines and smooth planes of his history" (1989, 214), and views with unease his desire to marry her, to enclose her life within the frame of a familiar social plot and traditional closure. At this point, out of the blue, an old friend from New York arrives and invites her to move with him to California, which she does. Mukherjee's subsequent gloss on this abrupt turn of affairs is revealing: "I didn't know she was going to leave Bud at the end of the novel. She just up and went! . . . She felt it was a regression, like going back to village life, a life of duty and devotion, to stay on caring for this crippled fellow. The frontier was out there, beckoning. She just left" (1990, 31). Mukherjee's account of her novel's "unplanned" and unlikely denouement is itself a bit abrupt, and reveals that though there is a logic that inspires the progression of fictional events, it is not the logic of probability. This also helps to explain her comment on the work's mode: "[I]t's not a realistic novel. It's meant to be a fable" (1990, 8).

The book's realism is often so powerful and convincing that one may to some extent sympathize with the critics and reviewers who were seduced by it and looked no further. But only to some extent. Sadly, much of *Jasmine*'s reception reenacts a familiar master narrative of literary criticism. As Nancy Miller states: "The attack on female plots and plausibilities assumes that women writers cannot or will not obey the rules of fiction" (1981, 46). Building on Miller's work, Molly Hite asserts that "there exist a number of structurally and stylistically interesting fictional works by female authors, works that might well be regarded as experimental if it were possible to discount the reviews and criticism that, with ingenuity and even sympathy, translate experimentalism into flawed realism (for example, faulting a utopian romance for being insufficiently plausible)" (1989, 17–18). It is imperative for criticism to accurately represent the achievement of female authors like Mukherjee. A causal analysis can help to clarify precisely what is—and what is not—central to the text's internal dynamics and to establish its appropriate affiliations in literary history. Whether we describe the novel as a fable, a utopian romance, or an ingenious postmodern narrative temporarily disguised as a work of realism, close attention to Mukherjee's deployment of causation can clarify the work's ontological self-situation and preclude invidious misreading.[9]

While *Jasmine* establishes a naturalistic frame and then deconstructs it through continued interjections of unlikely events, Angela Carter in *Wise Children* pursues an opposite strategy by evoking a chance world that is then for a considerable duration portrayed as uncannily realistic—until other ordering forces emerge. As the story begins, we are presented with a great number of chance events. The protagonists, Nora and Dora Chance ("Chance by name, Chance by nature," Dora observes [1992, 24]), are the twin daughters of Sir Melchior Hazard who, as chance would have it, has a twin brother; each man, furthermore, has fathered a pair of twins with other women, and one of those twins eventually goes on to father yet another brace of identical children. What is noteworthy about this unusual genealogy is that twins result from multiple or split eggs produced by the mother; had all this twinning been matrilineal it would have been perfectly plausible, if somewhat unusual. But since all the twins are born of different mothers, the coincidences are so egregious that it is immediately clear that the fictional world diverges greatly from the world of our experience, and indeed is much closer to the fantasy worlds of Shakespeare's early, farcical comedies of errors.

As the narrative gets underway, a curious transformation occurs. Extraordinary coincidences happen only intermittently. For the most part we are offered an extended account of the more or less plausible vagaries of the careers of several generations of actors and performers. Most of these events are admittedly picaresque, unexpected, unusual, or accidental, but they are the "normal" unexpected accidents that typically befall daring, high-strung, and ambitious actors in difficult and changing times—the usual rivalries, betrayals, sexual maneuverings, and sudden reversals of fortune that are endemic to the profession. Having established a completely unrealistic frame that suggests that the ensuing events transpire at and only at authorial whim, Carter goes on to record a sequence of events that by and large can be placed within a naturalistic framework and is for the most part suspiciously lacking in chance interventions.

Materialist readings of ostensibly fortuitous events are common: "I must tell you that our father had become a truly great man of the theatre. . . . Luck had a lot to do with it, not to mention the Lady A's private fortune financed his Shylock and his Richard III and his Macbeth" (89). This unexpected "reality effect" is no doubt enhanced by the retrospective nature of the narration. The book is presented as the memoirs-in-progress of Dora Chance on her seventy-fifth birthday. Accidents and coincidences said to have occurred in the past have a greater aura of verisimilitude than the same events set forth in the narrative present tense, or "first narrative" as Genette terms it.

Some of the twists of the plot do nevertheless defy probability. At regular intervals, an outrageously melodramatic incident takes place. During the first-night party after a production of *Othello*, old Ranulph Hazard finds his wife in bed with the actor who played Iago; he kills them both, then shoots himself. As young Tristram Hazard hosts a TV game show, his distraught lover staggers onto the scene, sings a mad song, and is later reported drowned. When Dora wants a special present for her seventeenth birthday, she pretends she is her twin sister and sleeps with her sister's unsuspecting lover. Two aging Hazard daughters produce a bubbling, unhealthful stew at a family reunion; as Tristram is about to have a bite, his doting aunt shouts out and slaps the food from his hand. As is probably quite evident by now, these scenes all come from the same source. Even in this summary account, parallels to corresponding encounters in *Othello, Hamlet, Measure for Measure, Macbeth,* and *Hamlet* (again) are readily discernible. The star-crossed twins motif that informs the novel appears in several Shakespearean plays; the "bed trick" happens twice in *Wise Children* and twice in the bard (*Measure for Measure* and *All's Well that End's Well*); and the conclusion of Carter's book reenacts the ending of *Cymbeline* and alludes to the final scenes of *Lear* and *The Winter's Tale*.

The metafictional causal setting implied by the opening sections of the narrative—a largely gratuitous assemblage of wildly improbable events—is soon tempered by two alternative ordering principles: the knockabout realism of the protagonists' diurnal experiences and the characters' unenviable fate of having to periodically relive climactic scenes from Shakespeare's plays. The interplay between these forces creates an engaging textual dynamic comparable to Stoppard's rather different dynamic of chance events, probabilistic expectations, and Shakespearean intertextuality. As the novel continues to progress, yet another governing pattern emerges: the rules of the genre of romance. Unknown and illegitimate relations seek final recognition, quests need to be completed, obscure events shout out for illumination, bonds must be restored, and poetic justice has yet to be meted out to the good and the evil. In Carter's hands, however, the romance is revolutionized, denuded of the inevitable marriage plot, and given a feminist twist throughout.

This may be brought into relief by a brief comparison with David

Lodge's superficially similar "academic romance," *Small World*, a novel that also juxtaposes naturalistic progressions, an impossible series of coincidences, and an ironic adherence to the conventions of the genre of romance. In Lodge's text, women function primarily as sexual objects, the goals of various quests, or mildly monstrous supernumeraries, and hope of marriage is the telos that powers the main plotline of the narrative. In contrast, Carter's novel can be seen as a feminist rewriting of Lodge's project. Her narrator and protagonists are female, stable communities of women take the place of rivalries between isolated males, and detail is lavished on makeup, perfume, and wardrobes rather than descriptions of the physical beauty of lithe young women. Concerning the female body, Carter is less interested in large breasts than in the effects of menstruation and menopause. That the Chance sisters started to menstruate the day their half-sisters were born is said to be a "[f]unny coincidence," a "sort of mean connection between their birth and our puberty" (74). Lodge's text follows several simultaneous narrative strands in a sequential manner; most of *Wise Children* is a series of flashbacks into different pockets of the past ("There I go again! Can't keep a story going in a straight line, can I. Drunk in charge of a narrative" [158]). But the most radical transformation of the genre of romance is the book's systematic indifference to and deprecation of marriage. Inverting the traditional patriarchal plot, it is the married women who wind up suffering, isolated, or insane, an inversion all the more conspicuous because of its placement within the romance genre.[10]

Toward the end of the novel, naturalistic orderings vanish, and an overdetermined metafictional pattern takes over as Shakespearean insets and revolutionized romance patterns merge with authorial contrivance. At Melchior Hazard's one-hundredth birthday celebration, his long-lost twin brother Peregrine, missing for decades and long presumed dead, suddenly appears, upstaging not only "his brother but also plausibility" (207). It also turns out that the Hazards (and the Chance sisters) were born on the same day as Shakespeare, 23 April. At the grandiose, extravagant, and melodramatic birthday party, the final secrets are revealed, the essential reconciliations occur, and the last narrative surprises are unveiled. The conflicting causal systems invoked at various points throughout the novel cease to collide, and novel attains its closure.

This account of contemporary deployments of causality in narrative, by disclosing the varied and wide-ranging role of chance, can help resolve the important theoretical question of the precise relation between chance and (fictional) narrative. In *Enlightenment and the Shadows of Chance: The Novel and the Culture of Gambling in Eighteenth-Century France*, Thomas M. Kavanagh asserts that "[t]he chance event is recalcitrant to narrative. A story exists, is cogent, and achieves meaning only to the extent that it coaxes its reader into discovering some coherence of cause and effect, some rationality of the narrated events" (1993, 113). He goes on to argue that authors like Crebillon and Diderot, by injecting chance events into their novels, rupture the false coherence and specious rationalism of narrative form as well as Enlightenment sensibility.

Leland Monk, on the other hand, shows that such a felicitous union does not come about so easily. In his book *Standard Deviations: Chance and the Modern British Novel*, Monk suggests that the phrase "chance in narrative" is somewhat "oxymoronic" (8), since the "disruptions occasioned by ostensible chance events in narrative are always and already in the process of being recuperated by *some* sense of formal coherence and design" (1993, 8). A perfect example of this process can, I believe, be found in *Jacques le fataliste*, a key text Kavanagh employs to illustrate his position. Kavanagh admits that the novel's "authorial voice will revel in its no longer secret power over the potential infinity of chance events inflecting the stories we read—'You see, reader, that I am well on my way, and that it is completely up to me whether I make you wait one year, two years, or three years for the story of Jacques' loves'" (1993, 232–33). This kind of starkly metafictional admission utterly destroys the illusion of a verisimilar representation of chance events in a world governed by our laws of probability; the world presented here follows whatever causal laws Diderot—and only Diderot—imposes. Chance is not represented, but recuperated as authorial caprice.

But if it is not as easy to embody chance in a narrative as Kavanagh assumes, it is surely not as difficult as Monk affirms. We may agree with Monk that there is a general tension between the novel's twin mandates—a realist impulse to portray "experience in all its contingency" and a generic or formal imperative to structure this material into a "unified representation" (1993, 153). But must we then conclude that "chance *always* takes on a necessarily fateful quality once it is represented in narrative" (2)? I hope this study corroborates Monk's sense of the elusive and paradoxical nature of chance in narrative fiction. On the other hand, I'd like to suggest that many of the examples identified above do effectively represent chance in its full disruptive power, untamed by earlier narrative conventions. The most straightforward instance of this is Murdoch's *An Accidental Man*, the most outrageous is the frame narrative of *Rosencrantz and Guildenstern Are Dead*, and the most unexpected the virtually causeless stream of events (that nevertheless have important ramifications) in Dorothy Richardson's *Pointed Roofs*. Together, these works demonstrate how chance can be authentically and even plausibly represented, in part because they resist the dichotomy Monk describes—in Richardson's text, contingency can be displayed in all its wayward variety, since both traditional and high-modernist versions of form and design are conspicuously absent; no formal constraint reins in its free play. In Murdoch's case, this comes about precisely because the author is consciously trying to defuse the opposition Monk describes so well; in an interview she states, "I would like to have much more accident in my work than I've yet managed to put in. That is, I would like to be a more realistic novelist than I am" (Bryden 1968, 434).

The analyses provided in this chapter can also provide a point of entry to many of the current theoretical debates on the status and trajectory of postmodernism. Most significantly, it tends to corroborate Brian McHale's conception of postmodern narrative as one that centers on and problematizes ontological issues, in distinction to the epistemological obsession of modernism.[11] Indeed, by following out the tangled skein of chance and cause, we can see precisely where different worlds are made to intersect. This in turn provides a keener focus for determining just what constitutes that increasingly baggy monster, the postmodern novel: the disruption and parody of the naturalistic causal system present in the works of David Lodge, Muriel Spark, Salman Rushdie, and Angela Carter mentioned above provide the crucial imprimatur of the postmodern; on the other hand, Iris Murdoch's fascinating play with chance events within a naturalistic frame should be seen as a brilliant development of the realist novel rather than as a foray into postmodernism.

But while this kind of analysis suggests a rift between the postmodern and the contemporary, it also implies a much stronger historical genealogy of postmodernism, and thereby can challenge the standard critical master narrative of twentieth-century literary history. The ontological conflations found in Stoppard and Ionesco derive from the origin of the theater of the absurd and its immediate predecessors in surrealist, expressionist, and Pirandellian dramas from the twenties and thirties. In fact, the first work that completely fits almost all of the various criteria of postmodernism that have been set forth is Alfred Jarry's 1896 *Ubu Roi*—a play Ionesco's *Macbett* clearly salutes. In the drama, postmodernism appears before modernism does.[12]

On the vexing and hotly debated subjects of the politics and gender of postmodernism, this study offers no easy answers. That postmodernist strategies can be intensely political is confirmed by Ionesco's stridently antiauthoritarian *Macbett*, which bitterly mocks any lingering royalism, hero-worship, or autocratic hierarchies that conservatives or sentimentalists of either the Left or the Right may wish to indulge. Stoppard's play, by contrast, is resolutely apolitical; by juggling alternate worlds and indulging in metadramatic paradoxes he displays, as he puts it, "the courage of [his] own lack of convictions" (R. Hayman 1982, 2), a charge frequently leveled against postmodern fabricators.[13] Mukherjee's work is more ambiguous: postmodern interjections of chance alter the novel's shape as a formal analogue of the protagonist's resistance to patriarchal cultural master narratives. The resulting message, however, can easily be recuperated as a facile valorization of traditional liberal notions of personal independence and self-realization in a largely open, tolerant, and progressive American society. From these examples, one must conclude that the political valence of postmodern narrative strategies is ambiguous—as ambiguous, perhaps, as realism, expressionism, and modernism seem to be. In the words of Linda Hutcheon: "[A]s can be seen by its recuperation (and rejection) by both the Right and the Left, post-modernism is politically ambivalent: its critique coexists with an equally real and equally powerful complicity with the cultural dominants within which it inescapably exists" (1991, 168).

Molly Hite's *The Other Side of the Story* is an answer to the rhetorical question, "Why don't women produce postmodernist fiction?" The analyses in this chapter, building on the work of Hite and other feminist narrative theorists, suggest that *Jasmine* should be read as a progressive postmodern narrative that also partakes of a long tradition of female reconfigurations of male standards of fictional probability. Similarly, Carter's *Wise Children* should be seen as a central text of what might be called feminist postmodernism: postmodern in its ontological fusions and slippages, feminist in its systematic elision of the conventional patriarchal features of the typical romance plot.[14] Postmodernism thus would seem to be in itself gender neutral; the ideological burden rests more on the critics, theorists, and literary historians whose job it is to survey the subject as accurately and thoroughly as possible.

Earlier, it was intimated that chance, so long suppressed in Western literary and philosophical discourse, is in danger of being dissolved into self-indulgent metafictional amusements, its destabilizing effects thoroughly tamed and entirely recuperated by constant authorial intervention that results, in the end, in a kind of "metafictional imperialism." Instead, we have seen how Stoppard, Mukherjee, and Carter, in very different ways, assemble naturalistic orders that serve as a challenge to and foil for the radical chance constructions that ultimately frame and transcend them. Though its deployment has evolved considerably in the last hundred years, chance remains a dynamic and dominant force in newly emerging fictional worlds.

Conclusion:
Language, Interpretation, and Causality in Twentieth-Century Narrative

Cause is the single most undertheorized aspect of the narrative transaction. In this work I have attempted to document the fundamental significance of causality in narrative and to identify its spacious parameters. Almost every fictional world contains, as part of its setting, a canon of probability that it adheres to or transforms. Characters and readers are frequently confronted by unusual sequences of events that demand to be placed within one of several competing causal systems. Philosophical and popular notions of causation are often embodied within individual narratives; to be fully appreciated, these must be understood within larger ideological contexts and also viewed from the perspective of a poetics of narrative setting. We find that causality may be seen as a foundational aspect of all narratives: without some causal connection, whether direct, oblique, or intersecting, no sequence of represented events can be called a narrative. It also becomes clear that the prevalent notion of representation, which reduces all representations to the generic category of fictions, is fundamentally flawed and needs to be rethought: some narrative universes are considerably more fictional than others.

Like time and space, cause is an integral element of the setting of any narrative. A fictional world may be supernatural, naturalistic, or governed by chance. Supernatural worlds may be fatalistic *(Oedipus Rex)* or allow for the workings of grace, providence, or free will *(Life is a Dream)*. Naturalistic worlds may be haphazard *(Roderick Random)*, reductionist *(Germinal)*, or overdetermined *(Miss Julie)*, while chance universes foreground in varying degrees the random and the coincidental ("weak" in *Ulysses*, "strong" in Borges). The activities of a number of characters often end in tragedy because of a failure to interpret—in time—the precise order of the universe they inhabit (Oedipus, Macbeth). Some fictions, including the later works of Beckett, have ambiguous or indeterminable causal laws, just as they lack a specific temporal and spatial setting *(The Unnamable, Ill Seen Ill Said)*. Others, like Hawthorne's *The House of the Seven Gables*, suggest at different points that different canons of probability govern the fictional world without ever showing any of them to be false. Thus, Hawthorne's readers will always be able to find the universe they prefer to see. In addition, the author or narrator may alter the causal laws of the invented cosmos, interposing a metafictional causal mode that can take the form of explicit frame-breaking *(Jacques le fatalist)*, a swerve into the improbable *(Jasmine)*, or a battle between antagonistic worlds *(Rosencrantz and Guildenstern Are Dead)*.

Philosophical notions of cause have been invoked at least since Chaucer's parody of Aristotle in the Tale of Melibee; they were continued in the works of Swift, Sterne, and Diderot, and have recently appeared in the fiction of Proust, Borges, Ellison, Beckett, and Calvino. These parodies, fabulations, or embodiments are most effectively analyzed as ideational constructs that are either confirmed or refuted by the causal system of the given fictional world. Similarly, prephilosophical notions of luck, destiny, fortune, and divine intervention are frequently expressed by characters only to be refuted by the events of the world that resists their egocentric expectations. At the same time, the material basis for the characters' struggle over the control of causal explanation is repeatedly exposed: the figure who can impose his interpretation of the pattern of events can also command the actions of others. As a character in Walter Scott's *Castle Dangerous* sagely observes: "I have seldom known an insurrection in Scotland but that it was prophesied by some old, forgotten rhyme, conjured out of dust and cobwebs, for the sake of giving courage to those North Country rebels who durst not otherwise have abidden the whistling of the grey-goose shaft" (chap. 8).

In the late-seventeenth and early-eighteenth centuries a major transformation in Western thought occurs, as the concept of chance is mathematically formulated and applied, and philosophical and literary articulations of chance begin to appear. Prior to this period, religion, philosophy, popular belief, and narrative practice all conspired to deny the existence of chance events; John Dennis went so far as to condemn episodic texts as implicitly heretical: "[P]romiscuous Events call the Government of Providence into Question, and by Scepticks and Libertines are resolv'd into Chance" (cited in Patey 1984, 121). Until the end of the seventeenth century, the modern meaning of the word coincidence—a "juxtaposition of chance events"—did not exist, as Keith Thomas notes in *Religion and the Decline of Magic* (1971, 655).

In a relatively short period of time, the implications of the phenomenon of chance would wreak havoc on universally held beliefs about the order of the cosmos. Lionel Trilling writes that

> perhaps the greatest distress associated with the evanescence of faith, more painful and disintegrating than can now be fully imagined, was the loss of the assumption that the universe is purposive. This assumption, which as Freud says, "stands and falls with the religious system," was, for those who held it, not merely a comfortable idea but nothing less than a category of thought; its extirpation was a psychic catastrophe. (1972, 116)

It is also important to observe that naturalistic varieties of causalism, which likewise attempted to subsume all events into an equally universal (though nonteleological) determinism, were similarly undermined by the role of the random.

Ever since the publication of *Tristram Shandy* the presence of chance events in narrative fiction has progressively increased to the point where one may identify modernist fictional worlds by the dominant role played by chance and coincidence: modernist stories are inherently unlikely ones. The proliferation of chance and coincidental events leads in turn to the more pronounced metafictional component typical of postmodernism: starkly improbable events in the story necessarily point back to the artificer who invented them; an accident in the fiction is read as a contrivance of the text.

Modern authors have not only conjoined absurd or random events but have also frequently juxtaposed seemingly unrelated blocks of independent narratives, thereby intensifying the drama of causal connection. Fictional events are unbelievably coincidental at the same time that textual constructions seem disturbingly unconnected. Robbe-Grillet described the response of the critic of *Le Monde* who, first encountering *La Jalousie*, thought that his copy had fallen apart and that the pages had somehow become rearranged:

> [A]ll he could perceive in dealing with an order which was not what he had expected was absolute chance. On the contrary, whatever one

may think of it from the standpoint of its beauty, *La Jalousie* is an ordered system of extremely high character, extreme complexity, and extreme interest in its opposition to society's view of narrative probability. (1977, 8)

Unnatural connections of events combine with provocative modes of sequencing to apparently produce, as it were, too much causality in the fiction and too little in the text. Both strategies serve to underscore the fictionality of fiction and the presence of the narrative's creator.

Explicit questions about causation have been frequently raised in narrative at least since Jocasta's fervid speeches on fate, chance, and predestination in *Oedipus Rex*. In prose fiction, such discussions stretch back to Petronius's *Satyricon*.[1] Chaucer, Shakespeare, Sterne, and Dickens pointedly and provocatively thematize cause; numerous other authors, many of whom have been discussed at some point in the preceding pages, could certainly be added to this list. I hope I have been able to show the intricate interweaving of character motivation, causal setting, narrative sequencing, interpretive conflict, and philosophical speculation present in each of the novels I have selected for sustained analysis, tracing at the same time a general diachronic (though nonteleological) progression that begins with the transgression of naturalistic canons of probability and, after the requisite amount of meandering and doubling back, ends with an almost ostentatious metafiction situated at the very boundary of narrative. It is also the case the we find numerous "untimely" causal settings that anticipate later theoretical developments (chance in *Antony and Cleopatra*, "early" postmodernism) or hark back to older aesthetics (the revival of supernatural agency in turn-of-the-century ghost stories or in some contemporary U.S. ethnic writers). For the most part however, innovative twentieth-century literature discloses a fascination with the unstable notion of chance, as the verisimilitudinous documentation of the improbable frequently leads to authorial contrivance, and an uncompromising realism shares the same spectrum as avowedly metafictional utterances.

In the typically modern works I have analyzed in this book, issues of causality and its interpretation confront characters and readers in analogous ways, as the act of reading virtually becomes a form of narrative construction. The characters' difficulties in comprehending the rules that order their existence become allegories of the audience's processing of the obscure patterns that govern the text, until the roles of author, agent, and reader become inextricably bound together in the hermeneutic circle of causality and its interpretation. Commenting on the work of H. G. Wells (who, coincidentally, wrote *The Wheels of Chance*, an early modern novel of the unlikely), Borges observes: "[I]t is a mirror that reflects the reader's own features and it is also a map of the world" (1981, 87). This statement is of course an excellent description of Borges's own fictions, and at the same time it may serve as a compelling parable of the nexus between causality and interpretation typical of modern narrative.

Notes

Introduction

1. For an account of the interplay between providence and naturalistic causal progressions in Dickens, see Vargish (1985, 89–134). Vargish discusses the passage I have cited on pages 95–96.

2. For important works on narrative temporality, see the bibliographies in Higdon (1977, 150–65) and in Kort (1985, 209–20). For works on space in narrative, see Suvin (1987, 331–34).

3. Northrop Frye's section on modes (1971, 33–67), Todorov's study of the fantastic (1975), and Martinez-Bonati's essay on the ontology of possible worlds (1983) provide important groundwork for causal investigations. Major studies of fate, luck, and fortune in antiquity and the Middle Ages include those by Patch (1927, 1935); Cioffari (1935, 1947, 1973); and Nussbaum (1986). Newsom (1988) analyzes the nature of fictional probability, Patey (1984) explores probability in seventeenth- and eighteenth-century literature, Barfoot (1982) discusses fate in Jane Austen, and Vargish (1985) studies providence in Victorian fiction. Both Walcutt (1956) and Mitchell (1989) examine determinism in American naturalism, Hornbeck (1971) outlines Hardy's use of coincidence, and Hayles (1990) and Natoli (1992) write on chaos, disorder, and postmodernism. Thomas Kavanagh (1993) and David F. Bell (1993) respectively investigate chance in eighteenth- and in nineteenth-century French fiction, Leland Monk (1993) traces the play of chance in British fiction from George Eliot to James Joyce, and Erich Köhler (1973) and Ernst Nef (1970) both provide brief general surveys of chance in literature. All of these studies can be recommended; each, however, tends to suffer to some extent from the absence of a general model of causation, which typically results in limiting binary oppositions and corresponding critical blind spots. In addition, Roy Jay Nelson has written an excellent introduction to the study of causal connection between discrete textual units (1990).

4. For additional material on the history of chance in philosophy, science, and literature, see Monk (1993, 15–45).

5. The most thorough studies of fortune, fate, and chance in antiquity and the Middle Ages include Vincenzo Cioffari's *Fortune and Fate from Democritus to St. Thomas Aquinas* (1935), Martha Nussbaum's *The Fragility of Goodness: Luck and Ethics in Greek Tragedy and Philosophy* (1986), Howard Patch's *The Goddess Fortuna in Medieval Literature* (1927), and W. Wallace's *Causality and Scientific Explanation* (1972,

vol. 1). For a succinct account of interesting differences between Roman, medieval, and Renaissance notions of fortune, see Pitkin (1984, 138–43).

6. See Patch (1935) for a detailed exposition of Boethius's ideas and influence.

7. *Eine Fratze* is the term he uses; see Sharp (1982, 89–92). Interestingly, Goethe's response to Schiller indicates a sympathy for the sense of pattern in the universe felt by the believer in astrology. This response is typical of Goethe's post-naturalistic position, as set forth in his discussion of games of skill and chance (1963).

8. These paradigm shifts were gradual, of course. On the providential background of the work of Congreve and Fielding, see the studies by Aubrey Williams (1971, 1979); on the struggle between providence and chance in Victorian fiction, see Thomas Vargish (1985).

9. Patey (1984, 266–73) provides a thorough critique of this position. A significant counterexample to Hacking's assertion can be found in *Othello*, which Joel B. Altman argues "is Shakespeare's inquiry into the nature of probability, and, more specifically, into what it might mean to be *improbable*—since this is the condition so energetically defended against by character and critic alike" (1987, 131).

10. See Alkon (1979, 36–37) and Patey (1984, 67–74).

11. Nonrandom elements of this novel are discussed by James H. Bunn (1981), Patey (1984, 179f.), and John Barrell (1983, esp. 176–87). Smollett himself defends the plausible and probabilistic features of his work in the preface to *Roderick Random*.

12. In his sermon "Time and Chance," Sterne directly confronts the disquieting implications of rise of the doctrine of chance: "Some, indeed, from a superficial view of this representation of things, have atheistically inferred,——that because there was so much of lottery in this life,——and mere casualty seemed to have such a share in the disposal of our affairs,——that the providence of GOD stood neuter and unconcerned in their several workings, leaving them to the mercy of time and chance to be furthered or disappointed as such blind agents directed." He goes on to argue that the opposite is in fact the case, and calling "on the Deity to untie this knot" (cited at Patey 1984, 69), he reasserts the standard Christian position formulated by Boethius—that apparent chance is ultimately ordered by God's providence. In *Tristram Shandy*, however, Sterne provides what is probably the first extended, explicit thematization of chance in fictional narrative, as his chapter of chances (vol. 4, chap. 9) discloses and enacts.

13. In the entry for "Concatenation of Events" in his *Philosophical Dictionary*, Voltaire affirms that every event clearly has its cause, going back from cause to cause into the abyss of eternity, and also asserts that the causal chain stretches synchronically from one end of the universe to the other.

14. See Wallace (1972, 2:39–40).

15. See Bataille (1945), Granier (1977), and Deleuze (1983, esp. 25–29).

16. Nietzsche notes: "Supreme fatalism, nonetheless identical with chance and creative activity," cited in Birault (1977, 229).

17. Moritz Schlick, following Russell, went so far as to affirm that "it is exactly the same whether we say the past determines the future or the future determines the past," cited in Wallace (1972, 2:183).

18. See Wallace (1972, 2:218–22) for a comparison of the positions of Bergson and Whitehead.

19. Chaos theory, though extremely interesting in itself, is not directly relevant to this study since it is concerned with elaborate causal chains that are partially or largely unknowable due to the great number, complexity, and variability of the elements that compose the causal web, rather than the play of chance per se.

Chapter 1. Philosophical Systems, Fictional Worlds, and Ideological Contestations

1. For the philosophically sophisticated, I will offer a more accurate (and technical) definition of cause as the totality of conditions sufficient for the occurrence of an event. The analysis that follows is not dependent on this definition and is indeed compatible with most other accounts, including causal realism, Mackie's theory of necessary and/or sufficient conditions, and even (with some maneuvering) Wesley Salmon's probabilistic account. Basic statements of all these positions can be found in Sosa (1993) and Tooley (1987). Poststructuralists suspicious of the idea of causality should recall that Jonathan Culler's attempt to deconstruct causality is followed by the caveat: "The concept of causation is not an error that philosophy could or should have avoided but is indispensable—to the argument of deconstruction as to other arguments" (1982, 87). Both these issues will be explored at greater length later in this chapter.

2. Sternberg observes: "There are some pieces of information, varying in number and nature from one work to another, that the reader cannot do without. He must usually be informed of the time and place of the action; of the nature of the fictive world peculiar to the work or, in other words, of the canons of probability operating within it; of the history . . . and habitual behavior of the dramatis personae; and of the relations between them" (1978, 1).

3. Lyotard, approaching the book from a very different perspective, nevertheless concurs with Genette: "[T]he unity of the book, the odyssey of that consciousness, even if it is deferred from chapter to chapter, is not seriously challenged: the identity of the writing with itself throughout the labyrinth of the interminable narration is enough to connote such unity, which has been compared to that of *The Phenomenology of Mind*" (1979, 80).

4. In particular, the play of chance in *Tom Jones* came under close scrutiny since Ian Watt first drew attention to its role. See Watt (1957, 252–54).

5. For a thorough account of Nietzsche's extensive pronouncements on causality, see Kaufmann (1974, 263–66).

6. For an additional critique of Culler that proceeds along comparable lines, see Jon-K. Adams (1989).

7. For a comparable discussion that does not rely on possible worlds theory, see Rabinowitz (1987, 100–101). There he argues that "novelists always require their readers to make inferences about characters and actions; those inferences are possible only if there are at least some points at which the novel's inner world . . . is congruent with the world of the authorial audience" (101).

8. For a discussion of this interaction in several decades of realist drama, see Richardson (1996).

9. Charles C. Walcutt, for example, "was led to conclude that, with the exception of Crane's fiction, most of the work by other naturalistic writers suffered because of a failure to reconcile a belief in progress through human initiative with a

philosophy of determinism. . . . Compounding the conflict between attitudes was a conflict between doctrines, for Walcutt saw surfacing within single works the doctrine of freedom of the will as well as that of determinism" (Conder 1984, 2). Several other approaches to these issues are also analyzed by Conder in his *American Literary Naturalism* (1984, 1–10, 209–11).

10.   The issue is in fact still more problematic than I have indicated: some recent philosophers have argued that the notion of free will *implies* determinism. See Peter van Inwagen, *An Essay on Free Will* (1983), for a comprehensive analysis of the subject.

11.   Kleist does, however, frequently play with curious causal progressions within the worlds of his fictions and, like many writers of his time, is particularly fascinated by a range of issues associated with questions of interpretation, explanation, and understanding. As Jeffrey M. Peck observes: "Almost all of Kleist's characters find themselves alien and unfamiliar. They experience the world as a challenging threat, as something chaotic and thus incomprehensible, which they must order and understand in order to survive" (1983, 107). Peck discusses *The Marquise of O . . .* as an example of what he calls "hermeneutic literature" (107–49, esp. 122–32).

12.   See Michael Dummett and Anthony Flew, "Can an Effect Precede Its Cause?" (1954). For an update on this debate, see Tooley (1987, 212–16).

13.   See my essay "Hours Dreadful and Things Strange': Inversions of Chronology and Causality in *Macbeth*" (1989).

14.   For a discussion of these issues, see Graves (1982).

15.   See Patch (1918, 1929).

16.   Hannah Pitkin, in her exhaustive study of Machiavelli's concept of fortune, frequently refers to *Il Mandragora*, but only once even mentions the idea of fortune in relation to the play's events (1984, 166). Pitkin does, however, find a metaphorical connection between Machiavelli's theory of fortune and the events of his play *Clezia* (118–20).

17.   For an excellent account of the larger historical and dramatic contexts of Glendower's prophecies, see Howard Dobin (1990, 154–65).

18.   In Sophocles' *Antigone,* Creon levels similar charges against Teiresias. Some characters never learn.

Chapter 2. A Poetics of Probability

1.   Other authors who discuss some aspect of this subject include Wolterstorff (1980, 106–97), Pavel (1986, esp. 105–13), Margolis (1983), Ryan (1991), Quigley (1985), and McHale (1987, esp. 43–130). For a review of recent developments in literary applications of possible worlds theory, see Ryan (1992).

2.   Roy Jay Nelson nevertheless provides a meticulous account of the nuances of causality in Zola's work (1990, 37–87).

3.   In *Shakespeare and the Mystery of God's Judgments* (1976), Robert G. Hunter describes the disparate cosmologies that govern the worlds of *Richard III, Hamlet, Othello, Macbeth,* and *King Lear.*

4.   Similarly, we will find in Tawfik al-Hakim's Islamic *Oedipus* that divine design triumphs over predestined determinism.

5. On the equivocation of the witches, see Henry N. Paul (1950, 237–47) and Steven Mullaney (1980).

6. The relation between fate and *Oedipus Rex* and providence in *Life is a Dream* is explored by Peter N. Dunn in "The Horoscope Motif in *La vida es sueño*" (1953).

7. A good account of the role of the supernatural in *Julius Caesar* can be found in Wilders (1978, 38–42, 65–66).

8. In *King Lear and the Gods* (1966), William R. Elton presents the most comprehensive and convincing discussion of these issues. For a comparable account of supernatural claims refuted by naturalistic events in Jonson's *Sejanus*, see Gary Hamilton (1971).

9. Wallace Martin's account of one facet of literary realism is relevant to this discussion: "[R]ealism involves a doctrine of natural causality, most accurately defined through reference to its opposite—the chance, fate, and providence of romantic fiction" (1986, 60). Wellek discusses this idea at greater length in *Concepts of Criticism* (1963, 222–55, esp. 240–41); see also Rabinowitz (1987, 104–9).

10. Fielding himself, it will be observed, attempted to frame his probabilistic fictions within a larger providential order, as Aubrey Williams has demonstrated (1971). See Sheldon Sacks (1964, 258–62) and Leopold Damrosch (1985, 281–89) for the historical context and critical implications of this practice.

11. Conrad's additional, modernist deployment of chance will be discussed in the section on *Nostromo* that follows.

12. Classic examples include the clergy in *The Red and the Black* and *Madame Bovary*. As we will see, this is also a common feature of much modern Asian, postcolonial, and U.S. ethnic narrative.

13. Lodge, though correct concerning Trollope, does not seem to have perceived the trajectory of providence that Vargish has shown to be present in Austen's fiction.

14. See Carla Peterson's *The Determined Reader* (1986, 132ff.).

15. For a comparable investigation of the role of chance in *The Ambassadors*, see Armstrong (1987, 93–94). For a general account of chance in James, see Monk (1993, 166–74).

16. Jean-Paul Sartre's *Nausea*, though somewhat out of critical fashion at the moment, nevertheless deserves a place in this genealogy for foregrounding a number of the issues involving chance that would soon be taken up by later writers and theorists. The novel's opening section points out the curious "series of coincidences" that the narrator cannot explain (1969, 2). He observes that people, while sitting down with friends, invariably tell "clear, plausible stories" that are suspicious precisely because they are too neat, too facile, and too devoid of the improbable to be true or accurate (7). The same distorting effects of narrativization also obscure the characters and events of historical writing, projecting a causal unity and teleology where none in fact exists. For a sustained account of Sartre's treatment of the theme of narrative in this text, see Prince (1992, 91–103).

17. As we will see, *Mrs. Dalloway* has its full share of deferred causal connections. Richardson's *Pilgrimage* is much more loosely conjoined, and for this reason incurred Woolf's censure (1980, 188–98).

18. For a very different and more daring reading of chance in *Ulysses*, see Monk (1993, 110–44).

19. Other writers who could be added to this list include Céline, Gombrowicz,

Cela, Blanchot, Canetti, and Bioy-Cesares. In addition, some of the works of Dostoevsky, Bataille, and Beckett could profit by being viewed from an expressionistic perspective. For an excellent study of expressionist fiction in North America, see Sherrill E. Grace (1989); for a discussion of the proper place of expressionist fiction in the history of twentieth-century literature, see my article, "Re-Mapping the Present" (forthcoming).

20. For lucid and concise account of Borges's deployments of philosophical themes, see Weber (1968) and Sturrock (1977, 20–30). Calvino's tales that are most pertinent for this study in addition to "t zero," include "The Chase," "The Night Driver," and "The Count of Monte Cristo."

21. Brian McHale offers a rather different perspective on the world(s) of this text, suggesting it is a kind of "displaced" fantastic tale, in which the mysteries of the text "are mysteries of language, not of [its] fictional worlds" (1987, 81).

22. There is also a linguistic component to causal relations in this work that should be identified. Probably the most significant connection is Deronda's successful quest for Mirah's brother. In London's Jewish ghetto, Deronda sees a sign that reads "Ezra Cohen"—the name of the missing brother. The shop is owned by an Ezra Cohen who is no relation to Mirah; but his lodger, called Mordecai, just happens to be the man Deronda seeks. In *Light in August*, a similar miracle of coincidence occurs: Lena Grove, searching for Lucas Burch, the father of her child, is directed to Byron Bunch, her future husband, who comments prophetically, "I don't recall none named Burch except me, and my name is Bunch" (1972, 46). Here again, the name is more seminal than the object; the signified alters while the signifier stays constant. And once more, the contingent slides toward the metafictional.

23. Scott writes: ". . . Fielding pauses to explain the principles of his art, and to congratulate himself and his readers on the felicity with which he conducts his narrative, or makes his characters evolve themselves in its progress. These appeals to the reader's judgment, admirable as they are, have sometimes the fault of being diffuse, and always to the great disadvantage, that they remind us we are perusing a work of fiction; and that the beings with whom we have been conversant during the perusal, are but a sort of evanescent phantoms, conjured up by a magician for our amusement." Cited in Allott (1959, 269–70).

24. Todorov (1971, 144–46) and Chambers (1984, 151–80) discuss this tale's reflexivity.

25. Pavel provides an equally suggestive example, the medieval quest for the Holy Grail: "[T]here should be little doubt that most of the adventures narrated were destined to be understood as allegorically fictional. The structure of the text openly points to its own fictionality by the addition, after virtually every episode, of a hermeneutic reading. The strong insistence on the moral and spiritual meaning of the events suggests that they function as invented exampla" (1986, 81). For allegories of reflexivity in postmodern fiction, see McHale (1987, 140–47).

26. See Borges's "On the Cult of the Books" (1965, 116–20); Curtius (1953, 302–47); Josipovici (1971); and Gellrich (1985, esp. 29–50).

27. Failure to perceive this has lead to some interesting confusions. Stanley Sultan (1964) sees the book's many coincidences as a demonstration of the existence of an ordering deity; in fact, all they confirm is the ubiquitous presence of a very human author "who art not in heaven." On the other hand, Muriel Spark combines Catholicism with overt metafiction.

28. These ideas stem directly from Nietzsche, and are discussed by Deleuze (1983, 25–29) and by Bataille in his 1945 book on Nietzsche.

29. For another discussion of this phenomenon from another theoretical framework, see Perry and Sternberg (1986).

CHAPTER 3. TEMPORAL SEQUENCE, CAUSAL CONNECTION, AND THE NATURE OF NARRATIVE

1. Derrida hastens to add that he does not have the intention or the means to answer these questions. Instead, he wishes to replace the *"question of narrative"* with an inquiry into the *"demand for narrative"* (1979, 87). The question ("What is a narrative?") does not go away so easily, however.

2. Two other accounts have recently been set forth that argue for considerably more elaborate and restrictive notions of narrative. Philip J. M. Sturgess calls for a highly idiosyncratic definition of narrativity as "the way in which a narrative *articulates* itself" (1992, 26) that is unique to each novel and governs many aspects of the narrative's organization; that is to say, he is seeking something like a book's governing compositional principles rather than what makes it a narrative. Monika Fludernik has just advanced a very ambitious and suggestive theory of narrative that insists on the presence of a teleology in genuine narratives and that therefore excludes historical writing and action reports. Teleology, however, may be more difficult to establish than causal connection; at the same time, it may be an insufficiently delimiting criterion: non-narrative films, after all, usually possess a teleology, albeit a non-narrative one.

3. Todorov's examples of these antinomic possibilities are highly suspect. *Ulysses* is certainly not an example of purely sequential occurrences, devoid of causal connection, as the ultimate intersection of the lives of Bloom, Stephen, and Molly should demonstrate. (A better example might be Dorothy Richardson's *Pilgrimage*, though here too Miriam Henderson's life is continually modified by the apparently gratuitous events she experiences.) Similarly, Kafka's "A Little Woman," adduced by Todorov as a specimen of purely causal relations, does imply numerous temporal progressions—above all, how the woman came to hate and vow to avenge herself on the narrator—even though the temporal setting of the work is a single unspecified moment.

4. As Wallace Martin notes: "The newspaper says that three people died in a car crash, two died in a riot, and about 10,000 are starving every month on another continent. Despite their temporal contiguity, these events cannot be joined together in a single history" (1986, 73).

5. Leitch concocts a similar example, conjoining Scarlett O'Hara's fate with Sam Spade's attempt to secure the Maltese Falcon. He concludes: "[S]urely no one would accept this example as a narrative; although it conforms to Prince's rules, it contains too much information for one story—how are the problems of Scarlett O'Hara and Sam Spade related?—but not enough for two" (1986, 10).

6. Meir Sternberg attempts to distinguish Forster's position from Aristotle's observations, claiming that "while Aristotle's application of this insight is confined to the differentiation between episodic chronicles and properly artistic wholes, Forster acutely realizes that both story and plot may well coexist as different 'aspects' of the same work" (1978, 11).

7. A similar point is made by Walter O'Grady: "By making the people who died a king and queen, Forster postulates for us a situation which, although exterior, has a direct bearing on the interest of the story" (1965, 108).

8. Roy Jay Nelson offers a different and more detailed typology that includes the terms rectilinear causation, explicitly branching structures, implicitly branching structures, curviform causation, parallel causal structures, fragmented structure, and nonlinear structure (1990, 222–25).

9. To this group we may add Pamela Caughie's much more helpful opposition of the unified and the aleatory in this novel (1991, 73–76).

10. Patricia Laurence has recently criticized "the bipolar categories of thinking of many critics of Woolf," offering instead "a third vision of alternation as a principle of her style" (1991, 192). I would suggest that the alternation in *Mrs. Dalloway* oscillates between order and fragmentation.

11. Another example of this unusual kind of union suggests a linguistic coupling: the phrase "How's Clarissa?," once spoken, "united Lady Bruton and Mrs. Dalloway, who seldom met, and appeared when they did meet indifferent and hostile, in a singular bond" (161).

12. This work, though originally written for the stage, first premiered on radio, a medium that would exacerbate still further the disjunctions of the play.

13. For an excellent study of multiple plots in Elizabethan and Jacobean drama, see Richard Levin (1971).

14. Even Pinter's better critics tend to presume some level of personal interaction. Quigley states: "Not everything they say derives from what the other has said—indeed, it often derives from what they themselves said in their previous remark—but the words the other person speaks do affect the development of each individual's speech" (1975, 236). Steven H. Gale, while noting that the stage directions make it clear that the two figures "are not communicating, maybe not even talking to each other" (1977, 176), nevertheless asserts that "Beth has withdrawn from life into her imagination and Duff is still involved in living and trying to reinvolve her" (177). Similarly, Kristin Morrison affirms that "Beth exists for Duff (when he says 'you' he means Beth). . . . These two people are physically present now in the same room, have for many years physically participated in the same life, yet for all that proximity they are worlds apart" (1983, 129). Each of these readings assumes a naturalistic relation between the two characters that the dialogue consistently undermines.

15. To cite only one example, Martin Esslin states: "Beth thus does not even try to communicate. She has shut herself off from the present, the world that now surrounds her. Duff, on the other hand, *wants* to tell *her* what he has been doing, and also, clearly, wants to elicit an answer from her" (1984, 175). By contextualizing the characters' relationship within such a naturalistic frame, Esslin's account precludes the possibility of any play with the limits of narrative form ever arising. On the other hand, his observations concerning the identity of the man on the beach are quite astute, and he quotes from a letter by Pinter that suggests the man was actually Duff. See 178–80.

16. For a stimulating account of the progression of this novel, see Phelan (1989, 155–59).

17. The standard critical account of this text is Joseph Moldenhauer's article, "Unity of Theme and Structure in *The Wild Palms*" (1960); for a contemporary analysis

that foregrounds the reader's desire to experience a single "narrative flow" that embraces both tales, see Minrose Gwin (1990, 122–52).

Chapter 4. Modernism's Unlikely Stories

1. This passage is cited and discussed by Paul Armstrong (1987, 115), who also notes the importance of chance in *The Ambassadors* (93–94), *Parade's End* (256–57), and, as we will see, *Nostromo* (169–71).

2. See Hawthorn (1979, 56–60) for a concise discussion of Conrad's knowledge of Marx and the parallels between the two men's worldviews.

3. Discussing agency in *Nostromo*, Armstrong observes: "Chance prevails, however, even when the will succeeds. Good fortune alone saves Monygham from Sotillo's noose or a stray bullet during Barrios' attack, and any one of a number of unlucky occurrences could have halted Nostromo's miraculous ride. Many characters in the novel, both villains and heroes, could be described with these words which summarize Sotillo's career: 'Nothing he had planned had come to pass' (p. 440)" (1987, 169).

4. Siegle for example insists that "when chance *is* the explanation, institutionalized as the operative principle, it is a first cause, a prime mover, and inverts the classic oppositions of reliable/unreliable, truth/fiction, rational discourse/imaginative narrative, order/chaos" (1986, 103). Siegle is surely overstating his case: that a chance event can engender a causal progression hardly threatens the foundations of Western thought—particularly since the science of probability can predict the statistical likelihood of such accidental causes. See Monk (1993, 75–109) for a more balanced account of chance in *Chance*.

5. Jameson offers a provocative account of Conrad's relation to romance (1981, 206–80).

6. Guerard states, "*Nostromo* does pursue *Lord Jim*'s interest in the 'dream,' in the ego-ideal and its aura of illusion. Each of the major characters is immersed in the 'destructive element,' and must idealize something—if only, as with Dr. Monygham, a conception of his disgrace" (1958, 177). See also Bonney (1980, 109–11, 118–24) and Raval (1986, 73–102).

7. Decoud's "death by silence" is discussed at length by Fogel (1985, 118–19, 124–30).

8. The sequencing of *Nostromo* is discussed in depth by Spatt (1976) and by Pettersson (1982, 110–37).

9. For a recent discussion of history in *Nostromo*, see Demory (1993).

10. For an intriguing though ultimately disappointing analysis of ideas of necessity and predestination in *As I Lay Dying*, see Palliser (1986).

11. For general accounts of the role of language in Faulkner's works, see Larsen (1967) and Matthews (1982). On speech and voice in *Light in August*, see Ruppersburg (1983, 30–56); Wadlington (1987, 131–69); and Ross (1989, 51–58, 147–54). The theme of interpretation is discussed by Vickery (1964) and Kartiganer (1979); compelling studies of Faulkner's characters as readers can be found in Zender (1980) and Krause (1984).

12. For a more extended account of the varieties of reflexivity in this text, see Richardson (1988).

13. Or, as Carolyn Porter states: "With the significant exceptions of Lena Grove and eventually Byron Bunch, the characters of *Light in August* are victims of ordering myths, of what Frank Kermode has called degenerate fictions" (1981, 246).

14. As Sherrill E. Grace observes: "This invisible man, after all, is cast as 'a disembodied voice' (503) who 'speaks' for and *to* us. Speech making, as the hero knows (331), started him off in life; and he has continued to act under the influence of Trueblood's, Bledsoe's, Norton's, Emerson's, and Jack's words. What he has misunderstood is that the 'magic in spoken words' (330) will not work properly if the words are merely borrowed" (1989, 223–24). See also Callahan (1988).

15. For a stimulating account of Ellison's engagement with history in this text, see Callahan (1987).

16. On the functions of narration in *Invisible Man*, see Valerie Smith (1988).

CHAPTER 5. *MOLLOY* AND THE LIMITS OF CAUSALITY

1. Centering on causal disjunctions provides a more precise focus than that afforded by other related but less specific terms, such as H. Porter Abbott's "disorder" (1973), David Hesla's "chaos" (1971), Ihab Hassan's "solipsism" (1967), or J. E. Dearlove's "nonrelation" (1982).

2. See, for example, Kenner (1968, 79–132); L. Harvey (1970, 3–66); Robinson (1969, 86–91, 164–67); Morot-Sir (1975); and Mooney (1978). Strangely enough, there is almost no mention of Hume in Beckett criticism.

3. Some important allusions still need to be discussed, however. Molloy's depiction of himself as "a lump of melting wax, so to speak" (47) points back to Descartes's use of the same image to explain his notion of matter in the Second Meditation. I do not believe that this reference has been previously identified. Others need to be stressed: Michael Mooney has shown how Molloy inverts Descartes's criterion for knowledge—the presence of clear and distinct ideas—and makes it instead the sign of falsehood (1978, 54). It should also be noted that several other references to this, the cornerstone of Descartes's epistemology, appear throughout the text of *Molloy* (1985, 47, 50, 88).

4. Moran is by no means unaware of the more absurd aspects of the voice that drives him: "For it is within me and exhorts me to continue to the end the faithful servant I have always been, of a cause that is not mine, and patiently fulfil in all its bitterness my calamitous part, as it was my will, when I had a will, that others should. And this with hatred in my heart, and scorn, of my master and his designs" (1965, 132).

5. On the oddities of *Molloy's* geography, see Fletcher (1970, 125–26).

6. Consider for example Molloy's admission, "I knew only in advance, for when the time came I knew no longer, you may have noticed it, or only when I made a superhuman effort, and when the time was past I no longer knew either, I regained my ignorance" (1965, 82). Other confessions of unreliability are noted by Hesla (1971, 89–93).

7. The most popular critical stance on this topic seems to be that Moran becomes Molloy, a position first articulated by Edith Kern (1959). For a critique of the kind of reading proposed by Hayman, see Robinson (1969, 153–63).

8. Similarly, Leslie Hill shrewdly notes: "What is left is a binary opposition

which invites or solicits interpretation, yet refuses any contextual framework for interpretation. The contrast becomes both crucial and indeterminate, significant yet devoid of meaning" (1990, 62).

9.   Employing Nelson's useful distinctions for discussing causal connection in narrated sequences of events, we can say that causality is absent in the *histoire*, contradictory in the *récit*, and somewhat dubiously inferred at the level of *narration*. See Nelson (1990, 88–99) for a discussion of these levels.

10.   Extended studies of various strands of Beckett's metafiction have been made by Bernal (1969) and Brienza (1987). For an astute account of the relation between perception, narrativization, and reception in *Molloy*, see Iser (1973, 164–69, 264–68); for a thorough examination of what it means for a character to exist as words, see Dearlove (1982, 61–74). There is to my knowledge no theoretical model that can embrace all the forms of reflexivity employed by Beckett.

11.   Some of these examples are noted by Solomon (1975, 98–102).

12.   What may be considered a sixth type, the *mise en abyme*, also appears as the indeterminable relation between the figures A and C that Molloy observes from a distance, an indeterminability that mirrors his own obscure relation to Moran.

13.   This paradox has also been discussed from a different perspective by Raymond Federman (1975).

CHAPTER 6. FORGOTTEN CAUSES

1.   For a more dialectical assessment of this text (which does not, however, dispute its supernatural claims) see Meese (1990, 38–49).

2.   It should be noted that the general theme of storytelling tends to dwarf the metaphysical contestations, and frequently the literal truth of the ancient legends is not insisted on. Consequently the possibility of a metaphorical reading of supernatural claims is always left at least partially open. This position is crystallized in Tayo's final, epiphanic realization "at finally seeing the pattern, the way all the stories fit together—the old stories, the war stories, their stories—to become the story that was still being told" (1978, 258).

3.   This feature is discussed at some length by Taiwo (1976, 116–18).

4.   For a thorough account of the notion of *chi*, see Wren (1980, 42–45).

5.   Ndebele's tale also contains historical resonances: in the beginning of the twentieth century, the Xhosa nation was nearly decimated after following a visionary's injunction to abandon all their material possessions.

6.   In the course of deluding the M.P., Jero does state "I saw this country plunged into strife. I saw the mustering of men, gathered in the name of peace through strength" (169) and concludes the account of his vision by "seeing" the legislator as minister of war. After the play was written, civil war broke out in Nigeria and a military regime came to power. In 1973 Soyinka wrote a sequel, *Jero's Metamorphosis*, in which Jeroboam, now known as General Jero, takes credit for having predicted the turmoil. As Eldred Durosimi Jones points out in his discussion of these plays: "Prophecy had in a sense been fulfilled, and whether the gullible and ambitious politician in *The Trials* got the job or no, someone had to function in Nigeria in the office, if not the designation, of Minister of War" (1988, 84).

7.   Narayan's view of astrology may stem from a biographical incident: his

own idyllic marriage was held up by an unfavorable astrological prognostication—at least until "a more favourable reading [was] obtained from another expert," as William Walsh recounts (1982, 19–20).

8. See Schueller (1989, 423–25) for a discussion of additional aspects of the text's reflexivity.

9. As Anuradha Dingwaney Needham observes, "[W]e run into some fundamental problems when we construct an analysis of a 'true' or 'authentic' 'Third World' culture and text as necessarily opposed to . . . the 'West.' Consider, for instance, that most 'Third World' texts available in the West are written by writers from formerly colonized formations, who were educated in the West or in schools set up by the colonizers. . . . Suddenly, the myth of primal innocence, a pristine 'Third World' untouched by, and in implacable opposition to, the West and vice versa seems not only absurd but false as well" (1992, 50–51).

10. Achebe elaborates this position in *Hopes and Impediments* (1988, 142–43).

CHAPTER 7. PLOTTING AGAINST PROBABILITY

1. This phenomenon is explored in Winsbro (1993).

2. For an excellent discussion of these issues, see John Hannay (1986).

3. See Hawkes 1964, 56–57 for another imagined alternative destiny.

4. Leland Monk perspicaciously identifies a significant corollary to this paradox: "The novel has always been of (at least) two minds, evidencing in its realist mandate a fidelity to experience in all of its contingency and, at the same time, obeying a generic imperative to structure its material in an aesthetically autonomous and unified representation. A novelistic concern with chance is then always engaged in a simultaneous affirmation and denial of its existence, the affirmation eliciting a new appreciation of the causal contingency of life while the denial helps to define a new sense of narrative coherence and design" (1993, 153). I will discuss these important claims later in this chapter.

5. As David Streitfeld comments on the change in the reception of Truman Capote's "Hand Carved Coffins" once it was discovered that the piece was largely fictional and not the nonfictional narrative it was presented as being: "[N]ow that 'Coffins' is no longer the piece of fine reportage many believed it was when it was first published; it's only a so-so piece of fiction. Contradictions and implausibilities that were acceptable because this was real life are now simply unbelievable" (1992, 15).

6. A similar point is made by Peter Burger. The employment of direct chance in composition leads to a subject "thrown back into an empty subjectivity. . . . [T]he result remains accidental in the bad sense of the word, i.e., arbitrary" (1984, 67).

7. Thomas Whitaker describes the conflict between the two worlds in the following terms: "From one point of view, our . . . protagonists will seem as free as we are: they will struggle to understand their predicament . . . and finally choose to make no effort to escape their doom. And yet they are obviously marked for death, subject to a fate that is doubly or triply 'written'" (1983, 39).

8. This process of reconstructing and renaming her self occurs throughout the text. As she states toward the end of the novel: "I have had a husband for each of the women I have been. Prakash for Jasmine, Taylor for Jase, Bud for Jane. Half-Face for Kali" (197).

9. For a complementary Deleuzian account of Jasmine, see Natoli (1992, 71–92).

10. For a thorough (and delightful) study of the connections between romance, feminism, and postmodern fiction, see Elam 1992.

11. McHale's position, and his discussion of other accounts of postmodernism, appear at McHale (1987, 3–11). McHale's meticulous analysis of the multiple worlds of postmodern fiction (26–83) is highly recommended.

12. For a more sustained account of the problems of the standard versions of modern literary history, see Richardson (forthcoming).

13. Stoppard's plays "Cahoot's Macbeth" and *Professional Foul*, both set in Czechoslovakia, are relentless in their denunciation of the Communist regime. Interestingly, these are two of Stoppard's most realistic works.

14. See Rawdon Wilson (1991) for additional discussion of Carter's postmodernism.

CONCLUSION

1. In this work, Petronius's aesthetic spokesman contends: "The poet must be given that freedom he needs to develop his poem to its own inner logic, to construct, if he wishes, sudden wrenching reversals of human fortune, to arrange for divine interventions, and so on; free in short to construct that whole, fabulous, complex allusive fabric that great epic at all times demands" (1960, 129).

Works Cited

PR 6003 .E28 Z5L Abbott, H. Porter. 1973. *The Fiction of Samuel Beckett: Form and Effect.* Berkeley: University of California Press.

Achebe, Chinua. 1988. *Hopes and Impediments.* New York: Doubleday.

———. [1958] 1989. *Things Fall Apart.* Reprint, London: Heinemann.

Adam, Jean-Michel. 1984. *Le Récit.* Paris: Presses Universitaires de France.

Adams, Hazard. 1990. *Antithetical Essays in Literary Criticism and Liberal Education.* Tallahassee: Florida State University Press.

———, ed. 1971. *Critical Theory Since Plato.* New York: Harcourt Brace Jovanovich.

Adams, Henry. [1907] 1961. *The Education of Henry Adams.* Reprint, Boston: Houghton Mifflin.

Adams, Jon-K. 1989. "Causality and Narrative." *Journal of Literary Semantics* 18:149–62.

Alkon, Paul K. 1979. "The Odds Against Friday: Defoe, Bayes, and Inverse Probability." In *Probability, Time, and Space in Eighteenth-Century Literature,* edited by Paula R. Backscheider, 29–61. New York: AMS Press.

Allen, Walter, ed. 1948. *Writers on Writing.* Boston: Writer, Inc.

Altman, Joel B. 1987. "'Preposterous Conclusions': Eros, *Enargeia,* and the Composition of *Othello.*" *Representations* 18:129–57.

Allott, Miriam, ed. 1959. *Novelists on the Novel.* New York: Columbia University Press.

Aristophanes. 1964. *The Complete Plays of Aristophanes.* Edited by Moses Hadas. Translated by B. B. Rogers and others. New York: Bantam.

Aristotle. 1971. "Poetics." In Hazard Adams 1971, 48–66.

Armstrong, Paul B. 1987. *The Challenge of Bewilderment: Understanding and Representation in James, Conrad, and Ford.* Ithaca: Cornell University Press.

Bal, Mieke. 1985. *Narratology: Introduction to the Theory of Narrative.* Toronto: University of Toronto Press.

Balakian, Anna. 1959. *Surrealism: The Road to the Absolute.* New York: Noonday.

Barfoot, C. C. 1982. *The Thread of Connection: Aspects of Fate in the Novels of Jane Austen and Others.* Amsterdam: Rodopi.

Barnes, Julian. [1984] 1990. *Flaubert's Parrot*. Reprint, New York: Random.

Barrell, John. 1983. *English Literature in History, 1730–80: An Equal, Wide Survey*. London: Hutchinson.

Barthes, Roland. 1972. *Critical Essays*. Evanston, Ill: Northwestern University Press.

———. 1974. *S/Z*. New York: Hill and Wang.

———. 1977. *Image-Music-Text*. New York: Hill and Wang.

Bataille, Georges. 1945. *Sur Nietzsche, volonté de chance*. Paris: Gallimard.

Beckett, Samuel. [1931] 1957. *Proust*. Reprint, New York: Grove.

———. 1965. *Three Novels by Samuel Beckett: Molloy, Malone Dies, The Unnamable*. New York: Grove.

Bédier, Joseph. 1945. *The Romance of Tristan and Iseult, as Retold by Joseph Bédier*. New York: Random.

Bell, Bernard W. 1987. *The Afro-American Novel and Its Tradition*. Amherst: University of Massachusetts Press.

Bell, David F. 1993. *Circumstances: Chance in the Literary Text*. Lincoln: University of Nebraska Press.

Bernal, Olga. 1969. *Langage et fiction dans le roman de Beckett*. Paris: Gallimard.

Birault, Henri. 1977. "Beatitude in Nietzsche." In *The New Nietzsche: Contemporapy Styles of Interpretation*, edited by David B. Allison, 219–31. New York: Dell.

Boethius. 1962. *The Consolation of Philosophy*. Translated by Richard Green. Indianapolis, Ind.: Bobbs-Merrill.

Bonaparte, Felicia. 1975. *Will and Destiny: Morality and Tragedy in George Eliot's Novels*. New York: New York University Press.

Bonney, William W. 1980. *Thorns and Arabesques: Contexts for Conrad's Fiction*. Baltimore: Johns Hopkins University Press.

Booth, Wayne C. 1983. *The Rhetoric of Fiction*. 2d ed. Chicago: University of Chicago Press.

Bordwell, David, and Kristin Thompson. 1979. *Film Art*. Reading, Mass.: Addison-Wesley.

Borges, Jorge Luis. 1964. *Labyrinths*. New York: New Directions.

———. 1965. *Other Inquisitions, 1937–1952*. New York: Simon and Schuster.

———. 1981. *Borges: A Reader*. New York: Dutton.

Bremner, Geoffrey. 1983. *Order and Chance: The Pattern of Diderot's Thought*. Cambridge: Cambridge University Press.

Brienza, Susan D. 1987. *Samuel Beckett's New Worlds: Style in Metafiction*. Norman: University of Oklahoma Press.

Breton, André. *Manifestoes of Surrealism*. Translated by Richard Seaver and Helen R. Lane. Ann Arbor: University of Michigan Press.

Bryden, Ronald. 1968. "Talking to Iris Murdoch." *The Listener*, 4 April, 434.

Bufkin, E. C. 1975. "Conrad, Grand Opera, and *Nostromo*." *Nineteenth-Century Fiction* 30:206–14.

Bunn, James H. 1981. "Signs of Randomness in *Roderick Random*." *Eighteenth-Century Studies* 14:452–69.

Bürger, Peter. 1984. *Theory of the Avant-Garde*. Translated by Michael Shaw. Minneapolis: University of Minnesota Press.

Callahan, John F. 1987. "Chaos, Complexity, and Possibility: The Historical Frequencies of Ralph Waldo Ellison." In *Speaking for You: The Vision of Ralph Ellison*, edited by Kimberley W. Bentson, 125–43. Washington, D.C.: Howard University Press.

———. 1988. "Frequencies of Eloquence: The Performance and Composition of *Invisible Man*." In *New Essays on Invisble Man*, edited by Robert O'Meally, 55–94. Cambridge: Cambridge University Press.

Camões, Luis de. 1963. *The Lusiads*. Translated by Richard Fanshawe. Carbondale: University of Southern Illinois Press.

Carlson, Marvin. 1984. *Theories of the Theatre*. Ithaca: Cornell University Press.

Carter, Angela. [1991] 1992. *Wise Children*. Reprint, New York: Farrar, Straus, & Giroux.

Caserio, Robert L. 1979. *Plot, Story, and the Novel*. Princeton: Princeton University Press.

Caughie, Pamela L. 1991. *Virginia Woolf and Postmodernism: Literature in Quest and Question of Itself*. Urbana: University of Illinois Press.

Chambers, Ross. 1984. *Story and Situation: Narrative Seduction and the Power of Fiction*. Minneapolis: University of Minnesota Press.

Chase, Cynthia. 1978. "The Decomposition of the Elephants: Double Reading *Daniel Deronda*." *PMLA* 93:215–27.

Chatman, Seymour. 1978. *Story and Discourse: Narrative Structure in Fiction and Film*. Ithaca: Cornell University Press.

Chesnutt, Charles W. [1899] 1969. *The Conjure Woman*. Reprint, Ann Arbor: University of Michigan Press.

Cicero, Marcus Tullius. 1948. *De oratore*. Translated by H. Rackham. Vol. 2. Loeb Classical Library. Cambridge: Harvard University Press.

Cioffari, Vincenzo. 1935. *Fortune and Fate from Democritus to St. Thomas Aquinas*. New York: Privately printed.

———. 1947. "The Function of Fortune in Dante, Boccaccio and Machiavelli." *Italica* 24:1–13.

———. 1973. "Fortune, Fate, and Chance." In *Dictionary of the History of Ideas*, edited by Philip Wiener. New York: Scribner.

Conder, John J. 1984. *Naturalism in American Fiction: The Classic Phase*. Lexington: University Press of Kentucky.

Connor, Steven. 1988. *Samuel Beckett: Repetition, Theory and Text*. Oxford: Blackwell.

Conrad, Joseph. 1960. *Nostromo: A Tale of the Seaboard*. New York: New American Library.

———. 1984. *The Collected Letters of Joseph Conrad*. Cambridge: Cambridge University Press

———. 1989. *Heart of Darkness*. New York: St. Martin's.

Crane, R. S. 1957. "The Concept of Plot and the Plot of *Tom Jones*." In *Critics and*

Criticism, edited by R.S. Crane, 62–93. Abridged ed. Chicago: University of Chicago Press.

Culler, Jonathan. 1982. *On Deconstruction: Theory and Criticism after Structuralism.* Ithaca: Cornell University Press.

Curtius, Ernst Robert. 1953. *European Literature and the Latin Middle Ages.* Princeton: Princeton University Press.

Daiches, David. 1942. *Virginia Woolf.* Norfolk, Conn: New Directions.

Damrosch, Leopold. 1985. *God's Plot and Man's Stories: Studies in the Fictional Imagination from Milton to Fielding.* Chicago: University of Chicago Press.

Dearlove, J. E. 1982. *Accommodating the Chaos: Beckett's Nonrelational Art.* Durham, N.C.: Duke University Press.

Deleuze, Gilles. 1972. *Proust and Signs.* New York: G. Braziller.

———. [1962] 1983. *Nietzsche and Philosophy.* New York: Columbia University Press.

de Man, Paul. 1979. *Allegories of Reading: Figural Language in Rousseau, Nietzsche, Rilke, and Proust.* New Haven: Yale University Press.

Demory, Pamela H. 1993. "*Nostromo*: Making History." *Texas Studies in Language and Literature* 35:316–46.

Derrida, Jacques. 1979. "Living On: Border Lines." In *Deconstruction and Criticism,* edited by Harold Bloom et al, 75–176. New York: Seabury.

———. 1984. "My Chances/*Mes Chances*: A Rendezvous with Some Epicurean Stereophonies." In *Psychiatry and the Humanities,* vol. 7, *Taking Chances: Derrida, Psychoanalysis, and Literature,* 1–32. Baltimore: Johns Hopkins University Press.

Descartes, René. 1971. *Philosophical Writings.* Edited and translated by Elizabeth Anscombe and Peter Geach. New York: Bobbs-Merrill.

Dobin, Howard. 1990. *Merlin's Disciples: Prophecy, Poetry, and Power in Renaissance England.* Stanford, Calif.: Stanford University Press.

Drabble, Margaret. 1977. *The Ice Age.* New York: Knopf.

Dreiser, Theodore. 1974. *Notes on Life.* Tuscaloosa: University of Alabama Press.

Dummett, Michael, and Anthony Flew. 1954. "Can an Event Precede Its Cause?" *Proc. Aristotelian Society,* supp. vol. 28:27–62.

Dunn, Peter N. 1953. "The Horoscope Motif in *La vida es sueño.*" *Atlante,* 187–201.

Eble, Kenneth E. 1982. *William Dean Howells.* 2d ed. Boston: Twayne.

Elam, Diane. 1992. *Romancing the Postmodern.* London: Routledge.

Elam, Keir. 1980. *The Semiotics of Theatre and Drama.* London: Methuen.

Eliot, George. *Daniel Deronda.* New York: Harper, 1961.

Ellison, Ralph. [1952] 1972a. *Invisible Man.* Reprint, New York: Random.

———. [1962] 1972b. *Shadow and Act.* Reprint, New York: Random.

Elton, William R. 1966. "*King Lear*" *and the Gods.* San Marino, Calif.: Huntington Library.

Emerson, Ralph Waldo. 1983. *Essays and Lectures.* New York: Library of America.

Engels, Friedrich. 1940. *Dialectics of Nature.* New York: International.

Esslin, Martin. 1984. *Pinter the Playwright.* 4th ed. London and New York: Methuen.

Faulkner, William. 1972. *Light in August*. New York: Random.

Federman, Raymond. 1975. "Samuel Beckett: The Liar's Paradox." In Morot-Sir, Harper, and McMillan 1975, 119–41.

Fielding, Henry. 1961. *Jonathan Wild*. New York: New American Library.

Fiore, Robert L. 1984. *Lazarillo de Tormes*. Boston: Twayne.

Fisher, Philip. 1982. "Acting, Reading, Fortune's Wheel: *Sister Carrie* and the Life History of Objects." In *American Realism: New Essays*, edited by Eric J. Sundquist, 259–77. Baltimore: Johns Hopkins University Press.

Flaubert, Gustave. 1964. *Oeuvres completes*. Edited by Bernard Masson. Vol. 1. Paris: Seuil.

Fletcher, John. 1970. *The Novels of Samuel Beckett*. 2d ed. New York: Barnes and Noble.

Fludernik, Monika. 1996. *Towards a "Natural" Narratology*. New York: Routledge.

Fogel, Aaron. 1985. *Coercion to Speak: Conrad's Poetics of Dialogue*. Cambridge: Harvard University Press.

Forster, E. M. 1927. *Aspects of the Novel*. New York: Harcourt, Brace, and World.

Friedman, Susan Stanford. 1989. "Lyric Subversion of Narrative in Women's Writing: Virginia Woolf and the Tyranny of Plot." In *Reading Narrative: Form, Ethics, Ideology*, edited by James Phelan, 162–85. Columbus: Ohio State University Press.

Frye, Joanne S. 1986. *Living Stories, Telling Lives: Women and the Novel in Contemporary Experience*. Ann Arbor: University of Michigan Press.

Frye, Northrop. [1957] 1971. *Anatomy of Criticism*. Reprint, Princeton: Princeton University Press.

Gale, Steven H. 1977. *Butter's Going Up: A Critical Analysis of Harold Pinter's Work*. Durham, N.C.: Duke University Press.

García Marquez, Gabriel. [1967] 1970. *One Hundred Years of Solitude*. Translated by Gregory Rabassa. New York: Avon.

Gellrich, Jesse M. 1985. *The Idea of the Book in the Middle Ages*. Ithaca: Cornell University Press.

Genette, Gérard. 1980. *Narrative Discourse: An Essay in Method*. Translated by Jane E. Lewin. Ithaca: Cornell University Press.

Goethe, Johann Wolfgang von. 1963. "Shakespeare ad Infinitum." In *Shakespeare in Europe*, edited by Oswald LeWinter, 57–69. Cleveland, Ohio: World.

Gombrowicz, Witold. 1978. *Ferdydurke, Pornografia, Cosmos*. New York: Grove.

Grace, Sherrill F. 1989. *Regression and Apocalypse: Studies in North American Literary Expressionism*. Toronto: University of Toronto Press.

Granier, Jean. 1977. "Nietzsche's Conception of Chaos." In *The New Nietzsche*, edited by David B. Allison, 135–41. New York: Dell.

Graves, Lila W. 1982. "Locke's *Essay* and Sterne's 'Work Itself.'" *Journal of Narrative Technique* 12:36–47.

Greene, Gayle. 1991. *Changing the Story: Feminist Fiction and the Tradition*. Bloomington: Indiana University Press.

Guerard, Albert J. 1958. *Conrad the Novelist*. Cambridge: Harvard University Press.

Guiguet, Jean. 1965. *Virginia Woolf and Her Works*. London: Hogarth.

Gwin, Minrose C. 1990. *The Feminine and Faulkner: Reading (Beyond) Sexual Difference*. Knoxville: University of Tennessee Press.

Hacking, Ian. 1975. *The Emergence of Probability: A Philosophical Study of Early Ideas about Probability, Induction, and Statistical Inference*. Cambridge: Cambridge University Press.

al-Hakim, Tawfik. 1981. *Plays, Prefaces and Postscripts of Tawfik al-Hakim*. Translated by W. M. Hutchins. Vol. 1. Washington, D.C.: Three Continents Press.

Hamilton, Gary D. 1971. "Irony and Fortune in *Sejanus*." *SEL* 11:265–81.

Hannay, John. 1986. *The Intertextuality of Fate: A Study of Margaret Drabble*. Columbia: University of Missouri Press.

Harper, Howard H. 1982. *Between Language and Silence: The Novels of Virginia Woolf*. Baton Rouge: Louisiana State University Press.

Harvey, Lawrence E. 1970. *Samuel Beckett: Poet and Critic*. Princeton: Princeton University Press.

Harvey, William J. 1962. "Chance and Design in *Bleak House*." In *Dickens in the Twentieth Century*, edited by John Gross and Gabriel Pearson, 145–57. London: Routledge and Kegan Paul.

———. 1965. *Character and the Novel*. Ithaca: Cornell University Press.

Hassan, Ihab. 1967. *The Literature of Silence: Henry Miller and Samuel Beckett*. New York: Knopf.

Hawkes, John. 1964. *Second Skin*. New York: New Directions.

Hawthorn, Jeremy. 1979. *Joseph Conrad: Language and Fictional Self-Consciousness*. London: Edward Arnold.

Hayles, N. Katherine. 1990. *Chaos Bound: Orderly Disorder in Contemporary Literature and Science*. Ithaca: Cornell University Press.

Hayman, David. 1970. "*Molloy* or the Quest for Meaninglessness: A Global Interpretation." In *Samuel Beckett Now*, edited by Melvin J. Friedman, 129–56. Chicago: University of Chicago Press.

Hayman, Ronald. 1982. *Tom Stoppard*. 4th ed. London: Heineman.

Hesla, David. 1971. *The Shape of Chaos: An Interpretation of the Art of Samuel Beckett*. Minneapolis: University of Minnesota Press.

Higdon, David Leon. 1977. *Time and English Fiction*. Totowa, N.J.: Rowman and Littlefield.

Hill, Leslie. 1990. *Beckett's Fiction: In Other Words*. Cambridge: Cambridge University Press.

Hite, Molly. 1989. *The Other Side of the Story: Structures and Strategies of Contemporary Feminist Narrative*. Ithaca: Cornell University Press.

Honeywell, J. Arthur. 1968. "Plot in the Modern Novel." In *Critical Approaches to Fiction*, edited by Shiv K. Kumar and Keith McKean, 45–55. New York: McGraw-Hill.

Horace. "Art of Poetry." In Hazard Adams 1971, 68–74.

Hornback, Bert G. 1971. *The Metaphor of Chance: Vision and Technique in the Works of Thomas Hardy*. Athens: Ohio University Press.

Hosain, Attia. [1953] 1989. *Phoenix Fled and Other Stories*. Reprint, New York: Penguin.

Howells, William Dean. [1890] 1965. *A Hazard of New Fortunes*. Reprint, New York: New American Library.

Hume, David. 1902. *Enquiries Concerning the Human Understanding, and Concerning the Principles of Morals*. Edited by L. A. Selby-Bigge. Oxford: Oxford University Press.

Hunter, Robert G. 1976. *Shakespeare and the Mystery of God's Judgments*. Athens: University of Georgia Press.

Hutcheon, Linda. [1980] 1984. *Narcissistic Narrative: The Metafictional Paradox.*. Reprint, London: Methuen.

———. 1991. "Circling the Downspout of Empire." In *Past the Last Post: Theorizing Post-colonialism and Post-modernism*, edited by Ian Adam and Helen Tiffin, 67–84. Calgary: University of Calgary Press.

Ionesco, Eugene. 1973. *Macbett*. Translated by Charles Marowitz. New York: Grove.

Irwin, John T. 1980. *American Hieroglyphics: The Symbol of the Egyptian Hieroglyphics in the American Renaissance*. New Haven: Yale University Press.

Iser, Wolfgang. 1974. *The Implied Reader: Patterns of Communication in Prose Fiction from Bunyan to Beckett*. Baltimore: Johns Hopkins University Press.

———. 1978. *The Act of Reading: A Theory of Aesthetic Response*. Baltimore: Johns Hopkins University Press.

Jackson, Robert Louis. 1968. "Chance and Design in *Anna Karenina*." In *The Disciplines of Criticism: Essays in Literary Theory, Interpretation, and History*, edited by Peter Demetz et al., 315–29. New Haven: Yale University Press.

James, Henry. 1972. *Theory of Fiction*. Edited by James E. Miller Jr. Lincoln: University of Nebraska Press.

———. 1973. *The Tales of Henry James*. Vol. 1, *1864–1869*. Edited by Maqbool Aziz. Oxford: Oxford University Press.

Jameson, Fredric. 1981. *The Political Unconscious: Narrative as a Socially Symbolic Act*. Ithaca: Cornell University Press.

Jauss, Hans Robert. 1982. *Aesthetic Experience and Literary Hermeneutics*. Minneapolis: University of Minnesota Press.

Johnson, Charles. [1986] 1987 *The Sorcerer's Apprentice: Tales and Conjurations*. Reprint, New York: Penguin.

Johnson, Samuel. 1960. *Samuel Johnson on Shakespeare*. Edited by W. K. Wimsatt Jr. New York: Hill and Wang.

Jones, Eldred Durosimi. 1988. *The Writing of Wole Soyinka*. 3d ed. London: James Currey.

Jones, Peter. 1975. *Philosophy and the Novel*. Oxford: Oxford University Press.

Josipovici, Gabriel. 1971. *The World and the Book: A Study of Modern Fiction*. Stanford, Calif.: Stanford University Press.

Kakutani, Michiko. 1989. "Third World Refugees Rootless in U.S." Review of *Jasmine*, by Bharati Mukherjee. *New York Times*, 19 September, C-18.

PN3491 .J913

Karl, Frederick R. 1979. *Joseph Conrad, the Three Lives: A Biography*. New York: Farrar, Straus, & Giroux.

Kartiganer, Donald M. 1979. *The Fragile Thread: The Meaning of Form in Faulkner's Novels*. Amherst: University of Massachusetts Press.

Kaufmann, Walter. 1974. *Nietzsche: Philosopher, Psychologist, Antichrist*. 4th ed. Princeton: Princeton University Press.

Kavanagh, Thomas M. 1993. *Enlightenment and the Shadows of Chance: The Novel and the Culture of Gambling in Eighteenth-Century France*. Baltimore: Johns Hopkins University Press.

Kelley, Alice van Buren. 1973. *The Novels of Virginia Woolf: Fact and Vision*. Chicago: University of Chicago Press.

Kenner, Hugh. 1968. *Samuel Beckett: A Critical Study*. 2d ed. Berkeley: University of California Press. *PR 6003 .E28 t7L*

Kermode, Frank. 1981. "Secrets and Narrative Sequence." In *On Narrative*, edited by W. J. T. Mitchell, 79–98. Chicago: University of Chicago Press.

Kern, Edith. 1959. "Moran-Molloy: The Hero as Author." *Perspective* 11:183–93.

Kingston, Maxine Hong. [1976] 1977. *The Woman Warrior: Memoirs of a Girlhood Among Ghosts*. Reprint, New York: Random.

Köhler, Erich. 1973. *Der literarische Zufall, das Mögliche und die Notwendigkeit*. Munich: Wilhelm Fink.

Kort, Wesley A. 1985. *Modern Fiction and Human Time: A Study in Narrative and Belief*. Tampa: University of South Florida Press.

Krause, David. 1984. "Reading Bon's Letter and Faulkner's *Absalom, Absalom!*" *PMLA* 99:225–41.

Kristeva, Julia. 1980. *Desire in Language: A Semiotic Approach to Literature and Art*. New York: Columbia University Press.

Larsen, Eric. 1967. "The Barrier of Language: The Irony of Language in Faulkner." *Modern Fiction Studies* 13:19–31.

Laurence, Patricia Ondek. 1991. *The Reading of Silence: Virginia Woolf in the English Tradition*. Stanford, Calif.: Stanford University Press.

Leitch, Thomas B. 1986. *What Stories Are: Narrative Theory and Interpretation*. University Park: Pennsylvania State University Press.

Lem, Stanislaw. 1984. *The Chain of Chance*. Translated by Louis Iribane. New York: Harcourt Brace Jovanovich.

Leong, Liew-Geok. 1991. "Bharati Mukherjee." In *International Literature in English: Essays on the Major Writers*, edited by Robert L. Ross, 487–500. New York: Garland.

Levi, Albert W. 1962. *Literature, Philosophy and the Imagination*. Bloomington: Indiana University Press.

Levin, Richard L. 1971. *The Multiple Plot in English Renaissance Drama*. Chicago: University of Chicago Press.

Lloyd, Michael. 1962. "Antony and the Game of Chance." *JEGP* 61:548–54.

Lodge, David. 1977. *The Modes of Modern Writing: Metaphor, Metonymy, and the Typology of Modern Literature*. Ithaca: Cornell University Press.

Lu Hsun. 1972. *Selected Stories of Lu Hsun*. Peking: Foreign Languages Press.

Lyotard, Jean-François. 1984. *The Postmodern Condition: A Report on Knowledge*. Minneapolis: University of Minnesota Press.

MacPhail, Eric. 1995." *Don Quixote* and the Plot of History." *Comparative Literature* 47:289–306.

Magnusson, Magnus. 1960. Introduction to *Njal's Saga*. London: Penguin.

Mallarmé, Stéphane. 1945. *Oeuvres complètes*. Paris: Gallimard.

Margolis, Joseph. 1983. "The Logic and Structures of Fictional Narrative." *Philosophy and Literature* 7:162–81.

Martin, Wallace. 1986. *Recent Theories of Narrative*. Ithaca: Cornell University Press.

Martinez-Bonati, Felix. 1983. "Towards a Formal Ontology of Fictional Worlds." *Philosophy and Literature* 7:182–95.

Matthews, John T. 1982. *The Play of Faulkner's Language*. Ithaca: Cornell University Press.

McHale, Brian. 1987. *Postmodernist Fiction*. London: Methuen.

Meese, Elizabeth. 1990. *(Ex) Tensions: Re-Figuring Feminist Criticism*. Urbana: University of Illinois Press.

Meisel, Perry. 1978. "Decentering *Heart of Darkness*." *Modern Language Studies* 8:20–28.

Melville, Herman. 1983. *Redburn, White-jacket, Moby Dick*. New York: Library of America.

Mendilow, Adam Abraham. 1952. *Time and the Novel*. London: P. Nevill.

Miller, J. Hillis. 1982. *Fiction and Repetition: Seven English Novels*. Cambridge: Harvard University Press.

Miller, Nancy K. 1981. "Emphasis Added: Plots and Plausibilities in Women's Fiction." *PMLA* 96:36–48.

Mitchell, Lee Clark. 1989. *Determined Fictions: American Literary Naturalism*. New York: Columbia University Press.

Moldenhauer, Joseph J. 1960. "Unity of Theme and Structure in *The Wild Palms*." In *William Faulkner: Three Decades of Criticism*, edited by Frederick J. Hoffman and Olga W. Vickery, 305–22. East Lansing: Michigan State University Press.

Monk, Leland. 1993. *Standard Deviations: Chance and the Modern British Novel*. Stanford, Calif.: Stanford University Press.

Monod, Jacques. 1972. *Chance and Necessity: An Essay on the Natural Philosophy of Modern Biology*. New York: Random.

Mooney, Michael. 1978. "*Molloy*, Part One: Beckett's 'Discourse on Method.'" *Journal of Beckett Studies* 3:40–55.

Morot-Sir, Eduoard. 1975. "Samuel Beckett and Cartesian Emblems." In Morot-Sir, Harper, and McMillan 1975, 25–104.

Morot-Sir, Eduoard, Howard Harper, and Douglas McMillan, eds. 1975. *Samuel Beckett: The Art of Rhetoric*. North Carolina Studies in the Romance Languages and Literature 5. Chapel Hill: University of North Carolina Department of Romance Languages.

Morrison, Kristin. 1983. *Canters and Chronicles: The Use of Narrative in the Plays of Samuel Beckett and Harold Pinter*. Chicago: University of Chicago Press.

Mukherjee, Bharati. 1989. *Jasmine*. New York: Grove Weidenfeld.

———. 1990. "An Interview with Bharati Mukherjee." *The Iowa Review* 20:7–32.

Mullaney, Steven. 1980. "Lying Like Truth: Riddle, Representation and Treason in Renaissance England." *ELH* 47:32–47.

Murdoch, Iris. [1971] 1973. *An Accidental Man*. Reprint, London: Penguin.

Nabokov, Vladimir. [1955] 1970. *The Annotated Lolita*. Reprint, New York: McGraw-Hill.

———. [1968] 1971. *The Portable Nabokov*. Reprint, New York: Random.

———. 1973. *Strong Opinions*. New York: McGraw-Hill.

———. 1984. *The Man from the U.S.S.R. and Other Plays*. Translated by Dmitri Nabokov. New York: Harcourt Brace Jovanovich.

Narayan, R. K. 1964. *An Astrologer's Day and Other Stories*. Mysore, India: Wesley Press.

Natoli, Joseph. 1992. *Mots D'Ordre: Disorder in Literary Worlds*. Albany: State University of New York Press.

Ndebele, Njabulo. [1983] 1986. *Fools and Other Stories*. Reprint, London: Readers International.

Needham, Anuradha D. 1992. "Reimagining Familiar Dichotomies in Reading 'Alternative' Texts." *The Journal of the Midwest Modern Language Association* 25:47–53.

Nef, Ernst. 1970. *Der Zufall in der Erzählkunst*. Bern: Franke.

Nelson, Roy Jay. 1990. *Causality and Narrative in French Fiction from Zola to Robbe-Grillet*. Columbus: Ohio State University Press.

Newsom, Robert. 1988. *A Likely Story: Probability and Play in Fiction*. New Brunswick, N.J.: Rutgers University Press.

Newton, William. 1951. "Chance as Employed by Hardy and the Naturalists." *Philological Quarterly* 30:154–75.

Nietzsche, Friedrich. 1965. *The Philosophy of Nietzsche*. Edited by Geoffrey Clive. New York: New American Library.

Nussbaum, Martha C. 1986. *The Fragility of Goodness: Luck and Ethics in Greek Tragedy and Philosophy*. Cambridge: Cambridge University Press.

O'Donnell, Patrick. 1982. *John Hawkes*. Boston: Twayne.

O'Grady, William. 1965. "On Plot in Modern Fiction: Hardy, James, and Conrad." *Modern Fiction Studies* 11:107–14.

Palliser, Charles. 1986. "Predestination and Freedom in *As I Lay Dying*." *American Literature* 58:557–73.

Patch, Howard R. 1927. *The Goddess Fortuna in Mediaeval Literature*. Cambridge: Harvard University Press.

———. 1929. "Troilus on Determinism." *Speculum* 6:225–43.

———. 1935. *The Tradition of Boethius: A Study of His Importance in Medieval Culture*. Oxford: Oxford University Press.

Patey, Douglas Lane. 1984. *Probability and Literary Form: Philosophic Theory and Literary Practice in the Augustan Age.* Cambridge: Cambridge University Press.

Paul, Henry N. 1950. *The Royal Play of Macbeth.* New York: Macmillan.

Pavel, Thomas. 1986. *Fictional Worlds.* Cambridge: Harvard University Press.

Peck, Jeffrey M. 1983. *Hermes Disguised: Literary Hermeneutics and the Interpretation of Literature.* Bern: Peter Lang.

Perry, Menahem, and Meir Sternberg. 1986. "The King Through Ironic Eyes: Biblical Narrative and the Literary Reading Process." *Poetics Today* 7:275–322.

Peterson, Carla L. 1986. *The Determined Reader: Gender and Culture in the Novel from Napoleon to Victoria.* New Brunswick, N.J.: Rutgers University Press.

Petronius Arbiter. 1960. *The Satyricon.* Translated by William Arrowsmith. New York: New American Library.

Pettersson, Torsten. 1982. *Consciousness and Time: A Study in the Philosophy and Narrative Technique of Joseph Conrad.* Abo, Sweden: Abo Akademi.

Phelan, James. 1989. *Reading People, Reading Plots: Character, Progression, and the Interpretation of Narrative.* Chicago: University of Chicago Press.

Pinsker, Sanford. 1978. *The Languages of Joseph Conrad.* Amsterdam: Rodopi.

Pinter, Harold. 1978. *Complete Works.* Vol. 3. New York: Grove.

Pitkin, Hanna. 1984. *Fortune Is a Woman: Gender and Politics in the Thought of Niccolo Machiavelli.* Berkeley: University of California Press.

Porter, Carolyn. 1981. *Seeing and Being: The Plight of the Participant Observer in Emerson, James, Adams, and Faulkner.* Middletown, Conn.: Wesleyan University Press.

Prince, Gerald. 1982. *Narratology: The Form and Functioning of Narrative.* Amsterdam: Mouton.

———. 1992. *Narrative as Theme: Studies in French Fiction.* Lincoln: University of Nebraska Press.

Pushkin, Alexander Sergeevich. 1983. *Complete Prose Fiction.* Translated by Paul Debreczeny. 2 vols. Stanford, Calif.: Stanford University Press.

Quigley, Austin E. 1975. *The Pinter Problem.* Princeton: Princeton University Press.

———. 1985. *The Modern Stage and Other Worlds.* London: Methuen.

Quilligan, Maureen. 1979. *The Language of Allegory: Defining the Genre.* Ithaca: Cornell University Press.

Rabinowitz, Peter J. 1987. *Before Reading: Narrative Conventions and the Politics of Interpretation.* Ithaca: Cornell University Press.

Raval, Suresh. 1986. *The Art of Failure: Conrad's Fiction.* Boston: Allen and Unwin.

Ray, Martin. 1984. "Language and Silence in the Novels of Joseph Conrad." *Conradiana* 16:19–41.

Reed, Joseph W. 1973. *Faulkner's Narrative.* New Haven: Yale University Press.

Reed, Walter L. 1977. "The Problem with a Poetics of the Novel." In *Towards a Poetics of Fiction,* edited by Mark Spilka, 62–74. Bloomington: Indiana University Press.

Richardson, Brian. 1988. "Death by Fiction in *Light in August.*" *The Faulkner Journal* 3.2:24–33.

———. 1989. "'Hours Dreadful and Things Strange': Inversions of Chronology and Causality in *Macbeth*," *Philological Quarterly* 68:283–94.

———. 1996. "The Struggle for the Real: Interpretive Conflict, Dramatic Method, and the Paradox of Realism." In *Realism and the American Dramatic Tradition*, edited by William Demastes, 1–17. Tuscaloosa: University of Alabama Press.

———. Forthcoming. "Re-Mapping the Present: The Master Narrative of Modern Literary History and the Lost Forms of Twentieth-Century Fiction." *Twentieth Century Literature.*

Richter, David H. 1974. *Fable's End: Completeness and Closure in Rhetorical Fiction.* Chicago: University of Chicago Press.

Rimmon-Kenan, Shlomith. 1983. *Narrative Fiction: Contemporary Poetics.* London: Methuen.

Robbe-Grillet, Alain. 1977. "Order and Disorder in Film and Fiction." *Critical Inquiry* 4:1–20.

Robinson, Michael. 1969. *The Long Sonata of the Dead: A Study of Samuel Beckett.* New York: Grove. *BFCPL PR 6003 . E28L*

Ruotolo, Lucio. 1986. *The Interrrupted Moment: A View of Virginia Woolf's Novels.* Stanford, Calif.: Stanford University Press.

Rusinko, Susan. 1986. *Tom Stoppard.* Boston: Twayne.

Ryan, Marie-Laure. 1991. *Possible Worlds, Artificial Intelligence, and Narrative Theory.* Bloomington: Indiana University Press.

———. 1992. "Possible Worlds in Recent Literary Theory." *Style* 26:528–53.

Sacks, Sheldon. 1964. *Fiction and the Shape of Belief.* Chicago: University of Chicago Press.

Said, Edward W. [1975] 1985. *Beginnings: Intention and Method.* Reprint, New York: Columbia University Press.

Sartre, Jean-Paul. 1969. *Nausea.* Translated by Lloyd Alexander. New York: New Directions.

Scholes, Robert. 1979. *Fabulation and Metafiction.* Urbana: University of Illinois Press.

———. 1982. *Semiotics and Interpretation.* New Haven: Yale University Press.

Schueller, Malini. 1989. "Questioning Race and Gender Definitions: Dialogic Subversions in *The Woman Warrior*." *Criticism* 31:421–37.

Searle, John R. 1983. "The World Turned Upside Down." *New York Review of Books,* 27 October, 74–79.

Senior, Olive. 1989. *The Arrival of the Snake Woman and Other Stories.* Harlow, U.K.: Longman.

Shakespeare, William. 1969. *The Complete Works.* Edited by Alfred Harbage. New York: Random.

Sharpe, Lesley. 1982. *Schiller and the Historical Character.* Oxford: Oxford University Press.

Siegle, Robert. 1986. *The Politics of Reflexivity: Narrative and the Constitutive Poetics of Culture.* Baltimore: Johns Hopkins University Press.

Silko, Leslie Marmon. [1977] 1978. *Ceremony*. Reprint, New York: New American Library.

Smith, Barbara Herrnstein. 1981. "Narrative Versions, Narrative Theories." In *On Narrative*, edited by W. J. T. Mitchell, 209–32. Chicago: University of Chicago Press.

Smith, Valerie. 1988. "The Meaning of Narration in *Invisible Man*." In *New Essays on "Invisible Man*," edited by Robert O'Meally, 25–53. Cambridge: Cambridge University Press.

Sollers, Philippe. 1983. *Writing and the Experience of Limits*. New York: Columbia University Press.

Soloman, Philip H. 1975. *The Life After Birth: Imagery in Samuel Beckett's Trilogy*. University: University of Mississippi Press.

Sophocles. 1959. *The Complete Greek Tragedies*. Vol. 2, *Sophocles*. Edited by David Grene and Richard Lattimore. Translated by David Grene and others. Chicago: University of Chicago Press.

Sosa, Ernest, and Michael Tooley, eds. 1993. *Causation*. Oxford: Oxford University Press.

Soyinka, Wole. 1974. *Collected Plays*. Vol. 2. Oxford: Oxford University Press.

Spatt, Harley S. 1976. "Nostromo's Chronology: The Shaping of History." *Conradiana* 8:37–46.

Stein, Gertrude. 1971. *Look at Me Now and Here I Am*. London: Penguin.

Sternberg, Meir. 1978. *Expositional Modes and Temporal Ordering in Fiction*. Baltimore: Johns Hopkins University Press.

Stoppard, Tom. [1967] 1968. *Rosencrantz and Guidenstern Are Dead*. Reprint, New York: Grove.

Strauss, Leo. 1959. *Thoughts on Machiavelli*. Glencoe, Ill.: Free Press.

Streitfeld, David. 1992. "Capote's 'Coffins'." *Washington Post Book World*, 19 July, 15.

Sturgess, Philip J. M. 1992. *Narrativity: Theory and Practice*. Oxford: Oxford University Press.

Sturrock, John. 1977. *The Ideal Fictions of Jorge Luis Borges*. Oxford: Oxford University Press.

Suleiman, Susan. 1983. *Authoritarian Fictions: The Ideological Novel as a Literary Genre*. New York: Columbia University Press.

Sultan, Stanley. 1964. *The Argument of Ulysses*. Columbus: Ohio State University Press.

Suvin, Darko. 1987. "Approach to Topoanalysis and to the Paradigmatics of Dramaturgic Space." *Poetics Today* 8:311–34.

Taiwo, Oladele. 1976. *Culture and the Nigerian Novel*. New York: St. Martin's.

Thomas, Keith. 1971. *Religion and the Decline of Magic*. New York: Scribner's.

Todorov, Tzvetan. [1970] 1975. *The Fantastic: A Structural Approach to a Literary Genre*. Reprint, Ithaca: Cornell University Press.

———. 1977. *The Poetics of Prose*. Ithaca: Cornell University Press.

BCCPL
PO 2003 .E378

―――. 1981. *Introduction to Poetics*. Minneapolis: University of Minnesota Press.

Tomashevsky, Boris. 1965. "Thematics." In *Russian Formalist Criticism: Four Essays*, edited by Lee T. Lemon and Marion J. Reis, 61–95. Lincoln: University of Nebraska Press.

Tooley, Michael. 1987. *Causation: A Realist Approach*. Oxford: Oxford University Press.

Trilling, Lionel. 1972. *Sincerity and Authenticity*. Cambridge: Harvard University Press.

Tyler, Anne. [1974] 1984. *Celestial Navigation*. Reprint, New York: Berkeley Books.

Van Inwagen, Peter. 1983. *An Essay on Free Will*. Oxford: Oxford University Press.

Vargish, Thomas. 1985. *The Providential Aesthetic in Victorian Fiction*. Charlottesville: University of Virginia Press.

Velie, Alan R. 1982. *Four American Indian Masters: N. Scott Momaday, James Welch, Leslie Marmon Silko, and Gerald Vizenor*. Norman: University of Oklahoma Press.

Vickery, Olga W. 1964. *The Novels of William Faulkner: A Critical Interpretation*. Baton Rouge: Louisiana State University Press.

Walcutt, Charles C. 1956. *American Literary Naturalism: A Divided Stream*. Minneapolis: University of Minnesota Press.

Wallace, William. 1972. *Causality and Scientific Explanation*. 2 vols. Ann Arbor: University of Michigan Press.

Walsh, William. 1982. *R. K. Narayan: A Critical Appreciation*. Chicago: University of Chicago Press.

Watt, Ian. 1957. *The Rise of the Novel*. Berkeley: University of California Press.

Watts, Harriett Ann. 1980. *Chance: A Perspective on Dada*. Ann Arbor, Mich.: UMI Research Press.

Weber, Frances Wyers. 1968. "Borges' Stories: Fiction and Philosophy." *Hispanic Review* 36:124–41.

Weinstein, Arnold. 1986. "Fusion and Confusion in *Light in August*." *The Faulkner Journal* 1:2–16.

Wellek, René. 1963. *Concepts of Criticism*. New Haven: Yale University Press.

Whitaker, Ruth. 1979. "'Angels Dining at the Ritz': The Faith and Fiction of Muriel Spark." In *The Contemporary English Novel*, edited by Malcolm Bradbury and David Palmer, 157–79. London: E. Arnold.

Whitaker, Thomas R. 1983. *Tom Stoppard*. New York: Grove.

White, Hayden. 1981. "The Value of Narrativity in the Representation of Reality." In *On Narrative*, edited by W. J. T. Mitchell, 1–23. Chicago: University of Chicago Press.

Wilder, Thornton. [1927] 1986. *The Bridge of San Luis Rey*. Reprint, New York: Harper and Row.

Wilders, John. 1978. *The Lost Garden: A View of Shakespeare's English and Roman History Plays*. Totowa, N.J.: Rowman and Littlefield.

Williams, Aubrey. 1971. "Interpositions of Providence and the Design of Fielding's Novels." *South Atlantic Quarterly* 70:265–86.

―――. 1979. *An Approach to Congreve*. New Haven: Yale University Press.

Winsbro, Bonnie. 1993. *Supernatural Forces: Belief, Difference, and Power in Contemporary Works by Ethnic Women*. Amherst: University of Massachusetts Press.

Wolff, Geoffrey. [1986] 1991. *Providence*. Reprint, New York: Random.

Wolterstorff, Nicholas. 1980 *Works and Worlds of Art*. Oxford: Oxford University Press.

Woolf, Virginia. [1925a] n.d. *The Common Reader: First Series*. Reprint, New York: Harcourt, Brace and World.

———. [1925b] n.d. *Mrs. Dalloway*. Reprint, New York: Harcourt Brace Jovanovich.

———. [1954] 1973. *A Writers' Diary*. Edited by Leonard Woolf. Reprint, New York: Harcourt Brace Jovanovich.

———. 1980. *Women and Writing*. Edited by Michele Barrett. New York: Harcourt Brace Jovanovich.

Wren, Robert M. 1980. *Achebe's World: The Historical and Cultural Context of the Novels*. Washington, D.C.: Three Continents.

Zender, Karl F. 1980. "Reading in 'The Bear.'" *Faulkner Studies* 1:91–99.

Index

3 5084 00328 8977

PR 478 .C38 R53 1997

Richardson, Brian, 1953-

Unlikely stories

CANISIUS COLLEGE LIBRARY
BUFFALO, N.Y.